SOFTWARE PROJECT PLANNING

SOFTWARE PROJECT PLANNING

PMI, IEEE-CS, SCRUM, and Hybrid Models

Moh'd A. Radaideh

MERCURY LEARNING AND INFORMATION
Boston, Massachusetts

MERCURY LEARNING AND INFORMATION
121 High Street, 3rd Floor
Boston, MA 02110
info@merclearning.com

M. Radaideh. *Software Project Planning: PMI, IEEE-CS, SCRUM, and Hybrid Models.*
ISBN: 978-1-5015-2321-2

Library of Congress Control Number: 2025943293

242526321   This book is printed on acid-free paper in the United States of America.

Our titles are available for adoption, license, or bulk purchase by institutions, corporations, etc.

All of our titles are available in digital format at various digital vendors.

This book is dedicated to my late father Ahmad's and late son Ahmad's memories.

CONTENTS

PREFACE

As I was wondering what else I could add to my recent textbook entitled *"Software Project Management: With PMI, IEEE-CS, and AGILE-Scrum,"* I thought of asking my students to work on a lengthy assignment to tune the Scrum project management by injecting the IEEE-CS classification of software requirements (*e.g., software product functional requirements, software product non-functional requirements, system and software requirements, software project and process requirements, software product technology constraints, and software product quality of service constraints*) into it. Thus, I drafted an early descriptive version of that assignment, which led me to consider working out a mathematical description (*e.g., an early draft model*) that revises the Scrum project management methodology. Then, I took that draft into further revisions with further enhancements to the point where I started to think that a new hybrid software project management methodology could emerge by (i) injecting the IEEE-CS classification of requirements into Scrum and (b) reforming/restructuring the Scrum project management and its processes. The new hybrid model makes it more structured and process-oriented and helps overcome the shortcomings of the traditional project management methods (*e.g., phased project management*) and the modern ones (*e.g., Agile methods including Scrum*).

Around the time I was excited about my *"being-explored hybrid model,"* I received an email from Steven Elliot asking if I was thinking of writing a second book, but this time for professionals (*e.g., not a textbook for academicians*). I said yes and shared with him a preliminary table of contents with the latest-at-that-time version of that assignment document. All that emerged into this book that I am presenting to information technology and software professionals, and I hope all will find it helpful.

THE PURPOSE OF THIS BOOK

This book mainly serves software project management and IT/Software industry consulting professionals. However, it can still be used for senior graduate courses in software project management (*e.g., project management, project planning, planning tools, etc.*).

This book is meant to present:

1. An overview of the IEEE-CS software engineering management method (*e.g., as in Chapter 2*) and the Scrum software project management methodology (*e.g., as in Chapter 3*). It also proposes models for their planning phases and symbolic case studies.

2. The author's proposed RHSI software project management methodology (*e.g., as in Chapter 4*), along with a model for it (*e.g., as in Chapter 5*) and a symbolic case study (*e.g., as in Chapter 6*). RHSI stands for *Rationale-Hybrid-Scrum-IEEE*.

THE ORGANIZATION OF THIS BOOK

This book is organized into several chapters as follows:

- The first chapter overviews the project planning, a function crucial to any project management methodology.

- The second chapter overviews the IEEE-CS software project management methodology. It also presents a proposed model for its planning function and a symbolic case study.

- The third chapter overviews the Scrum project management methodology. It also presents a proposed model for its planning function and a symbolic case study.

- The fourth chapter describes the author's proposed RHSI software project management methodology.

- The fifth chapter presents a proposed model for the RHSI planning function.

- The sixth chapter presents a symbolic RHSI case study.

ACKNOWLEDGMENTS

I want to thank Mercury Learning and Information (*a subsidiary of DE GRUYTER BRILL*), notably Steven Elliot, for allowing me to publish this book through them. I also want to thank Jennifer Blaney of Mercury Learning and Information for taking care of the production process of this book.

I want to thank my university, Jordan University of Science and Technology (JUST), for their ongoing support.

After all, I want to thank my wife, Rawiah, and sons/daughters Saeb, Ahmad, Saleh, Khaled, Abdul-Kareem, Haneen, and Ro'yah for their ongoing love and support. My mother, Sameeha, and late father, Sheikh Dr. Ahmad Radaideh, deserve the dedication of this book to their memory.

Kindest regards,

Moh'd A. Radaideh, Ph.D., MCPM
Department of Software Engineering
Faculty of Computer and Information Technology
Jordan University of Science and Technology, Irbid, Jordan
Email: maradaideh@just.edu.jo / radaideh03@gmail.com
Website: https://www.just.edu.jo/~maradaideh
YouTube: https://www.youtube.com/@radaideh03
LinkedIn: https://www.linkedin.com/in/radaideh03

1

SOFTWARE PROJECT PLANNING

1.1 OVERVIEW

This section illustrates the purpose of this chapter, its contributions, and its organization.

1.1.1 The Purpose of This Chapter

This chapter is meant to briefly describe software project planning in several traditional and modern software project management methodologies, including the method of the *Project Management Institute* (*PMI*), the approach of the *Institute of Electrical and Electronics Engineering Computer Society* (*IEEE-CS*), the Scrum methodology (*Scrum*), and the RHSI method, a new method proposed by the author (*RHSI* stands for *Rationale Hybrid Scrum IEEE*).

1.1.2 The Organization of This Chapter

This chapter is organized as follows: Section 1.1 depicts the purpose of this chapter and its organization. Section 1.2 describes software project management and planning in general. Section 1.3 overviews software project planning in IEEE-CS and PMI. Section 1.4 overviews the software planning functions with the Scrum methodology and the RHSI method.

1.2   SOFTWARE PROJECT PLANNING BACKGROUND

This section overviews the subjects of software project management and software project planning.

1.2.1   Software Project Management

Software project management is the utilization of knowledge, methods, and tools to carry out the tasks and activities of a software project such that the software requirements are met and satisfied at the end of that project.

It involves planning, organizing, and controlling resources to achieve specific goals and objectives. It encompasses *scope management*, which defines the project scope, goals, and deliverables; *time management*, which creates schedules, sets deadlines, and allocates tasks; *cost management*, which establishes budgets, tracks expenses, and ensures cost-effectiveness; *quality management*, which provides the project meets the required standards, specifications, and quality attributes; *resource management*, which allocates and manages team members, vendors, and stakeholders; *risk management*, which identifies, assesses, and mitigates potential risks and issues; and *communication management*, which coordinates and facilitates communication among stakeholders.

1.2.2   Software Project Planning

Software project planning is where you define the project objectives, scope, and approach. It involves *project initiation*, which describes project goals, objectives, and scope; the *project scope statement*, which outlines project deliverables, boundaries, and constraints; *work breakdown structure (WBS)*, which decomposes the project scope into manageable tasks and activities; *Gantt charts and schedules*, which create visual representations of project timelines and milestones; *resource allocation*, which assigns team members and resources to specific tasks and activities; *risk management planning*, which identifies potential risks and develops mitigation strategies; and *budgeting and cost estimation*, which establish project budgets and estimate costs.

Software project planning outputs include, but are not limited to, the project objectives, scope, requirements, WBS, schedule, resource allocations, and project management plan.

1.2.3 Benefits of Effective Software Project Management and Planning

The cornerstone of software project management is its initiation and planning stages. Therefore, when a software project management methodology is applied effectively, the project is managed and completed satisfactorily, meeting its business objectives, satisfying its stakeholders' expectations, managing its change requests, and handling its issues/risks/threats. Meanwhile, poor software project management fails to accomplish the project's objectives, disturbs its schedule, misses its deadlines, disturbs its budget and expenditure, and fails to meet the targeted product's predefined specifications.

In summary, effective software project management and planning result in several benefits, including *improved project delivery*, which indicates that the project is completed on time per its predefined schedule, within its predetermined budget, and with its outcome software product meeting the predetermined quality standards; *enhanced team productivity*, which indicates that the project's goals, roles, and responsibilities are clear and well defined in advance; *better risk management*, which suggests that the project's potential risks are proactively identified and mitigated; *increased stakeholder satisfaction*, which indicates that communication across the project team and its stakeholders is clear and articulated, and their expectations are well managed; and *reduced costs*, which shows that project's resources are well allocated, and its costs are well managed.

1.2.4 Best Practices for Software Project Management and Planning

Best software project management and planning practices include, but are not limited to, *Agile methodologies,* including Scrum and RHSI, which embrace iterative and incremental approaches; *continuous improvement*, which embraces regular reviews and refinement processes; *collaboration*, which fosters open communication among team members and stakeholders; *risk-based planning*, which prioritizes tasks and activities based on risk and impact; and *metrics-driven decision-making*, which uses data to inform project decisions.

In summary, applying these best practices can leverage the software project management and planning skills and ensure successful project outcomes.

1.3   PLANNING WITH THE TRADITIONAL METHODS

In this book, traditional project management includes the IEEE-CS software engineering management approach explained in the author's earlier textbook [Ref#3] and the PMI phased project management methodology described in the author's earlier textbook [Ref#3].

1.3.1   Planning with the IEEE-CS Approach

As detailed in Section 2.3, the IEEE-CS initiation and planning phases each involve a set of processes in sequence as follows:

- The *initiation and scope definition* phase is concerned with setting up the stage for a software project opportunity, defining its scope of work, assessing that opportunity, and deciding on accepting it by involving the following processes in sequence:
  - *[P1] Determination and Negotiation of Requirements.* This process involves eliciting, analyzing, specifying, and validating the project's software requirements so that its scope becomes well defined and determined to meet its objectives and satisfy its constraints.
  - *[P2] Feasibility Analysis.* This process helps determine whether the proposed project is feasible while considering its constraints related to technology, resources, finances, etc. It also helps prepare, estimate, and determine the project's scope, deliverables, duration, and resources needed.
  - *[P3] Review and Revision of Requirements.* This process enables the stakeholders to review the software product scope and requirements and ensure the revised scope and requirements comply with the stakeholders' expectations.
- The *software project planning* phase is concerned with creating a detailed plan for managing the software project opportunity in terms of its execution, evaluation, deployment, etc., by involving the following processes:
  - *[P4] Process Planning.* This process defines and articulates the entire set of processes required throughout the project lifecycle.
  - *[P5] Determine Deliverables.* This process determines, defines, and articulates the deliverables throughout the project lifecycle.
  - *[P6] Effort, Schedule, and Cost Estimation.* This process estimates the effort needed to carry out the project's activities, schedules them, and assesses and estimates their cost.

- *[P7] Resource Allocation*. This process allocates equipment, facilities, and people to the activities throughout the project lifecycle.
- *[P8] Risk Management*. This process identifies and assesses potential risks and uncertainties and plans for resolving them throughout the project lifecycle. Uncertainties are typically the result of incomplete information, while risks are the probabilities of unexpected events that can negatively impact a project.
- *[P9] Quality Management*. This process identifies and defines the software quality requirements.
- *[P10] Plan Management*. This process prepares, reviews, validates, and manages a complete project plan, including the WBS, schedule, resource allocation, deliverables, milestones, and all subsidiary plans.

The IEEE-CS's overall process interactions during the initiation and planning phases can be summarized as follows:

[P1] ⬌ *[P2]* ⬌ *[P3]* ⬅==➔ *[P4]* ⬌ *[P5]* ⬌ *[P6]* ⬌ *[P7]* ⬌ *[P8]* ⬌ *[P9]* ⬌ *[P10]*

1.3.2 Planning with the PMI Methodology

Table 1.1 presents the PMI initiation and planning processes based on Chapter 3 of the author's earlier textbook [Ref#3].

Table 1.2 shows the sequence in which these processes are involved during the initiation and planning phases. Things start with the *[P1-1] Develop Project Charter* process and end with the *[P1-2] Develop Project Management Plan* process. Both belong to the PMI's project integration management knowledge area (e.g., *KA1*).

It is noticeable that:

- The *[P2-1] Plan Scope Management* (followed by *[P2-2]*, *[P2-3]*, and *[P2-4]*), *[P3-1] Plan Schedule Management*, *[P4-1] Plan Cost Management*, *[P5-1] Plan Quality Management*, *[P6-1] Plan Resource Management*, *[P7-1] Plan Communications Management*, *[P8-1] Plan Risk Management* (followed by *[P8-2]*), *[P9-1] Plan Procurement Management*, and *[P10-1] Identify Stakeholders* (followed by *[P8-2]*) processes are carried out in parallel right after the *[P1-1] Develop Project Charter* process is completed.
- The *[P3-2] Define Activities* (followed by *[P3-3]*, *[P3-4]*, and *[P3-5]*) and *[P6-2] Estimate Activity Resources* processes are carried out in parallel

right after the batch of *[P2-1]*, *[P3-1]*, *[P4-1]*, *[P5-1]*, *[P6-1]*, *[P7-1]*, *[P8-1]*, *[P9-1]*, and *[P10-1]* parallel processes are completed.

▪ The *[P4-2] Estimate Costs* (followed by *[P4-2]*) and *[P8-3]* (followed by *[P8-4]* and *[P8-5]*) are carried out in parallel right after the batch of *[P3-2]* and *[P6-2]* parallel processes are completed.

▪ The *[P1-2] Develop Project Management Plan* process is carried out after all other initiation and planning processes are completed.

TABLE 1.1 The PMI initiation and planning processes

PMI knowledge area (KA)	PMI initiation and planning processes				
[KA1] Project integration management	[P1-1] Develop Project Charter	[P1-2] Develop Project Management Plan			
[KA2] Project scope management	[P2-1] Plan Scope Management	[P2-2] Collect Requirements	[P2-3] Define Scope	[P2-4] Create WBS	
[KA3] Project schedule management	[P3-1] Plan Schedule Management	[P3-2] Define Activities	[P3-3] Sequence Activities	[P3-4] Estimate Activity Durations	[P3-5] Develop Schedule
[KA4] Project cost management	[P4-1] Plan Cost Management	[P4-2] Estimate Costs	[P4-3] Determine Budget		
[KA5] Project quality management	[P5-1] Plan Quality Management				
[KA6] Project resource management	[P6-1] Plan Resource Management	[P6-2] Estimate Activity Resources			
[KA7] Project communications management	[P7-1] Plan Communications Management				
[KA8] Project risk management	[P8-1] Plan Risk Management	[P8-2] Identify Risks	[P8-3] Perform Qualitative Risk Analysis	[P8-4] Perform Quantitative Risk Analysis	[P8-5] Plan Risk Responses
[KA9] Project procurement management	[P9-1] Plan Procurement Management				
[KA10] Project stakeholder management	[P10-1] Identify Stakeholders	[P10-2] Plan Stakeholder Engagement			

TABLE 1.2 The PMI initiation and planning processes' sequencing

[P1-1] →	[P2-1] → [P2-2] → [P2-3] → [P2-4] →	→	→	[P1-2]
	P[3-1] →	[P3-2] → [P3-3] → [P3-4] → [P3-5] →	→	
	P[4-1] →	→	[P4-2] → [P4-3] →	
	[P5-1] →	→	→	
	[P6-1] →	[P6-2] →	→	
	[P7-1] →	→	→	
	[P8-1] → [P8-2] →	→	[P8-3] → [P8-4] → [P8-5] →	
	[P9-1] →	→	→	
	[P10-1] → [P10-2] →	→	→	

1.4 PLANNING WITH THE MODERN METHODOLOGIES

In this book, *modern project management* refers to the Scrum methodology explained in Chapter 5 of the author's earlier textbook [Ref#3] and Chapter 3 of this book, as well as the author's proposed RHSI methodology explained in Chapters 4–6.

1.4.1 Planning with the Scrum Methodology

The processes of the Scrum initiation and planning phases can be depicted as follows (Chapter 3 provides further details on these processes):

▪ The Scrum *initiate phase* incorporates six processes: *[SP1] Create Project Vision*, *[SP2] Identify Scrum Master and Stakeholders*, *[SP3] Form Scrum Team*, *[SP4] Develop Epics*, *[SP5] Create Prioritized Product Backlog*, and *[SP6] Conduct Release Planning*.

▪ The Scrum *plan-and-estimate phase* incorporates five processes: *[SP7] Create User Stories*, *[SP8] Approve/Estimate/Commit User Stories*, *[SP9] Create Tasks*, *[SP10] Estimate Tasks*, and *[SP11] Create Sprint Backlog*.

These initiation and planning processes interact as in the diagram in Figure 1.1.

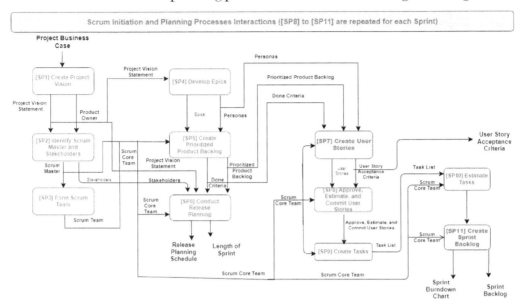

FIGURE 1.1 Scrum initiation and planning processes' interactions

1.4.2 Planning with the RHSI Methodology

This section briefly describes the author's proposed RHSI methodology and its initiation and planning phases. The proposed RHSI methodology reforms Scrum using the IEEE-CS classification of software requirements and expands and restructures its processes. Therefore, it is called RHSI, a Rationale and Hybrid Scrum-IEEECS methodology.

As the IEEE classification of software requirements sounds comprehensive and satisfactory for managing the requirements of any software project, and given the importance of Scrum and its commonality in the information technology and software industry, a hybrid model can be derived and introduced by considering the IEEE-CS classification of software requirements and by expanding and restructuring the Scrum processes to dramatically enhance the usefulness and comprehensiveness of the project planning and execution management.

The IEEE classification of software requirements comprises six classes: *software product functional requirements (SPFRs), software product non-functional requirements (SPNFRs), system requirements and software requirements (SRSRs), software project and process requirements (SPPRs), software product technology constraints (SPTCs), and software product quality of service constraints (SPQSCs).*

TABLE 1.3 The RHSI initiation and planning processes

Batch #1: Initiation/setup processes [P1] to [P23]		
[P1] Create Project Vision [P2] Identify RHSI Master and Stakeholders [P3] Form RHSI Team [P4] Develop Epics [P5] Create SPFUSs [P6] Extract SPFRs [P7] Create SPFR PPBacklog [P8] Create SPNFUSs [P9] Extract SPNFRs	[P10] Create SPNFR PPBacklog [P11] Create SSUSs [P12] Extract SRSRs [P13] Create SRSR PPBacklog [P14] Create SPPUSs [P15] Extract SPPRs [P16] Create SPPR PPBacklog	[P17] Create SPTCUSs [P18] Extract SPTCs [P19] Create SPTC PPBacklog [P20] Create SPQSCUSs [P21] Extract SPTCs [P22] Create SPQSC PPBacklog [P23] Create an overall deliverables release schedule
Batch #2: Sprint planning processes [P24] to [P35]		
[P24] Create/Approve SPFR-S-Backlog [P25] Create/Estimate/Commit SPFR-S-Backlog Tasks [P26] Create/Approve SPNFR-S-Backlog [P27] Create/Estimate/Commit SPNFR-S-Backlog Tasks [P28] Create/Approve SRSR-S-Backlog [P29] Create/Estimate/Commit SRSR-S-Backlog Tasks		[P30] Create/Approve SPPR-S-Backlog [P31] Create/Estimate/Commit SPPR-S-Backlog Tasks [P32] Create/Approve SPTC-S-Backlog [P33] Create/Estimate/Commit SPTC-S-Backlog Tasks [P34] Create/Approve SPQSC-S-Backlog [P35] Create/Estimate/Commit SPQSC-S-Backlog Tasks

Table 1.3 presents only the RHSI initiation and planning processes (e.g., *[P1]* to *[P23]*, and *[P24]* to *[P35]*) of the RHSI's entire fifty-seven processes (as presented in Table 4.4). These processes interact as in the diagram of Figure 1.2. Processes *[P24]* to *[P35]* are repeated for each Sprint. Chapters 4–6 provide the details of the proposed RHSI methodology.

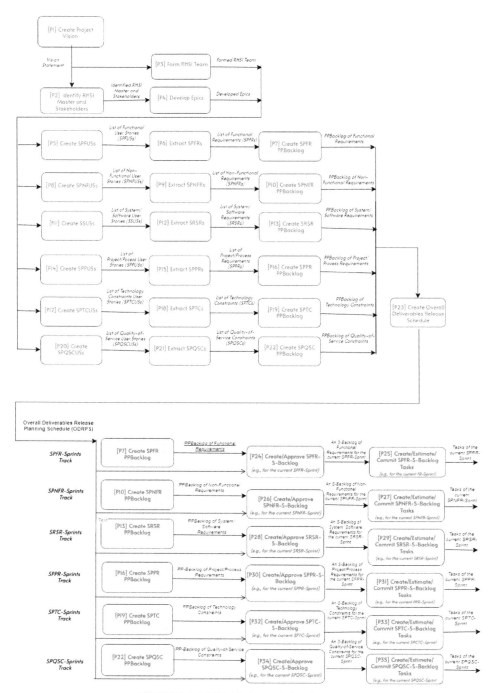

FIGURE 1.2 RHSI initiation and planning processes' interactions

1.5   SUMMARY

This chapter overviewed the planning function in several traditional and modern software project management methodologies, including the IEEE-CS, PMI, Scrum, and RHSI methodologies as follows:

- Section 1.1 described the purpose of this chapter and its organization.
- Section 1.2 provided an introductory background of the software project planning function.
- Section 1.3 elaborated on the planning function in some traditional methodologies. The planning with the IEEE-CS methodology was briefly described in section 1.3.1, and the planning with the PMI methodology was briefly described in section 1.3.2.
- Section 1.4 elaborated on the planning function in some modern methodologies. The planning with the Scrum methodology was briefly described in section 1.4.1. Meanwhile, section 1.4.2 elaborated on the author's proposed RSHI methodology, including why it was introduced, its initiation and planning processes, and their interactions.
- Section 1.5 is this summary section.

2

IEEE-CS SOFTWARE PROJECT MANAGEMENT

2.1 OVERVIEW

This section outlines the purpose of this chapter, its key contributions, and its organizational structure.

2.1.1 The Purpose of This Chapter

This chapter overviews the IEEE-CS software project management approach in terms of its phases and processes. It also presents and models the IEEE-CS classification of software requirements [Ref#2]. The said classification of software requirements and the Scrum project management (Chapter 3) form the foundation for the author's hybrid software project management methodology (e.g., the RHSI method, as in Chapters 4–6).

2.1.2 The Contributions of This Chapter

This chapter makes the following contributions:

1. Section 2.2 overviews the IEEE-CS classification of software requirements into six classes: *software project and process requirements (SPPRs), system and software requirements (SRSRs), software product functional requirements (SPFRs), software product non-functional requirements (SPNFRs), software product technology constraints (SPTCs),* and *software product quality of service constraints (SPQSCs).*

2. Section 2.3 overviews the six IEEE-CS phases and their processes as follows:

   - The *initiation and scope definition* phase and its processes: *[P1] Determination and Negotiation of Requirements*, *[P2] Feasibility Analysis*, and *[P3] Review and Revision of Requirements*.

   - The *software project planning* phase and its processes: *[P4] Process Planning*, *[P5] Determine Deliverables*, *[P6] Effort/Schedule/Cost Estimation*, *[P7] Resource Allocation*, *[P8] Risk Management*, *[P9] Quality Management*, and *[P10] Plan Management*.

   - The *software project execution* phase and its processes: *[P11] Implement Plans*, *[P12] Software Acquisition and Supplier Contract Management*, *[P13] Implementation of the Measurement Process*, *[P14] Monitoring Process*, *[P15] Control Process*, and *[P16] Reporting*.

   - The *software review and evaluation* phase and its processes: *[P17] Determining Satisfaction of Requirements*, and *[P18] Reviewing and Evaluating Performance*.

   - The *closure* phase and its processes: *[P19] Determining Closure,* and *[P20] Closure Activities*.

   - The *software engineering measurement* phase and its processes: *[P21] Establish and Sustain Measurement Commitment*, *[P22] Plan the Measurement Process*, *[P23] Perform the Measurement Process*, and *[P24] Evaluate Measurement*.

3. Section 2.4 overviews the interactions among these processes: *[P1]* to *[P24]*.

4. Section 2.5 proposes a model for the IEEE-CS planning function.

5. Section 2.6 provides a symbolic IEEE-CS case study.

2.1.3 The Organization of This Chapter

This chapter comes in several sections, including the following:

- Section 2.1 elaborates on the purpose of this chapter, its contributions, and its organization.

- Section 2.2 elaborates on the IEEE-CS classification of software requirements.

- Section 2.3 elaborates on the IEEE-CS phases and their processes.

- Section 2.4 elaborates on the interactions between the IEEE-CS processes.
- Section 2.5 presents a proposed model for the IEEE-CS planning function.
- Section 2.6 presents a proposed symbolic IEEE-CS planning case study.
- Section 2.7 summarizes this chapter.

2.2 THE IEEE-CS CLASSIFICATION OF SOFTWARE REQUIREMENTS

Software project management uses various management activities (e.g., planning, coordination, measurement, monitoring, controlling, reporting, etc.) to ensure that software products, solutions, and services are delivered effectively and efficiently to benefit stakeholders.

In their latest version of the software engineering body of knowledge [Ref#2], the IEEE-CS addressed the software requirements from the perspectives of the needs and constraints imposed on the targeted software product and the activities required to develop and maintain the functional and non-functional requirements for that targeted software product. Accordingly, and as depicted in Figure 2.1, the software requirements are classified into the following classes:

1. *SPPRs*. This class includes the processes and requirements needed throughout the project lifecycle.

2. *SRSRs*. This class includes the software tools used to carry out the project activities and tasks, as well as the system infrastructure used throughout the project lifecycle.

3. *SPFRs*. This class includes all functional requirements that must be considered throughout the project lifecycle.

4. *SPNFRs*. This class includes all non-functional requirements concerning the software product, such as its performance, scalability, maintainability, availability, reliability, etc.

5. *SPTCs*. This class includes all functionalities, strengths, boundaries, and limitations of all technological tools required to complete the project throughout its lifecycle.

6. *SPQSCs.* This includes all quality requirements and restrictions that must be considered and satisfied throughout the project lifecycle.

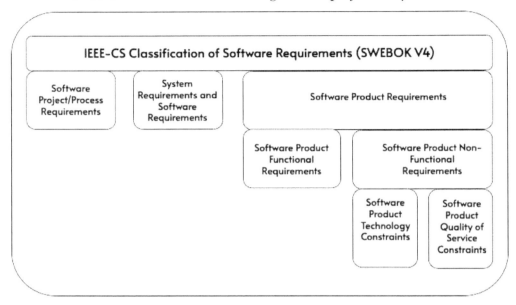

FIGURE 2.1 IEEE-CS classification of software requirements

2.3   THE IEEE-CS PHASES AND PROCESSES

As shown in Figure 2.2, software project management incorporates six phases:

1. The *initiation and scope definition* phase. This phase is concerned with setting the stage for the software project opportunity by defining its scope of work, assessing that opportunity, and deciding whether to accept it. It involves the following processes:

   • *[P1] Determination and Negotiation of Requirements.* This process involves eliciting, analyzing, specifying, and validating the project's software requirements. Its scope becomes well defined and determined to meet its objectives and satisfy its constraints.

   • *[P2] Feasibility Analysis.* This process helps determine whether the proposed project is the best choice while considering its potential constraints (e.g., constraints of technology, resources, finances, etc.). It also helps prepare, estimate, and determine the project's scope, deliverables, duration, and resources needed.

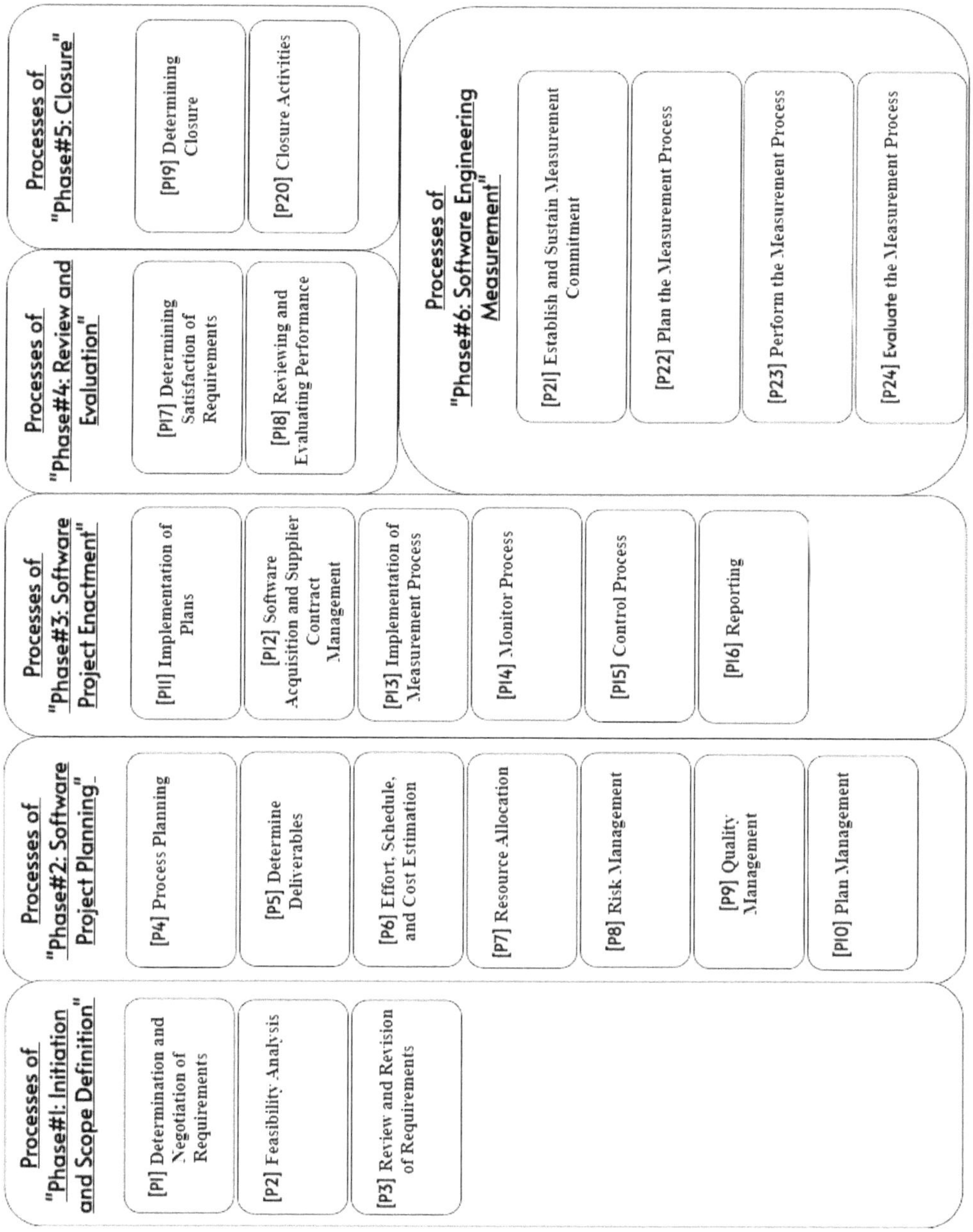

Processes of "Phase#1: Initiation and Scope Definition"

[P1] Determination and Negotiation of Requirements

[P2] Feasibility Analysis

[P3] Review and Revision of Requirements

Processes of "Phase#2: Software Project Planning"

[P4] Process Planning

[P5] Determine Deliverables

[P6] Effort, Schedule, and Cost Estimation

[P7] Resource Allocation

[P8] Risk Management

[P9] Quality Management

[P10] Plan Management

Processes of "Phase#3: Software Project Enactment"

[P11] Implementation of Plans

[P12] Software Acquisition and Supplier Contract Management

[P13] Implementation of Measurement Process

[P14] Monitor Process

[P15] Control Process

[P16] Reporting

Processes of "Phase#4: Review and Evaluation"

[P17] Determining Satisfaction of Requirements

[P18] Reviewing and Evaluating Performance

Processes of "Phase#5: Closure"

[P19] Determining Closure

[P20] Closure Activities

Processes of "Phase#6: Software Engineering Measurement"

[P21] Establish and Sustain Measurement Commitment

[P22] Plan the Measurement Process

[P23] Perform the Measurement Process

[P24] Evaluate the Measurement Process

FIGURE 2.2 The IEEE-CS phases and their processes

- *[P3] Review and Revision of Requirements.* This process enables the stakeholders to review and revise the software product scope and requirements. Such review and revision will ensure that the revised scope and requirements meet the stakeholders' expectations.

2. The *software project planning* phase. This phase concerns creating a detailed plan for managing the software project opportunity (e.g., its execution, evaluation, deployment, etc.). It involves the following processes:

   - *[P4] Process Planning.* This process defines and articulates the entire set of processes required throughout the project lifecycle.
   - *[P5] Determine Deliverables.* This process determines, defines, and articulates the various deliverables (e.g., product increments) throughout the project lifecycle.
   - *[P6] Effort, Schedule, and Cost Estimation.* This process estimates the effort needed to carry out the project's activities, schedule them, and assess and estimate their cost.

   The following processes existed in the *Software Engineering Body of Knowledge* (*SWEBOK*) V3 [Ref#1] but were discontinued in the SWEBOK V4 [Ref#2]. The author includes them here due to their importance:

   - *[P7] Resource Allocation.* This process allocates equipment, facilities, and people to the activities throughout the project lifecycle.
   - *[P8] Risk Management.* This process identifies and assesses potential risks and uncertainties and plans for resolving them throughout the project lifecycle. Uncertainties are typically the result of incomplete information, while risks are the probabilities of unexpected events that can negatively impact a project.
   - *[P9] Quality Management.* This process identifies and defines the software quality requirements.
   - *[P10] Plan Management.* This process prepares, reviews, validates, and manages a complete project plan, including the core plan (e.g., work breakdown structure, schedule, resource allocations, deliverables, milestones, etc.) and its subsidiary plans.

3. The *software project execution* phase. This phase involves executing, monitoring, and controlling the software project opportunity and testing the resulting software solution. It involves the following processes:

   - *[P11] Implementation of Plans.* The project plan and its subsidiary plans should involve activities to utilize the project's resources and generate products.

- *[P12] Software Acquisition and Supplier Contract Management*. This process involves contracting with the customers who acquire the products and with the needed suppliers.
- *[P13] Implementation of Measurement Process*. This process ensures that only relevant and valuable data is collected.
- *[P14] Monitor Process*. This process assesses the project plan at predetermined intervals. It maps to the monitoring fold of the *monitoring and control* phase in the traditional phased project management approaches.
- *[P15] Control Process*. The process carries on the control fold of the *monitoring and control* phase in the traditional phased project management approaches.
- *[P16] Reporting*. This process reports on the progress within the organization and to the project's stakeholders.

4. The *software review and evaluation* phase. This phase is concerned with reviewing and assessing the outcome of a software product, solution, or service to ensure that the entire set of activities carried out during the software project execution phase was satisfied reasonably from the technical, schedule, cost, and quality perspectives. It involves the following processes:

- *[P17] Determining Satisfaction of Requirements*. This process ensures that all requirements are carefully considered and stakeholders are satisfied.
- *[P18] Reviewing and Evaluating Performance*. This process reviews the performance of the project's staff members.

5. The *closure* phase. This phase ensures the completion of activities throughout the project's lifecycle, including deploying the software product, solution, or service at the customer's site. It involves the following processes:

- *[P19] Determining Closure*. This process confirms that the project has been closed (e.g., the tasks have been completed, leading to satisfactory completion).
- *[P20] Closure Activities*. Closure activities should have been conducted and completed when the closure is confirmed.

6. The *software engineering measurement* phase. This phase ensures that the organization's measurement programs are implemented to take the necessary proactive actions once potential problems are identified. An example is noticing a performance degradation after the number of students accessing their university admission and registration system exceeds a predefined threshold. That way, the system will notify the students to access it at other times or scale up the system by increasing its processing and storage capacities. It involves the following processes:

   - *[P21] Establish and Sustain Measurement Commitment.* This process establishes the targeted measurement's requirements, scope, team commitment, and resources.

   - *[P22] Plan the Measurement Process.* This process characterizes the organizational unit, identifies information needs, and selects measures. It also defines data collection, analysis, and reporting procedures. In addition, it selects criteria for evaluating the information products, provides resources for measurement tasks, identifies resources to be made available for implementing the planned and approved measurement tasks, and acquires and deploys all needed supporting technologies.

   - *[P23] Perform the Measurement Process.* This process integrates measurement procedures with relevant software processes, collects data, and communicates results.

   - *[P24] Evaluate Measurement Process.* This process evaluates information products and the measurement process against specified evaluation criteria to determine the strengths and weaknesses of the information products or process, identify potential improvements, and communicate proposed improvements to the measurement process owner and stakeholders for their review and approval.

2.4   THE IEEE-CS PROCESSES' INTERACTIONS

Figure 2.3 illustrates the interactions among the various processes as explained in the following:

1. The *initiation and scope definition* phase's process interactions are as follows:

   - *[P1]* determines and negotiates the software requirements.
   - *[P2]* analyzes them and assesses their feasibility.

- If the feasibility analysis finds something unclear in the requirements, it will revert to *[P1]* to revise and update them accordingly.
- Once the feasibility of the requirements is determined, they are passed to *[P3]* for review and modification if needed.
- If the review finds any of these requirements unclear or requires updates, it will revert to *[P2]* and, if necessary, to *[P1]* to clarify them.
- Once [P3] finalizes and endorses the requirements, they are passed on to *[P4]* (e.g., the entry process in phase 2).

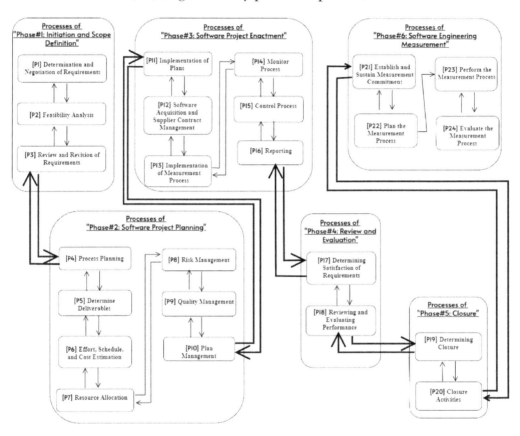

FIGURE 2.3 The IEEE-CS processes interactions

The overall interaction among the processes of phase 1 goes in a sequence such as:

$$[P1] \leftrightarrow [P2] \leftrightarrow [P3] \leftrightarrow [P4]$$

2. The *software project planning* phase's process interactions are as follows:

   - [P4] plans the subsidiary plans required throughout the project lifecycle. [P4] then passes to [P5] to determine the project deliverables. If necessary, [P5] reverts to [P4]. Otherwise, it passes to [P6] to estimate project tasks, activities, schedule, and cost.

   - Once this is done (e.g., given the schedule and cost constraints), [P6] passes over to [P7] to assign the needed resources to carry on the project tasks and activities.

   - Once [P7] is completed, it passes over to [P8] to create a subsidiary plan for risk management, and then to [P9] to create a subsidiary plan for quality management before a complete project management plan is developed by possessing [P10]. Then, [P10] passes over to [P11] (e.g., the entry process in phase 3).

     The overall interaction among the processes of phase 2 goes in a sequence such as:

$$[P3] \leftrightarrow [P4] \leftrightarrow [P5] \leftrightarrow [P6] \leftrightarrow [P7] \leftrightarrow [P8] \leftrightarrow [P9]$$
$$\leftrightarrow [P10] \leftrightarrow [P11]$$

3. The *software project execution* phase's process interactions are as follows:

   - This phase starts with [P11], which coordinates the implementation of the complete project management plan and its subsidiaries.

   - [P12] is carried out in parallel with [P11], which is carried out to conduct all required acquisitions of software tools and subcontractors and the necessary contractual agreements.

   - [P13] then performs all the needed measurements, enabling [P14] to carry on all monitoring and quality assurance activities and preparing the stage for [P15] to carry on all required formal testing and quality control activities.

   - [P16] is then carried on to report on all activities during phase 2 and all outcomes and deliverables produced during that phase.

- Once all project tasks and activities are executed and their associated outcomes and deliverables are produced and reported, *[P16]* passes over to *[P17]* (e.g., the entry process in phase 4).

  The overall interaction among the processes of phase 3 goes in a sequence such as:

$$[P10] \leftrightarrow [P11] \leftrightarrow [P12] \leftrightarrow [P13] \leftrightarrow [P14] \leftrightarrow [P15]$$
$$\leftrightarrow [P16] \leftrightarrow [P17]$$

4. The *review and evaluation* phase's process interactions are as follows:

- This phase starts with *[P17]*, determining whether the resulting software product satisfies the original requirements. If the requirements are not satisfied with the outcome of the software product, *[P17]* then reverts to the previous phase (e.g., phase 3, *software project execution*) with the found issues to be handled and fixed in the software product. Otherwise, *[P17]* passes to *[P18]* to review and evaluate its performance.

- If the software product's performance is not as expected, *[P18]* will revert to *[P17]* and/or earlier processes from phase 3 to revisit the software product and enhance its performance. Otherwise, *[P18]* passes to *[P19]* of phase 5.

  The overall interaction among the processes of phase 4 goes in a sequence such as:

$$[P16] \leftrightarrow [P17] \leftrightarrow [P18] \leftrightarrow [P19]$$

5. The *closure* phase's process interactions are as follows:

- This phase starts with *[P19]*, which checks whether all tasks and activities throughout the project lifecycle were carried out successfully and identifies the actions that must be taken to close the project. If *[P19]* succeeds, it passes over to *[P20]* to conduct the closure actions identified by the previous process, *[P19]*.

  The overall interaction among the processes of phase 5 goes in a sequence such as:

$$[P18] \leftrightarrow [P19] \leftrightarrow [P20] \leftrightarrow [P21]$$

6. The *software engineering measurement* phase's process interactions are as follows:

- This phase starts with *[P21]*, establishing the sustained software measurement commitments. Then, it passes over to *[P22]* to plan for carrying out these measurement commitments.

- *[P22]* then passes over to *[P23]* to perform these measurements before passing over to *[P24]* to evaluate them and conclude on their results.

The overall interaction among the processes of phase 6 goes in a sequence such as:

$$[P20] \leftrightarrow [P21] \leftrightarrow [P22] \leftrightarrow [P23] \leftrightarrow [P24]$$

2.5 A PROPOSED IEEE-CS PLANNING MODEL

This section presents the various aspects of the proposed IEEE-CS planning model, including its software requirements identification, overall work breakdown structure, and overall deliverables.

2.5.1 The Requirements in the Proposed IEEE-CS Planning Model

This section presents a proposed IEEE-CS planning model. Table 2.1 provides a generic, self-explanatory, and simplified tabular representation of the software requirements according to the IEEE-CS classification of software requirements as in their SWEBOK V4 [Ref#2].

Table 2.2 provides representations for the IEEE-CS categorized requirements: SPPRs, SRSRs, SPFRs, SPNFRs, SPTCs, and SPQSCs.

TABLE 2.1 The requirements in the proposed IEEE-CS planning model

	SPPR.ID	SPPRs contain O requirements.	
Software project and process requirements (SPPRs)	$SPPR_1$	Software project/process requirement #1	SPPR.ID: Software product and process requirement identification. Product requirements refer to what should be in the targeted product, including the constraints imposed on the product by the customer.
	$SPPR_2$	Software project/process requirement #2	
	...	...	
	$SPPR_O$	Software project/process requirement #O	
	SRSR.ID	**SRSRs contain N requirements.**	
System and software requirements (SRSRs)	$SRSR_1$	System/software requirement #1	SRSR.ID: System and software requirement identification. A system is a composition of many hardware, software, firmware, people, information, techniques, tools, facilities, and services components.
	$SRSR_2$	System/software requirement #2	
	...	...	
	$SRSR_N$	System/software requirement #N	
	SPFR.ID	**SPFRs contain L requirements.**	
Software product functional requirements (SPFRs)	$SPFR_1$	Software product functional requirement #1	SPFR.ID: Software product functional requirement identification. SPFRs include the functionalities of the targeted software solution.
	$SPFR_2$	Software product functional requirement #2	
	...	...	
	$SPFR_L$	Software product functional requirement #L	
	SPNFR.ID	**SPNFRs contain M requirements.**	
Software product non-functional requirements (SPNFRs)	$SPNFR_1$	Software product non-functional requirement #1	SPNFR.ID: Software product non-functional requirement identification. Software product non-functional requirements involve quality factors such as performance, privacy, security, safety, scalability, maintainability, supportability, availability, interoperability, and reliability associated with their quality metrics to assess and evaluate the solution.
	$SPNFR_2$	Software product non-functional requirement #2	
	...	...	
	$SPNFR_M$	Software product non-functional requirement #M	
	SPTC.ID	**SPTCs contain P requirements.**	
Software product technology constraints (SPTCs)	$SPTC_1$	Software product technology constraint #1	SPTC.ID: Software product technology constraints identification. SPTCs are the ones that a single system component cannot address. Rather, they depend on how the software components interoperate.
	$SPTC_2$	Software product technology constraint #2	
	...	...	
	$SPTC_P$	Software product technology constraint #P	

(Continued)

	SPQSC.ID	SPQSCs contain Q requirements.	
Software product quality of service constraints (SPQSCs)	$SPQSC_1$	Software product quality of service constraint #1	SPQSC.ID: Software product quality of service constraint identification.
	$SPQSC_2$	Software product quality of service constraint #2	SPQSCs refer to the SPNFRs that should be precise, verified, clear, unambiguous, qualitative, and quantitative.
	...	...	
	$SPQSC_Q$	Software product quality of service constraint #Q	

TABLE 2.2 The requirements and tasks in the proposed IEEE-CS planning model

Requirements		Associated tasks	Dependencies
SPPRs	$SPPR_1$	$SPPR_1.Tasks = [SPPR_1.T_1, SPPR_1.T_2, ...]$	$SPPR_1.DP = [SPPR_1.Task_1.DP, SPPR_1.Task_2.DP ...]$
	$SPPR_2$	$SPPR_2.Tasks = [SPPR_2.T_1, SPPR_2.T_2, ...]$	$SPPR_2.DP = [SPPR_2.Task_1.DP, SPPR_2.Task_2.DP ...]$
	...	......	......
	$SPPR_O$	$SPPR_O.Tasks = [SPPR_O.T_1, SPPR_O.T_2, ...]$	$SPPR_O.DP = [SPPR_O.Task_1.DP, SPPR_O.Task_2.DP ...]$
SRSRs	$SRSR_1$	$SRSR_1.Tasks = [SRSR_1.T_1, SRSR_1.T_2, ...]$	$SRSR_1.DP = [SRSR_1.Task_1.DP, SRSR_1.Task_2.DP ...]$
	$SRSR_2$	$SRSR_2.Tasks = [SRSR_2.T_1, SRSR_2.T_2, ...]$	$SRSR_2.DP = [SRSR_2.Task_1.DP, SRSR_2.Task_2.DP ...]$
	...	......	......
	$SRSR_N$	$SRSR_N.Tasks = [SRSR_N.T_1, SRSR_N.T_2, ...]$	$SRSR_N.DP = [SRSR_N.Task_1.DP, SRSR_N.Task_2.DP ...]$
SPFRs	$SPFR_1$	$SPFR_1.Tasks = [SPFR_1.T_1, SPFR_1.T_2, ...]$	$SPFR_1.DP = [SPFR_1.Task_1.DP, SPFR_1.Task_2.DP ...]$
	$SPFR_2$	$SPFR_2.Tasks = [SPFR_2.T_1, SPFR_2.T_2, ...]$	$SPFR_2.DP = [SPFR_2.Task_1.DP, SPFR_2.Task_2.DP ...]$
	...	......	......
	$SPFR_L$	$SPFR_L.Tasks = [SPFR_L.T_1, SPFR_L.T_2, ...]$	$SPFR_L.DP = [SPFR_L.Task_1.DP, SPFR_L.Task_2.DP ...]$
SPNFRs	$SPNFR_1$	$SPNFR_1.Tasks = [SPNFR_1.T_1, SPNFR_1.T_2, ...]$	$SPNFR_1.DP = [SPNFR_1.Task_1.DP, SPNFR_1.Task_2.DP ...]$
	$SPNFR_2$	$SPNFR_2.Tasks = [SPNFR_2.T_1, SPNFR_2.T_2, ...]$	$SPNFR_2.DP = [SPNFR_2.Task_1.DP, SPNFR_2.Task_2.DP ...]$
	...	......	......
	$SPNFR_M$	$SPNFR_M.Tasks = [SPNFR_M.T_1, SPNFR_M.T_2, ...]$	$SPNFR_M.DP = [SPNFR_M.Task_1.DP, SPNFR_M.Task_2.DP ...]$

(Continued)

Requirements		Associated tasks	Dependencies
SPTCs	$SPTC_1$	$SPTC_1.Tasks = [SPTC_1.T_1, SPTC_1.T_2, ...]$	$SPTC_1.DP = [SPTC_1.Task_1.DP, SPTC_1.Task_2.DP ...]$
	$SPTC_2$	$SPTC_2.Tasks = [SPTC_2.T_1, SPTC_2.T_2, ...]$	$SPTC_2.DP = [SPTC_2.Task_1.DP, SPTC_2.Task_2.DP ...]$
	...	......	......
	$SPTC_P$	$SPTC_P.Tasks = [SPTC_P.T_1, SPTC_P.T_2, ...]$	$SPTC_P.DP = [SPTC_P.Task_1.DP, SPTC_P.Task_2.DP ...]$
SPQSCs	$SPQSC_1$	$SPQSC_1.Tasks = [SPQSC_1.T_1, SPQSC_1.T_2, ...]$	$SPQSC_1.DP = [SPQSC_1.Task_1.DP, SPQSC_1.Task_2.DP ...]$
	$SPQSC_2$	$SPQSC_2.Tasks = [SPQSC_2.T_1, SPQSC_2.T_2, ...]$	$SPQSC_2.DP = [SPQSC_2.Task_1.DP, SPQSC_2.Task_2.DP ...]$
	...	......	......
	$SPQSC_Q$	$SPQSC_Q.Tasks = [SPQSC_Q.T_1, SPQSC_Q.T_2, ...]$	$SPQSC_Q.DP = [SPQSC_Q.Task_1.DP, SPQSC_Q.Task_2.DP ...]$

Legend

- SPFRs: Software product functional requirements
- SPNFRs: Software product non-functional requirements
- SRSRs: System/software requirements
- SPPRs: Software project/process requirements
- SPTCs: Software product technology constraints
- SPQSCs: Software product quality of service constraints

- L: Number of the SPFRs
- M: Number of the SPNFRs
- N: Number of the SRSRs
- O: Number of the SPPRs
- P: Number of the SPTCs
- Q: Number of the SPQSCs

- $SPFR_I$: The Ith SPFR requirement
- $SPNFR_I$: The Ith SPNFR requirement
- $SRSR_I$: The Ith SRSR requirement
- $SPPR_I$: The Ith SPPR requirement
- $SPTC_I$: The Ith SPTC requirement
- $SPQSC_I$: The Ith SPQSC requirement

- $SPFR_I.Task_J$: The Jth task in the Ith SPFR-related tasks
- $SPNFR_I.Task_J$: The Jth task in the Ith SPNFR-related tasks
- $SRSR_I.Task_J$: The Jth task in the Ith SRSR-related tasks
- $SPPR_I.Task_J$: The Jth task in the Ith SPPR-related tasks
- $SPTC_I.Task_J$: The Jth task in the Ith SPTC-related tasks
- $SPQSC_I.Task_J$: The Jth task in the Ith SPQSC-related tasks

- $SPFR_I.DLVS$: The deliverables out of the Ith SPFR-related tasks
- $SPNFR_I.DLVS$: The deliverables out of the Ith SPNFR-related tasks
- $SRSR_I.DLVS$: The deliverables out of the Ith SRSR-related tasks

- $SPPR_I.DLVS$: The deliverables out of the Ith SPPR-related tasks
- $SPTC_I.DLVS$: The deliverables out of the Ith SPTC-related tasks
- $SPQSC_I.DLVS$: The deliverables out of the Ith SPQSC-related tasks

- SPFR.WBS: Software product functional requirements work breakdown structure
- SPNFR.WBS: Software product non-functional requirements work breakdown structure
- SRSR.WBS: System/software requirements work breakdown structure
- SPPR.WBS: Project/process requirements work breakdown structure

(Continued)

Requirements	Associated tasks	Dependencies
– SPTC.WBS: Software product technology constraints work breakdown structure – SPQSC.WBS: Software product quality of service constraints work breakdown structure – WBS: Work breakdown structure		– UNION: This function unites the six sub-WBSs (e.g., SPFR.WBS, SPNFR.WBS, SRSR.WBS, SPPR.WBS, SPTC.WBS, and SPQSC.WBS) into the overall work breakdown structure (e.g., WBS)

2.5.2 The Work Breakdown Structures in the Proposed IEEE-CS Planning Model

Table 2.3 provides representations for the work breakdown structures as follows:

1. The *work breakdown structure of the software product functional requirements (SPFR.WBS)*

2. The *work breakdown structure of the software product non-functional requirements (SPNFR.WBS)*

3. The *work breakdown structure of the system and software requirements (SRSR.WBS)*

4. The *work breakdown structure of the software project and process requirements (SPPR.WBS)*

5. The *work breakdown structure of the software product technology constraints (SPTC.WBS)*

6. The *work breakdown structure of the software product quality of services constraints (SPQSC.WBS)*

TABLE 2.3 The work breakdown structures in the proposed IEEE-CS planning model

Work breakdown structure of SPPRs (SPPR.WBS)	$SPPR.WS = \{SPPR_1.Tasks, SPPR_2.Tasks, \ldots, SPPR_N.Tasks\}$
Work breakdown structure of SRSRs (SRSR.WBS)	$SRSR.WBS = \{[SRSR_1.Tasks], [SRSR_2.Tasks], \ldots, [SRSR_N.Tasks]\}$
Work breakdown structure of SPFRs (SPFR.WBS)	$SPFR.WBS = \{[SPFR_1.Tasks], [SPFR_2.Tasks], \ldots, [SPFR_L.Tasks]\}$
Work breakdown structure of SPNFRs (SPNFR.WBS)	$SPNFR.WBS = \{[SPNFR_1.Tasks], [SPNFR_2.Tasks], \ldots, [SPNFR_M.Tasks]\}$
Work breakdown structure of SPTCs (SPTC.WBS)	$SPTC.WBS = \{[SPTC_1.Tasks], [SPTC_2.Tasks], \ldots, [SPTC_O.Tasks]\}$
Work breakdown structure of SPQSCs (SPQSC.WBS)	$SPQSC.WBS = \{[SPQSC_1.Tasks], [SPQSC_2.Tasks], \ldots, [SPQSC_Q.Tasks]\}$
Overall work breakdown structure (WBS)	$WBS = UNION(SPFR.WBS, SPNFR.WBS, SRSR.WBS, SPPR.WBS, SPTC.WBS, SPQSC.WBS)$

(Continued)

Legend		
- SPFRs: Software product functional requirements - SPNFRs: Software product non-functional requirements - SRSRs: System/software requirements - SPPRs: Software project/process requirements - SPTCs: Software product technology constraints - SPQSCs: Software product quality of service constraints	- L: Number of the SPFRs - M: Number of the SPNFRs - N: Number of the SRSRs - O: Number of the SPPRs - P: Number of the SPTCs - Q: Number of the SPQSCs	SPFR$_I$: The Ith SPFR SPNFR$_I$: The Ith SPNFR SRSR$_I$: The Ith SRSR SPPR$_I$: The Ith SPPR SPTC$_I$: The Ith SPTC requirement SPQSC$_I$: The Ith SPQSC requirement
- SPFR$_I$.Task$_J$: The Jth task in the Ith SPFR-related tasks - SPNFR$_I$.Task$_J$: The Jth task in the Ith SPNFR-related tasks - SRSR$_I$.Task$_J$: The Jth task in the Ith SRSR-related tasks	- SPPR$_I$.Task$_J$: The Jth task in the Ith SPPR-related tasks - SPTC$_I$.Task$_J$ The Jth task in the Ith SPTC-related tasks - SPQSC$_I$.Task$_J$: The Jth task in the I^{-h} SPQSC-related tasks	
- SPFR$_I$.DLVS: The deliverables out of the Ith SPFR-related tasks - SPNFR$_I$.DLVS: The deliverables out of the Ith SPNFR-related tasks - SRSR$_I$.DLVS: The deliverables out of the Ith SRSR-related tasks	- SPPR$_I$.DLVS: Deliverables of the Ith SPPR-related tasks - SPTC$_I$.DLVS: Deliverables of the Ith SPTC-related tasks - SPQSC$_I$.DLVS: Deliverables of the Ith SPQSC-related tasks	
- SPFR.WBS: Software product functional requirements work breakdown structure - SPNFR.WBS: Software product non-functional requirements work breakdown structure - SRSR.WBS: System/software requirements work breakdown structure - SPPR.WBS: Project/process requirements work breakdown structure	- SPTC.WBS: Software product technology constraints work breakdown structure - SPQSC.WBS: Software product quality of service constraints work breakdown structure - WBS: Overall work breakdown structure - UNION: This function unites the six sub-work breakdown structures (e.g., SPFR.WBS, SPNFR.WBS, SRSR.WBS, SPPR.WBS, SPTC.WBS, and SPQSC.WBS) into the overall work breakdown structure (e.g., WBS)	

2.5.3 The Deliverables in the Proposed IEEE-CS Planning Model

Given Table 2.4, which provides representations for the deliverables release schedule, the following assumptions are taken into consideration:

- The sets of tasks in the current WBS's tasks (e.g., SPFR.WBS's tasks, SPNFR.WBS's tasks, SRSR.WBS's tasks, SPPR.WBS's tasks, SPTC.WBS's tasks, and SPQSC.WBS's tasks) are executed concurrently, but each in its own task sequencing.

- The sets of deliverables of WBS in the current WBS (e.g., SPFR.WBS deliverables, SPNFR.WBS's tasks, SRSR.WBS deliverables, SPPR.WBS deliverables, SPTC.WBS deliverables, and SPQSC.WBS deliverables) are handled (e.g., created, reviewed, and deployed) concurrently, but each in its own deliverable sequencing.

TABLE 2.4 The deliverables in the proposed IEEE-CS planning model

SPPRs	List of SPPRs	$SPPRs = [SPPR_1, SPPR_2, ..., SPPR_O]$
	SPPR.WBS	$SPPR.WBS = \{[SPPR_1.Tasks], [SPPR_2.Tasks], ..., [SPPR_O.Tasks]\}$
	SPPR.WBS deliverables	$SPPR.DLVS = \{[SPPR_1.DLVS], [SPPR_2.DLVS], ..., [SPPR_O.DLVS]\}$
SRSRs	List of SRSRs	$SRSRs = [SRSR_1, SRSR_2, ..., SRSR_N]$
	SRSR.WBS	$SRSR.WBS = \{[SRSR_1.Tasks], [SRSR_2.Tasks], ..., [SRSR_N.Tasks]\}$
	SRSR.WBS deliverables	$SRSR.DLVS = \{[SRSR_1.DLVS], [SRSR_2.DLVS], ..., [SRSR_N.DLVS]\}$
SPFRs	List of SPFRs	$SPFRs = [SPFR_1, SPFR_2, ..., SPFR_L]$
	SPFR.WBS	$SPFR.WBS = \{[SPFR_1.Tasks], [SPFR_2.Tasks], ..., [SPFR_L.Tasks]\}$
	SPFR.WBS deliverables	$SPFR.DLVS = \{[SPFR_1.DLVS], [SPFR_2.DLVS], ..., [SPFR_L.DLVS]\}$
SPNFRs	List of SPNFRs	$SPFRs = [SPFR_1, SPFR_2, ..., SPFR_M]$
	SPNFR.WBS	$SPNFR.WBS = \{[SPNFR_1.Tasks], [SPNFR_2.Tasks], ..., [SPNFR_M.Tasks]\}$
	SPNFR.WBS deliverables	$SPNFR.DLVS = \{[SPNFR_1.DLVS], [SPNFR_2.DLVS], ..., [SPNFR_M.DLVS]\}$
SPTCs	List of SPTCs	$SPTCs = [SPTC_1, SPTC_2, ..., SPTC_P]$
	SPTC.WBS	$SPTC.WBS = \{[SPTC_1.Tasks], [SPTC_2.Tasks], ..., [SPTC_P.Tasks]\}$
	SPTC.WBS deliverables	$SPTC.DLVS = \{[SPTC_1.DLVS], [SPTC_2.DLVS], ..., [SPTC_P.DLVS]\}$
SPQSCs	List of SPQSCs	$SPQSCs = [SPQSC_1, SPQSC_2, ..., SPQSC_Q]$
	SPQSC.WBS	$SPQSC.WBS = \{[SPQSC_1.Tasks], [SPQSC_2.Tasks], ..., [SPQSC_Q.Tasks]\}$
	SPQSC.WBS deliverables	$SPQSC.DLVS = \{[SPQSC_1.DLVS], [SPQSC_2.DLVS], ..., [SPQSC_Q.DLVS]\}$

Legend

- SPFRs: Software product functional requirements
- SPNFRs: Software product non-functional requirements
- SRSRs: System/software requirements
- SPPRs: Software project/process requirements
- SPTCs: Software product technology constraints
- SPQSCs: Software product quality of service constraints

- L: Number of the SPFRs
- M: Number of the SPNFRs
- N: Number of the SRSRs
- O: Number of the SPPRs
- P: Number of the SPTCs
- Q: Number of the SPQSCs

- $SPFR_I$: The Ith SPFR
- $SPNFR_I$: The Ith SPNFR
- $SRSR_I$: The Ith SRSR
- $SPPR_I$: The Ith SPPR
- $SPTC_I$: The Ith SPTC requirement
- $SPQSC_I$: The Ith SPQSC requirement

- $SPFR_I.Task_J$: The Jth task in the Ith SPFR-related tasks
- $SPNFR_I.Task_J$: The Jth task in the Ith SPNFR-related tasks
- $SRSR_I.Task_J$: The Jth task in the Ith SRSR-related tasks

- $SPPR_I.Task_J$: The Jth task in the Ith SPPR-related tasks
- $SPTC_I.Task_J$: The Jth task in the Ith SPTC-related tasks
- $SPQSC_I.Task_J$: The Jth task in the Ith SPQSC-related tasks

(Continued)

- SPFR$_I$.DLVS: The deliverables out of the Ith SPFR-related tasks - SPNFR$_I$.DLVS: The deliverables out of the Ith SPNFR-related tasks - SRSR$_I$.DLVS: The deliverables out of the Ith SRSR-related tasks	SPPR$_I$.DLVS: The deliverables out of the Ith SPPR-related tasks SPTC$_I$.DLVS: The deliverables out of the Ith SPTC-related tasks SPQSC$_I$.DLVS: The deliverables out of the Ith SPQSC-related tasks
- SPFR.WBS: Software product functional requirements work breakdown structure - SPNFR.WBS: Software product non-functional requirements work breakdown structure - SRSR.WBS: System/software requirements work breakdown structure - SPPR.WBS: Project/process requirements work breakdown structure	- SPTC.WBS: Software product technology constraints work breakdown structure - SPQSC.WBS: Software product quality of service constraints work breakdown structure - WBS: Overall work breakdown structure - UNION: This function unites the above six sub-work breakdown structures (e.g., SPFR.WBS, SPNFR.WBS, SRSR.WBS, SPPR.WBS, SPTC.WBS, and SPQSC.WBS) into the overall work breakdown structure (e.g., WBS)

2.6 IEEE-CS PLANNING—A SYMBOLIC CASE STUDY

This section presents the given artifacts of the concerned symbolic case study (Section 2.6.1), the action plan for the first alternative in this case study (Section 2.6.2), the action plan for the second alternative in this case study (Section 2.6.3), and the action plan for the third alternative in this case study (Section 2.6.4).

2.6.1 The Given Artifacts—IEEE-CS Planning Symbolic Case Study

Table 2.5 presents the assumed artifacts for the case study. Tables 2.6–2.8 present the plans for the three options (e.g., alternatives) of the concerned symbolic IEEE-CS case study in this section.

TABLE 2.5 The given artifacts—an IEEE-CS planning symbolic case study

Work Breakdown Structure	- The plan has two categories (requirements). - Each category has five tasks. - The first category has tasks T1–T5. - The second category has tasks T6–T10.
Resources and Their Competencies	- In addition to the project manager (PM), the project team includes four technical staff members (R1, R2, R3, and R4) with similar experience, competencies, and salaries (e.g., each of them can do any of the given ten tasks).
Financials	- The monthly salary of each of the team members (R1, R2, R3, and R4) is $3,000. - The monthly salary of the PM is $5,000.
Tasks Durations	- Each task takes 1 month to complete.

(Continued)

	Alternative #1	Alternative #2	Alternative #3
Dependencies	- T1 and T6: START-START dependency	- T6 STARTS after T1 ENDS - T7 STARTS after T2 ENDS - T8 STARTS after T3 ENDS - T9 STARTS after T4 ENDS - T10 STARTS after T5 ENDS	- T6 STARTS after T1 ENDS - T8 STARTS after T3 ENDS - T10 STARTS after T5 ENDS
Project Management	The PM must be fully assigned to the project.		
Start Date	February 1, 2025		

2.6.2 Alternative #1—An IEEE-CS Planning Symbolic Case Study

Table 2.6 presents the action plan for Alternative #1 of the symbolic IEEE-CS case study considered in this section.

TABLE 2.6 Alternative #1—an IEEE-CS planning symbolic case study

Dependencies	**T1 and T6 have a START-START dependency.**					
	Task Name	Start Date	End Date	Dependency	Resource	Cost
Work Breakdown Structure	Project Management	1/2/2025	30/4/2025		PM	3*$5,000.00 = $15,000.00
	Requirement #1	1/2/2025	30/4/2025		---	$15,000.00
	T1	1/2/2025	28/2/2025	SS-T6	R1	$3,000.00
	T2	1/2/2025	28/2/2025		R3	$3,000.00
	T3	1/3/2025	31/3/2025		R1	$3,000.00
	T4	1/3/2025	31/3/2025		R3	$3,000.00
	T5	1/4/2025	30/4/2025		R1	$3,000.00
	Requirement #2	1/2/2025	30/4/2025		----	$15,000.00
	T6	1/2/2025	28/2/2025	SeS-T1	R2	$3,000.00
	T7	1/2/2025	28/2/2025		R4	$3,000.00
	T8	1/3/2025	31/3/2025		R2	$3,000.00
	T9	1/3/2025	31/3/2025		R4	$3,000.00
	T10	1/4/2024	30/4/2024		R2	$3,000.00
Calculations	Period	- Project Start Date: 1/2/2025 ←→ End Date: 30/4/2025 → 3 months				
	Overall Base Cost	- Project Management Base Cost = $15,000.00 - Tasks Base Cost = $15,000.00 + $15,000.00 = $30,000.00 - Project Overall Base-Cost = $15,000.00 + $30,000.00 = $45,000.00 - Risks Contingency Fund = %5 * $45,000.00 = $2,250.00 - Overhead Cost = 1% *$45,000.00 = $450.00 - Overall Cost = $45,000.00 + $2,250.00 + $450.00 = $47,700.00 - Price = Overall Cost + Profit = $47,700.00 + (%20 = $9.540.00) = $57,240.00				

2.6.3 Alternative #2—An IEEE-CS Planning Symbolic Case Study

Table 2.7 presents the action plan for Alternative #2 of the symbolic IEEE-CS case study considered in this section.

TABLE 2.7 Alternative #2—an IEEE-CS planning symbolic case study

Dependencies	T6 STARTS after T1 ENDS + T7 STARTS after T2 ENDS + T8 STARTS after T3 ENDS + T9 STARTS after T4 ENDS + T10 STARTS after T5 ENDS					
	Task Name	Start Date	End Date	Dependency	Resource	Cost
Work Breakdown Structure	Project Management	1/2/2025	31/5/2025		PM	4*5,000.00 = $20,000.00
	Requirement #1	1/2/2025	30/4/2025		---	$15,000.00
	T1	1/2/2025	28/2/2025		R1	$3,000.00
	T2	1/2/2025	28/2/2025		R2	$3,000.00
	T3	1/2/2025	28/2/2025		R3	$3,000.00
	T4	1/2/2025	28/2/2025		R4	$3,000.00
	T5	1/4/2024	30/4/2025		R1	$3,000.00
	Requirement #2	1/3/2025	31/5/2025		---	$15,000.00
	T6	1/3/2025	31/3/2025	SE T1	R1	$3,000.00
	T7	1/3/2025	31/3/2025	SE T2	R2	$3,000.00
	T8	1/3/2025	31/3/2025	SE T3	R3	$3,000.00
	T9	1/3/2025	31/3/2025	SE T4	R4	$3,000.00
	T10	1/5/2025	31/5/2025	SE T5	R1	$3,000.00
Calculations	Period	Project Start Date: 1/2/2025 ⬅➡ End Date: 31/5/2025 ➔ 4 months				
	Overall Base Cost	Project Management Base Cost = $20,000.00 Tasks Base Cost = $15000 + $15000 = $30,000.00 Project Overall Base Cost = $20000 + $30,000.00 = $50,000.00 Risks Contingency Fund = %5 * $50,000.00 = $2,500.00 Overhead Cost = 1% *$50,000.00 = $500.00 Overall Cost = $50,000.00+ $2,500.00 + $500.00 = $5,300.00 Price = Overall Cost + Profit = $53,000.00 + (%20 = $10,600.00) = $63,600.00				

2.6.4 Alternative #3—An IEEE-CS Planning Symbolic Case Study

Table 2.8 presents the action plan for Alternative #3 of the symbolic IEEE-CS case study considered in this section.

TABLE 2.8 Alternative #3—an IEEE-CS planning symbolic case study

Dependencies	T6 STARTS WITH T1 + T8 STARTS WITH T3 + T10 STARTS WITH T5					
	Task Name	Start Date	End Date	Dependency	Resource	Cost
	Project Management	1/2/2025	30/4/2025		PM	3*$5,000.00 = $15,000.00
	Requirement #1	1/2/2025	30/4/2025		--	$15,000.00
	T1	1/2/2025	28/2/2025	SS T6	R1	$3,000.00
	T2	1/3/2025	31/3/2025	--	R3	$3,000.00
	T3	1/2/2025	28/2/2025	SS T8	R3	$3,000.00
Work Breakdown Structure	T4	1/4/2025	30/4/2025	--	R1	$3,000.00
	T5	1/3/2025	31/3/2025	SS T10	R1	$3,000.00
	Requirement #2	1/2/2025	30/4/2025	--	--	$15,000.00
	T6	1/2/2025	28/2/2025	SS T1	R2	$3,000.00
	T7	1/3/2025	31/3/2025	--	R4	$3,000.00
	T8	1/2/2025	28/2/2025	SS T3	R4	$3,000.00
	T9	1/4/2025	30/4/2025	---	R2	$3,000.00
	T10	1/3/2023	31/3/2025	SS T5	R2	$3,000.00
Calculations	Period	Project Start Date: 1/2/2025 ←→ End Date: 30/4/2025 → 3 months				
	Overall Base Cost	Project Management Base Cost = $15,000.00 Tasks Base Cost = $15,000.00 + $15,000.00 = $30,000.00 Project Overall Base Cost = $15,000.00 + $30,000.00 = $45,000.00 Risks Contingency Fund = %5 * $45,000.00 = $2,250.00 Overhead Cost = 1% *$45000 = $450.00 Overall Cost = $45,000.00 + $2,250.00 + $450.00 = $47,700.00 Price = Overall Cost + Profit = $47,700.00 + (%20 = $9,540.00) = $57,240.00				

2.7 SUMMARY

This chapter briefly described the IEEE-CS software project management methodology, laying the groundwork for software project processes, the IEEE-CS software project planning modeling, and a symbolic case study.

The key contributions made in this chapter included the following:

- A comprehensive exploration of the IEEE-CS phases and processes (Section 2.3) and a proposed model for their interaction (Section 2.4)

- A proposed model for the IEEE-CS planning (Section 2.5), including the software requirements sub-model (Section 2.5.1), the work breakdown structures sub-model (Section 2.5.2), and the deliverables sub-model (Section 2.5.3)

- A proposed symbolic case study (Section 2.6) providing an example of IEEE-CS planning through multiple action plans (Sections 2.6.2–2.6.4) based on given artifacts

These contributions collectively enhance the understanding and application of the IEEE-CS methodology in software project management contexts.

3

SCRUM PROJECT MANAGEMENT

3.1 OVERVIEW

This section illustrates the purpose of this chapter, its contributions, and its organization.

3.1.1 The Purpose of This Chapter

This chapter describes the Scrum project management methodology, its model, and a symbolic case study as proposed by the author. Along with the IEEE-CS classification of software requirements, Scrum forms the foundation for the author's proposed software project management methodology, which is presented and demonstrated in Chapters 4–6.

3.1.2 The Contributions of This Chapter

This chapter makes the following contributions:

1. Section 3.2 overviews the three areas of the Scrum project management methodology as follows:

   * Section 3.2.2 overviews the Scrum *principles* area, covering the *empirical process control* principle, which incorporates the concepts of transparency, inspection, and adaptation; the *self-organization* principle; the *collaboration* principle; the *value-based prioritization* principle; the *time-boxing* principle; and the *iterative development* principle.

- Section 3.2.3 overviews the Scrum *aspects* area, covering the *organization* aspect, which describes the Scrum roles of Product Owner, Scrum Master, Scrum Team, *Scrum of Scrums* (*SoS*), and Scrum portfolios and programs; the *business justification* aspect, which explains how Scrum projects should be justified; the *quality management* aspect, which explains how Scrum perceives and manages quality; the *change management* aspect, which describes how Scrum perceives and manages changes; and the *risk management* aspect, which shows how risks are identified, assessed, prioritized, mitigated, communicated, and minimized.

- Section 3.2.4 overviews the Scrum phases and their processes, covering the *initiate* phase and its processes, the *plan and estimate* phase and its processes, the *implement* phase and its processes, the *review and retrospect* phase and its processes, and the *release* phase and its processes.

2. In Sections 3.3 to 3.5, the chapter proposes a Scrum process interaction model, a Scrum processes/meetings model, and a Scrum planning model.

3. Section 3.6 provides a symbolic Scrum case study to help understand Scrum planning.

3.1.3 The Organization of This Chapter

This chapter comes in several sections as follows:

- Section 3.1 presents the purpose of this chapter, its contributions, and its organization.

- Section 3.2 overviews the Scrum project management methodology, including its six principles, five aspects, and five phases, along with their processes.

- Section 3.3 presents the proposed model for the Scrum processes' overall interaction structure.

- Section 3.4 presents the proposed Scrum processes/meetings structure model.

- Section 3.5 presents the proposed Scrum planning model.

- Section 3.6 provides a symbolic Scrum case study.

- Section 3.7 summarizes this chapter.

3.2   THE SCRUM METHODOLOGY

This section overviews the Scrum project management methodology, including its principles, aspects, phases, and processes.

3.2.1   Scrum Background

Scrum is an adaptive, iterative, fast, flexible, and effective methodology designed to deliver value deliverables. Scrum supports creating products, solutions, and services. A Scrum project involves collaboratively creating a new product, solution, or service based on a predetermined vision statement. Many constraints may impact projects including time, cost, scope, quality, resources, and organizational structures.

Figure 3.1 shows that a Scrum project starts with a stakeholder meeting to create the project vision. The Product Owner then develops a *prioritized product backlog* (*PPBacklog*), which includes a list of prioritized user stories.

A Sprint lasts 1–6 weeks and begins with a Sprint Planning meeting to select the user stories with the highest priority from the PPBacklog and include them in the current Sprint backlog.

During a Sprint, the Scrum Team creates a set of predefined deliverables for that Sprint. The team conducts standup meetings to enable members to discuss their daily progress.

Shortly before the end of that Sprint, a Sprint Review meeting is held to present and demonstrate the deliverables to the Product Owner and stakeholders. In turn, the Product Owner accepts the deliverables if and only if they meet the predefined deliverable acceptance criteria. If accepted, they will be shipped to the customer and implemented for them.

A Sprint lifecycle ends with a Sprint Retrospective meeting to enable the team to improve their processes and performance before they move on to the next Sprint. Using Scrum in software development and project management has many benefits, such as ensuring and promoting adaptability, transparency, continuous feedback, continuous improvement, continuous delivery of effective deliverables, motivation among employees, and fast problem-solving throughout the project lifecycle.

A Sprint Lifecycle

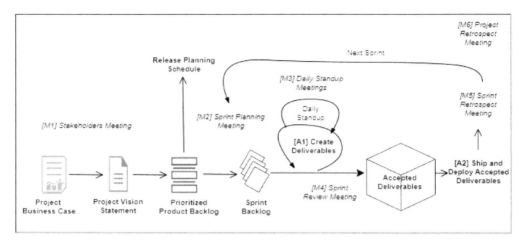

Scrum Meetings - Involved Scrum Processes

	[SP1]	[SP2]	[SP3]	[SP4]	[SP5]	[SP6]	[SP7]	[SP8]	[SP9]	[SP10]	[SP11]	[SP12]	[SP13]	[SP14]	[SP15]	[SP16]	[SP17]	[SP18]	[SP19]
[M1]	Yes	Yes	Yes	Yes	Yes	Yes	Yes												
[M2]								Yes	Yes	Yes	Yes								
[M3]													Yes						
[M4]															Yes	Yes			
[M5]													Yes				Yes		
[M6]																			Yes
[A1]												Yes							
[A2]																	Yes		

Scrum Processes

[SP1] Create Project Vision	[SP2] Identify Scrum Master and Stakeholders	[SP3] Form Scrum Team
[SP4] Develop Epics		
[SP5] Create Prioritized Product Backlog	[SP6] Conduct Release Planning	[SP7] Create User Stories
[SP8] Approve, Estimate, and Commit User Stories		
[SP9] Create Tasks	[SP10] Estimate Tasks	[SP11] Create Sprint Backlog
[SP12] Create Deliverables		
[SP13] Conduct Daily Standup Meetings	[SP14] Groom Prioritized Product Backlog	[SP15] Convene Scrum of Scrums
[SP16] Demonstrate and Validate Sprint		
[SP17] Ship Deliverables	[SP18] Sprint Retrospect	[SP19] Retrospect Project

FIGURE 3.1 Scrum flow diagrams—Sprint flow diagram and meetings

Figure 3.2 illustrates how Scrum is divided into three areas (principles, aspects, and phases), along with their processes.

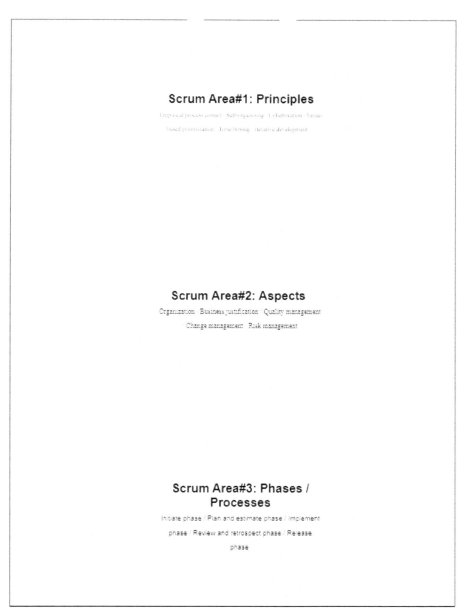

Scrum Area#1: Principles

Empirical process control / Self-organizing / Collaboration / Value-based prioritization / Time-boxing / Iterative development

Scrum Area#2: Aspects

Organization / Business justification / Quality management / Change management / Risk management

Scrum Area#3: Phases / Processes

Initiate phase / Plan and estimate phase / Implement phase / Review and retrospect phase / Release phase

FIGURE 3.2 Scrum areas—principles, aspects, and processes

3.2.2 Scrum Principles Area

This section presents the six principles of Scrum (Sections 3.2.2.1 to 3.2.2.6).

3.2.2.1 Principle #1: Empirical Process Control

This principle describes Scrum from the transparency, inspection, and adaptation perspectives:

- *Transparency*: This implies that Scrum processes and activities are observable to anyone involved in the project. As shown in Figure 3.3, transparency can be achieved by making the details of the project vision statement, PPBacklog, user stories, release planning schedule, team progress visibility, daily standup meetings, and Sprint Review meetings available to all personnel involved in a Scrum project.

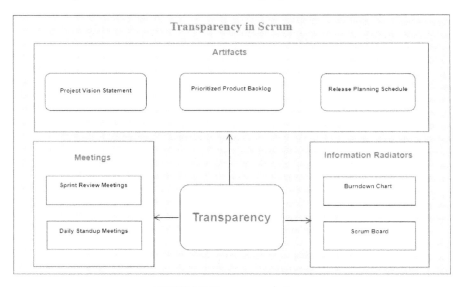

FIGURE 3.3 Transparency in Scrum

- *Inspection*: As shown in Figure 3.4, the inspection can be conducted using a standard Scrum board and other information radiators to show the team's progress with the current sprint.

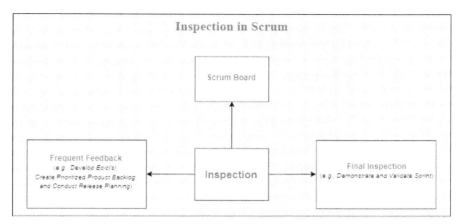

FIGURE 3.4 Inspection in Scrum

▪ *Adaptation*: As shown in Figure 3.5, the team and stakeholders adapt to the project environment and circumstances by improving their work during the daily standup meetings, using the identified risks as inputs to many Scrum processes.

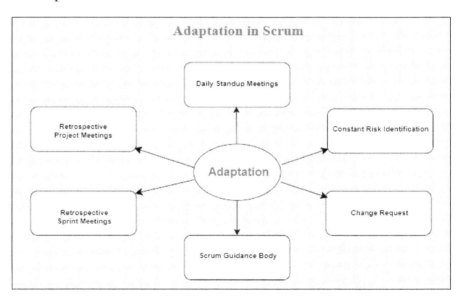

FIGURE 3.5 Adaptation in Scrum

3.2.2.2 Principle #2: Self-Organization

This principle indicates that if the team members are focused and self-organized, they can produce high-value deliverables. Figure 3.6 shows the main objectives of a self-organizing team.

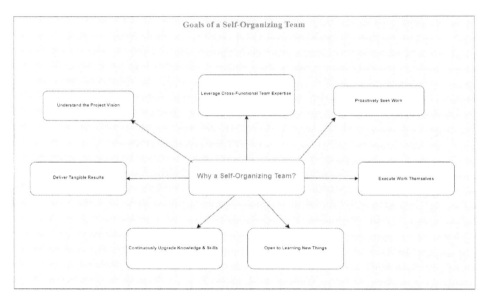

FIGURE 3.6 Self-organizing in Scrum

3.2.2.3 Principle #3: Collaboration

This principle involves the dimensions of collaboration regarding awareness, articulation, and appropriation:

- *Awareness*: Each team member should be aware of the duties, tasks, and activities carried out by their colleagues in the team.
- *Articulation*: During a Sprint, the work must be divided carefully among the team members so that their outcomes can be easily integrated as presented.
- *Appropriation*: Resources must be used appropriately, such that no or minimal efforts and time are wasted.

3.2.2.4 Principle #4: Value-Based Prioritization

This principle indicates that the team should focus on delivering the highest possible business value throughout the project lifecycle.

As shown in Figure 3.7, the Product Owner interprets the stakeholders' needs while prioritizing the user stories in the PPBacklog. Prioritization is based on the risks associated with each user story, its value and impact, and its dependencies.

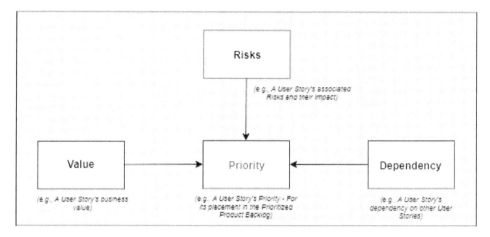

FIGURE 3.7 Value-based prioritization of user stories in Scrum

3.2.2.5 Principle #5: Time-Boxing

This principle indicates the time constraints in Scrum and how they can be used to manage the project planning and execution. As shown in Figure 3.8, the time boxes in Scrum are as follows:

- *Sprint*: A Sprint lasts 1–6 weeks.
- *Daily standup meetings*: A daily standup meeting lasts 15 minutes.
- *Sprint Planning meetings*: A Sprint Planning meeting lasts 8 hours
- *Sprint Review meetings*: A Sprint Review meeting lasts 4 hours.
- *Sprint Retrospective meetings*: A Sprint Retrospective meeting lasts 4 hours.

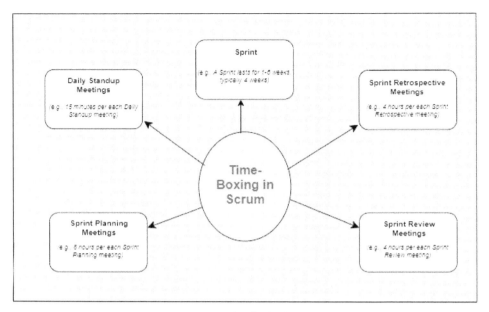

FIGURE 3.8 Time-boxing in Scrum

3.2.2.6 Principle #6: Iterative Development

This principle describes the iterative development in Scrum and shows how to manage changes and build products.

3.2.3 Scrum Aspects Area

This section presents the five aspects of Scrum (Sections 3.2.3.1 to 3.2.3.5).

3.2.3.1 Aspect #1: Organization

Sub-tables 3.1.1 to 3.1.19 present the various roles in Scrum projects (Product Owner, Scrum Master, and Scrum Team) and their responsibilities across the Scrum processes.

TABLE 3.1 Core roles and their responsibilities across the processes

Sub-Table 3.1.1: [SP1] Create Project Vision	
Product Owner	The Product Owner defines the project vision and facilitates the creation of the project charter and budget.
Scrum Master	-
Scrum Team	-
Sub-Table 3.1.2: [SP2] Identify Scrum Master and Stakeholders	
Product Owner	The Product Owner helps select a Scrum Master and identify the stakeholders.
Scrum Master	The Scrum Master helps the Product Owner identify the stakeholders.
Scrum Team	-
Sub-Table 3.1.3: [SP3] Form Scrum Team	
Product Owner	The Product Owner selects the Scrum Team and develops the collaboration and team-building plan jointly with the Scrum Master.
Scrum Master	The Scrum Master facilitates the selection of the Scrum Team and creates team collaboration, plans for building, etc.
Scrum Team	The Scrum Team helps create the collaboration and team-building plans.
Sub-Table 3.1.4: [SP4] Develop Epics	
Product Owner	The Product Owner creates a set of epics that can be used to develop and promote the targeted product.
Scrum Master	The Scrum Master helps the Product Owner create the project epics.
Scrum Team	The Scrum Team must clearly understand epics.
Sub-Table 3.1.5: [SP5] Create the Prioritized Product Backlog	
Product Owner	The Product Owner prioritizes the user stories in the PPBacklog.
Scrum Master	The Scrum Master helps the Product Owner create the PPBacklog, define the deliverables and acceptance criteria, etc.
Scrum Team	The Scrum Team must clearly understand the user stories in the PPBacklog.
Sub-Table 3.1.6: [SP6] Conduct Release Planning	
Product Owner	The Product Owner creates the release planning schedule to help determine the Sprint's time-boxing.
Scrum Master	The Scrum Master coordinates the creation of the release planning schedule and determines the Sprint's time-boxing.
Scrum Team	The Scrum Team considers and agrees on the Sprint's time-boxing as proposed by the Scrum Master.
Sub-Table 3.1.7: [SP7] Create User Stories	
Product Owner	The Product Owner helps create the user stories and define their acceptance criteria.
Scrum Master	The Scrum Master helps the Product Owner create and implement the user stories.
Scrum Team	The Scrum Team helps the Product Owner create the user stories.

(*Continued*)

Sub-Table 3.1.8: [SP8] Approve, Estimate, and Commit User Stories	
Product Owner	The Product Owner approves the user stories and encourages the Scrum Team to commit to these user stories.
Scrum Master	The Scrum Master facilitates the Scrum Team meetings to estimate and plan for implementing user stories.
Scrum Team	The Scrum Team estimates the effort and time required for each task.
Sub-Table 3.1.9: [SP9] Create Tasks	
Product Owner	The Product Owner explains the user stories to the Scrum Team and then lets the team decide on the tasks and activities needed to complete each user story.
Scrum Master	The Scrum Master helps the Scrum Team identify and create the task list for the current Sprint.
Scrum Team	The Scrum Team decides on and develops the task list for each user story.
Sub-Table 3.1.10: [SP10] Estimate Tasks	
Product Owner	The Product Owner guides the Scrum Team and helps them estimate and decide on the efforts required to complete the tasks and activities needed to complete each user story.
Scrum Master	The Scrum Master helps the team estimate the needed effort to complete the current Sprint.
Scrum Team	The Scrum Team estimates the effort and time for each task.
Sub-Table 3.1.11: [SP11] Create Sprint Backlog	
Product Owner	The Product Owner clarifies the user stories to the Scrum Team.
Scrum Master	The Scrum Master helps the Scrum Team select the correct user stories from the PPBacklog to include in the backlog of the current Sprint.
Scrum Team	The Scrum Team selects user stories from the PPBacklog and puts them into the incoming Sprint backlog.
Sub-Table 3.1.12: [SP12] Create Deliverables	
Product Owner	The Product Owner clarifies business requirements for the Scrum Team and provides them with a list of the required deliverables for each Sprint.
Scrum Master	The Scrum Master helps the Scrum Team create the current Sprint's deliverables and update the Scrum board and the "impediment log" file.
Scrum Team	The Scrum Team creates the deliverables, identifies risks, implements necessary mitigation plans, and updates the "impediment log" file.
Sub-Table 3.1.13: [SP13] Conduct Daily Standup	
Product Owner	-
Scrum Master	The Scrum Master updates the Scrum board and the "impediment log" files.
Scrum Team	The Scrum Team updates the burndown chart, Scrum board, and "impediment log" file, discusses any issues the participating team members raised, identifies risks, and submits change requests whenever necessary.
Sub-Table 3.1.14: [SP14] Groom Prioritized Product Backlog	
Product Owner	The Product Owner grooms the PPBacklog according to the feedback and recommendations made during the Retrospective meetings at the end of each Sprint.
Scrum Master	The Scrum Master facilitates the Sprints' Review and Retrospective meetings to update the Product Backlog.

(Continued)

Scrum Team	The Scrum Team participates in Sprint Review meetings to update the Product Backlog.
Sub-Table 3.1.15: [SP15] Convene Scrum of Scrums	
Product Owner	-
Scrum Master	The Scrum Master participates in the SoS meetings and discusses and resolves any issues affecting their team.
Scrum Team	The Scrum Team provides the Scrum Master with the necessary inputs on issues to be discussed and resolved at the SoS meetings.
Sub-Table 3.1.16: [SP16] Demonstrate and Validate Sprint	
Product Owner	The Product Owner accepts or rejects each Sprint's proposed deliverables, provides feedback to the Scrum Master and Scrum Team, and updates the release plan and the Product Backlog.
Scrum Master	The Scrum Master enables the Scrum Team to demonstrate the current Sprint's deliverables to the Product Owner for endorsement before shipping them to the customer.
Scrum Team	The Scrum Team demonstrates the completed deliverables to the Product Owner and seeks their approval.
Sub-Table 3.1.17: [SP17] Sprint Retrospect	
Product Owner	-
Scrum Master	The Scrum Master and Scrum Team improve the work environment of the incoming Sprints based on the lessons learned.
Scrum Team	The Scrum Team provides the Product Owner and Scrum Master with suggestions for improvements that benefit the incoming Sprints.
Sub-Table 3.1.18: [SP18] Ship Deliverables	
Product Owner	The Product Owner facilitates the deployment of the product releases in coordination with the customer.
Scrum Master	-
Scrum Team	The Scrum Team deploys the product releases.
Sub-Table 3.1.19: [SP19] Retrospect Project	
Product Owner	The Product Owner participates in all Retrospective meetings.
Scrum Master	The Scrum Master improves the work environment for future projects based on the lessons learned.
Scrum Team	The Scrum Team participates in the project Retrospective meeting.

3.2.3.2 Aspect #2: Business Justification

Scrum business justification involves justifying the endorsement of a Scrum project by answering questions such as *"Why is this project necessary?"*

The responsibilities of the various Scrum roles in this respect are as follows:

- *Portfolio Product Owner*: The portfolio Product Owner is responsible for justifying the projects in their portfolio and guiding and approving the justification of all projects in their respective programs.

- *Program Product Owner*: The program Product Owner is responsible for delivering value-creating business justifications for their program and guiding and approving business justifications for the projects under their program.

- *Scrum Master*: The Scrum Master is responsible for facilitating the creation of the project deliverables and managing risks and change requests.

- *Scrum Team*: The Scrum Team creates the project deliverables, demonstrates them to the Product Owner, and implements them at the customer's site.

- *Stakeholders*: The stakeholders (e.g., customers, users, and sponsors) are responsible as follows:

  - Sponsors are responsible for funding their Scrum projects and monitoring them to confirm that they realize their benefits.

  - Customers and users define the prioritized list of user stories in the PPBacklog.

The process for justifying a business need is based on many factors, such as the following:

- *Project reasoning*: The project must be justifiable and meaningful.

- *Business needs*: The needed business outcomes of the project must be based on its vision statement.

- *Project benefits*: The benefits must be achieved, such as achieving a measurable improvement in the product.

- *Risks*: Risks must be prepared for, such as any uncertainties or events that were not planned for.

- *Project timescales*: The project schedule must be well defined.

- *Project cost*: The cost of investment and development of a project must be well estimated.

The process for justifying a business need for a Scrum project goes through three steps:

1. Assessing and presenting the project's business case

2. Maintaining an ongoing justification of the project's value

3. Maintaining an ongoing confirmation of the project's benefits

3.2.3.3 Aspect #3: Quality Management

Quality management ensures that the deliverables of a Scrum project satisfy the project's predefined acceptance criteria and that the project's business value meets the customer's expectations.

The responsibilities of the Scrum roles in this respect are as follows:

- *Portfolio Product Owner*: The portfolio Product Owner sets the acceptance criteria and reviews the portfolio deliverables.
- *Portfolio Scrum Master*: The portfolio Scrum Master is responsible for ensuring that a sustainable focus is maintained on the quality of the overall portfolio features.
- *Program Product Owner*: The program Product Owner is responsible for setting the program's acceptance criteria and reviewing the program deliverables.
- *Program Scrum Master*: The program Scrum Master focuses on the quality of the program's overall features.
- *Product Owner*: The Product Owner is responsible for stating the business needs and requirements in the PPBacklog, ensuring that deliverables satisfy the quality requirements, setting the entire project acceptance criteria, facilitating the creation of the user story acceptance criteria, and reviewing and validating the deliverables.
- *Scrum Master*: The Scrum Master is responsible for estimating the obstacles that may impact the quality of the deliverables and processes, focusing on the overall quality of the project features, and ensuring that the Scrum Team follows the Scrum processes.
- *Scrum Team*: The Scrum Team is responsible for developing and maintaining all deliverables, encouraging effective communications, sharing knowledge, benefiting from others' experience, and making appropriate and smooth changes to the deliverables.

- *Scrum Guidance Body (SGB)*: The SGB provides a framework for developing the acceptance criteria.
- *Stakeholders*: The stakeholders review and accept the deliverables.

3.2.3.4 Aspect #4: Change Management

Change management ensures that change requests from the stakeholders are welcomed and endorsed. Figure 3.9 shows how change requests are received, approved, and implemented.

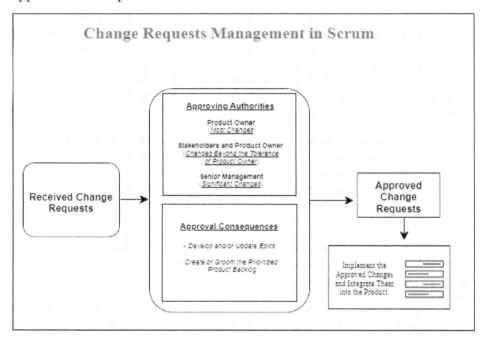

FIGURE 3.9 A sample Scrum change approval process

The responsibilities of the Scrum roles in this respect are as follows:

- *Portfolio Product Owner*: The portfolio Product Owner is responsible for providing the portfolio-level change requests and approving the amended, removed, and added products per the portfolio requirements.
- *Portfolio Scrum Master*: The portfolio Scrum Master facilitates identifying, assessing, and managing portfolio-level change requests.

- *Program Product Owner*: The program Product Owner is responsible for providing the program-level change requests and approving the amended, removed, and added products per the program requirements.
- *Program Scrum Master*: The program Scrum Master facilitates identifying, assessing, and managing program-level change requests.
- *Product Owner*: The Product Owner is responsible for providing project-level change requests, assessing the impact of the portfolio, program, and project change requests, and prioritizing the user stories in the PPBacklog.
- *Scrum Master*: The Scrum Master facilitates identifying, assessing, and escalating the team's change requests.
- *Scrum Team*: The Scrum Team suggests changes during the *Create deliverables* and *Conduct daily standup* processes.
- *Stakeholders*: The stakeholders are responsible for providing change requests and helping prioritize them.
- *SGB*: The SGB guides the change management procedures throughout the project lifecycle.

3.2.3.5 Aspect #5: Risk Management

A risk is an unexpected and uncertain event that can impact the project objectives. If its impact is negative, then that risk is a threat. If the effect is positive, then that risk is an opportunity:

- *Risk identification*: The Scrum Team identifies all risks impacting their project. Risk identification can be achieved in one or more of the following ways:
  - Through reviewing the lessons learned from the Sprint/project Retrospective meeting outcomes
  - From the risk checklists
  - From the risk prompt lists
  - From the brainstorming sessions
  - Through deriving a *risk breakdown structure* (*RBS*)
- *Risk assessment*: The Scrum Team assesses all potential risks impacting the project.
- *Risk prioritization*: Risks are considered while creating or updating the PPBacklog (e.g., during the *Create prioritized product backlog* or *Groom prioritized product backlog* processes).

- *Risk mitigation*: Scrum allows for early detection of failures. Thus, it has a natural mitigation feature built in. Risks can be mitigated by implementing several proactive and reactive responses. When a risk event occurs, a reactive response is formulated and used. Risks are accepted when their probabilities and impacts are too low.
- *Risk communication*: It is important to communicate information related to the risks to the stakeholders.
- *Risk minimization*: The Scrum framework minimizes risks using the Agile, iterative process.

The responsibilities of the Scrum roles in this respect are as follows:

- *Portfolio Product Owner*: The portfolio Product Owner is responsible for capturing and assessing the portfolio risks, prioritizing them, and communicating them to the stakeholders and the team.
- *Portfolio Scrum Master*: The portfolio Scrum Master is responsible for helping identify, assess, and communicate the portfolio risks.
- *Program Product Owner*: The program Product Owner is responsible for capturing and assessing the program risks, prioritizing them, and communicating them to the stakeholders and the team.
- *Program Scrum Master*: The program Scrum Master is responsible for helping identify, assess, and escalate the program risks.
- *Product Owner*: The Product Owner is responsible for capturing and assessing the project risks, prioritizing and communicating them to the stakeholders and the team, and ensuring the project risk levels are acceptable.
- *Scrum Master*: The Scrum Master is responsible for helping identify and escalate project risks to the team.
- *Scrum Team*: The Scrum Team identifies project risks during product development and implements management activities as the Product Owner advises.
- *Stakeholders*: The stakeholders are responsible for interacting with the team and providing input on project risk management.
- *SGB*: The SGB guides the risk management procedures.

3.2.4 Scrum Phases and Processes Area

This section presents the five phases in Scrum and their associated processes (Sections 3.2.4.1 to 3.2.4.5).

3.2.4.1 Scrum Initiate Phase and Its Processes

This section elaborates on the processes of the Scrum *initiate* phase, including their data flow and interactions.

As shown in Figure 3.10, the *initiate* phase incorporates the following six processes: *[SP1] Create Project Vision, [SP2] Identify Scrum Master and Stakeholders, [SP3] Form Scrum Team, [SP4] Develop Epics, [SP5] Create Prioritized Product Backlog,* and *[SP6] Conduct Release Planning.*

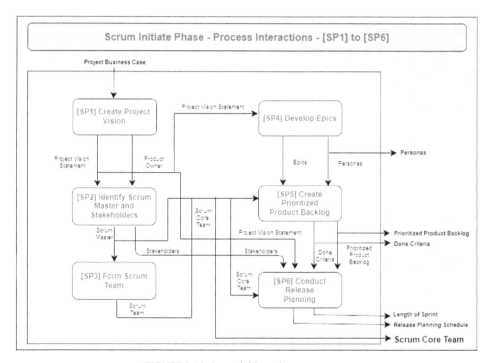

FIGURE 3.10 Scrum initiate phase—processes

Figure 3.11 presents the interactions among these processes. Please refer to Section 5.9 in the author's earlier textbook entitled *"Software Project Management: With PMI, IEEE-CS, and Agile-SCRUM"* [Ref#3] for details on these processes.

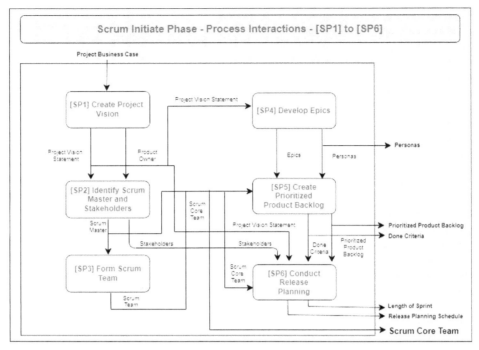

FIGURE 3.11 Scrum initiate phase—process interactions

3.2.4.2 Scrum Plan and Estimate Phase and Its Processes

This section elaborates on the processes of the Scrum *plan and estimate* phase. In addition, it elaborates on their data flow and interactions.

As shown in Figure 3.12, the *plan and estimate* phase incorporates the following five processes: *[SP7] Create User Stories*, *[SP8] Approve, Estimate, and Commit User Stories*, *[SP9] Create Tasks*, *[SP10] Estimate Tasks*, and *[SP11] Create Sprint Backlog*.

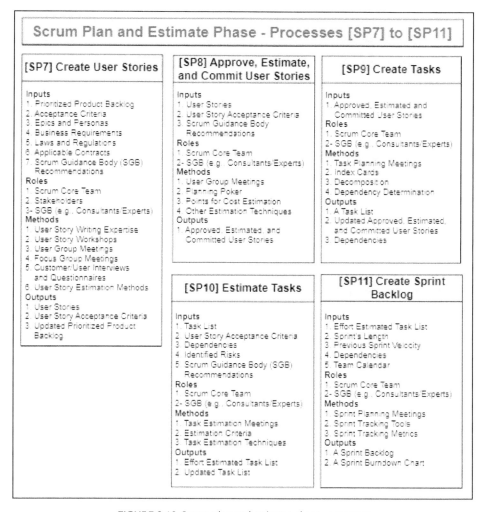

FIGURE 3.12 Scrum plan and estimate phase—processes

Figure 3.13 presents the interactions among these processes. For the details of these processes, please refer to Section 5.10 in the author's earlier textbook [Ref#3].

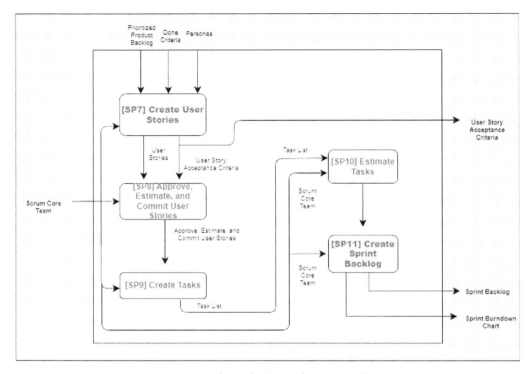

FIGURE 3.13 Scrum plan and estimate phase—process interactions

3.2.4.3 Scrum Implement Phase and Its Processes

This section elaborates on the processes of the Scrum *implement* phase, including their data flow and interactions.

As shown in Figure 3.14, the *implement* phase incorporates the following three processes: *[SP12] Create Deliverables*, *[SP13] Conduct Daily Standup Meetings*, and *[SP14] Groom Prioritized Product Backlog*.

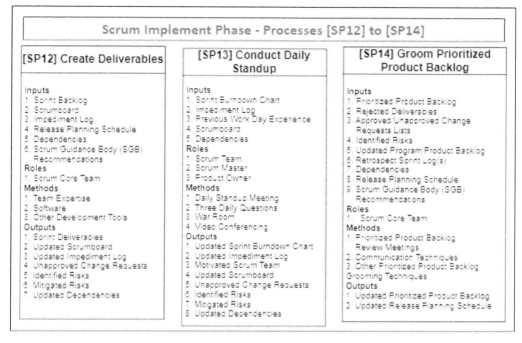

FIGURE 3.14 Scrum implement phase—processes

Figure 3.15 presents the interactions among these processes. For the details of these processes, please refer to Section 5.11 in the author's earlier textbook [Ref#3].

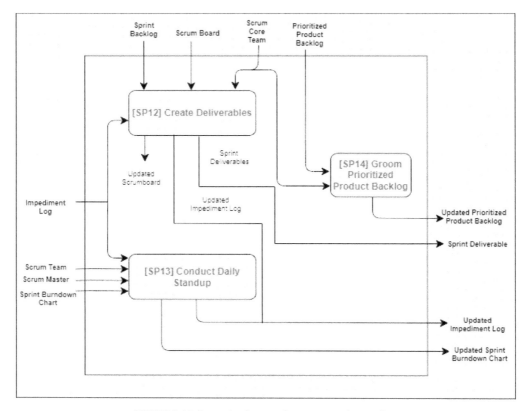

FIGURE 3.15 Scrum implement phase—process interactions

3.2.4.4 Scrum Review and Retrospect Phase and Its Processes

This section elaborates on the processes of the Scrum *review and retrospect* phase. In addition, it elaborates on their data flow and interactions.

As shown in Figure 3.16, the *review and retrospect* phase incorporates the following three processes: *[SP15] Convene Scrum of Scrums*, *[SP16] Demonstrate and Validate Sprint*, and *[SP18] Sprint Retrospect*.

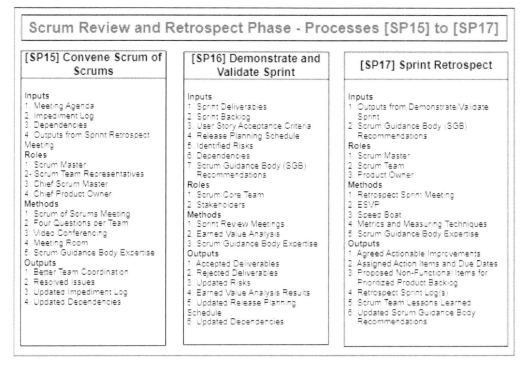

FIGURE 3.16 Scrum review and retrospect phase—processes

Figure 3.17 presents the interactions among these processes. For the details of these processes, please refer to Section 5.12 in the author's earlier textbook [Ref#3].

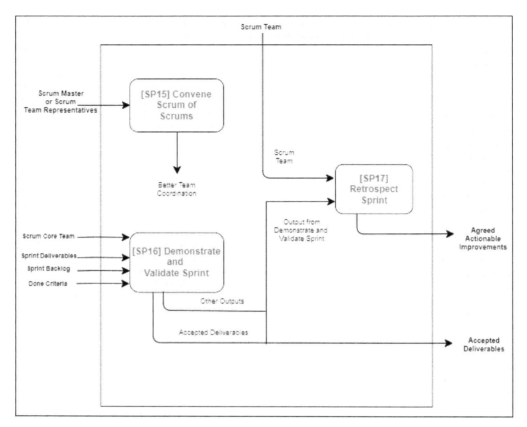

FIGURE 3.17 Scrum review and retrospect phase—process interactions

3.2.4.5 Scrum Release Phase and Its Processes

This section elaborates on the processes of the Scrum *release* phase, including their data flow and interactions.

As shown in Figure 3.18, the *release* phase incorporates the following two processes: *[SP17] Ship Deliverables* and *[SP19] Retrospect Project*.

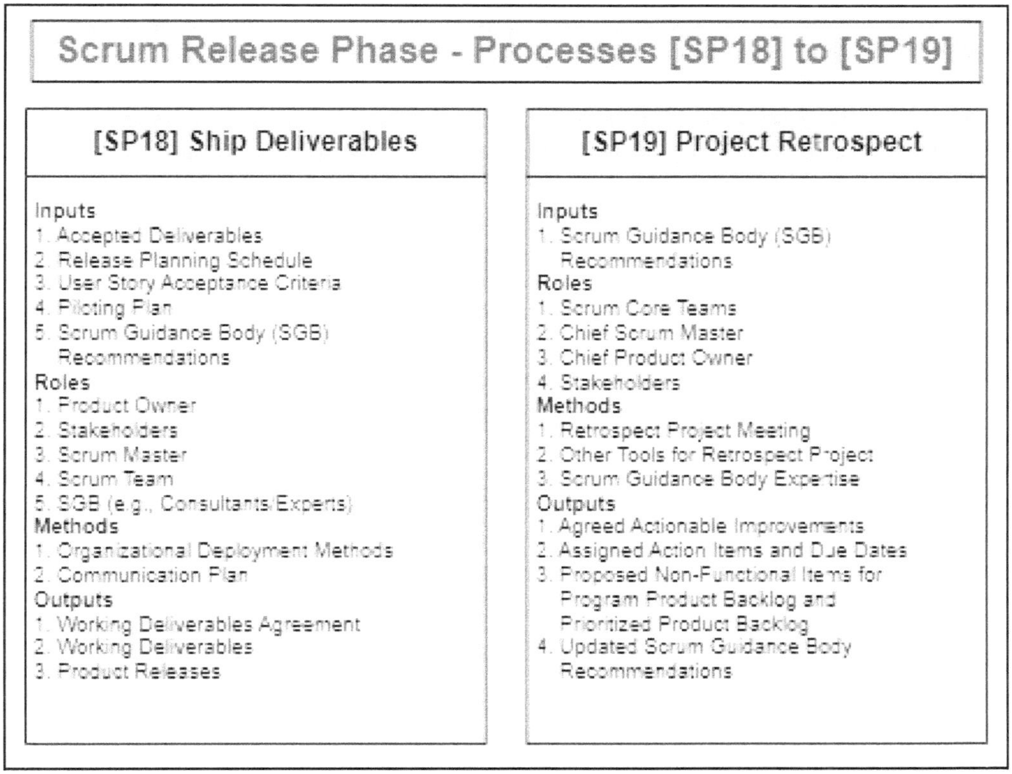

Scrum Release Phase - Processes [SP18] to [SP19]

[SP18] Ship Deliverables

Inputs
1. Accepted Deliverables
2. Release Planning Schedule
3. User Story Acceptance Criteria
4. Piloting Plan
5. Scrum Guidance Body (SGB)
   Recommendations
Roles
1. Product Owner
2. Stakeholders
3. Scrum Master
4. Scrum Team
5. SGB (e.g., Consultants/Experts)
Methods
1. Organizational Deployment Methods
2. Communication Plan
Outputs
1. Working Deliverables Agreement
2. Working Deliverables
3. Product Releases

[SP19] Project Retrospect

Inputs
1. Scrum Guidance Body (SGB)
   Recommendations
Roles
1. Scrum Core Teams
2. Chief Scrum Master
3. Chief Product Owner
4. Stakeholders
Methods
1. Retrospect Project Meeting
2. Other Tools for Retrospect Project
3. Scrum Guidance Body Expertise
Outputs
1. Agreed Actionable Improvements
2. Assigned Action Items and Due Dates
3. Proposed Non-Functional Items for
   Program Product Backlog and
   Prioritized Product Backlog
4. Updated Scrum Guidance Body
   Recommendations

FIGURE 3.18 Scrum release phase—processes

Figure 3.19 presents the interactions among these processes. For the details of these processes, please refer to Section 5.13 in the author's earlier textbook [Ref#3].

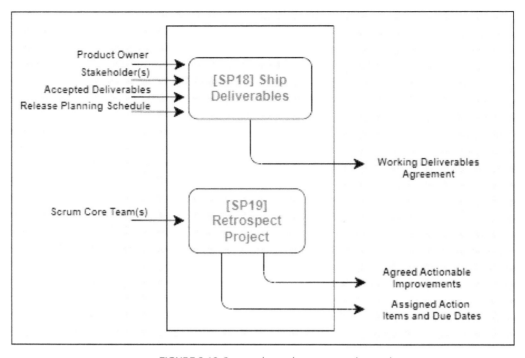

FIGURE 3.19 Scrum release phase—process interactions

3.3   A PROPOSED SCRUM PROCESS-INTERACTION MODEL

The self-explanatory Figure 3.20 illustrates the overall interactions of the Scrum processes in terms of setting up the project stage, the lifecycle of a Sprint, and the overall project lifecycle.

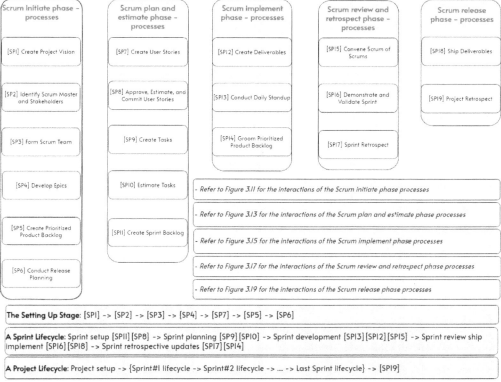

FIGURE 3.20 Scrum processes—overall interactions

3.3.1 The Setting Up Stage

Figure 3.20 shows the setting up stage for a Scrum project. The setting up stage starts by holding a stakeholders meeting that will then be followed by carrying on the following processes (i.e., *[SP1]* → *[SP2]* → *[SP3]* → *[SP4]* → *[SP7]* → *[SP5]* → *[SP6]*) in sequence:

- *[SP1] Create Project Vision*: This process produces the project vision statement and is carried out once during the project lifecycle.

- *[SP2] Identify Scrum Master and Stakeholders*: This process identifies a Scrum Master and a set of project stakeholders and is carried out once during the project lifecycle.

- *[SP3] Form Scrum Team*: This process leads to forming a Scrum Team for the project and is carried out once during the project lifecycle.

- *[SP4] Develop Epics*: This process produces a set of epics that will then be used to generate a set of user stories for the project and is carried out once during the project lifecycle.

- *[SP5] Create User Stories*: This process produces a set of user stories based on the stakeholders' needs and the epics of the preceding process and is carried out once during the project lifecycle.

- *[SP6] Create Prioritized Product Backlog*: This process prioritizes the user stories of the preceding process and includes them in a PPBacklog. It is carried out once during the project lifecycle.

- *[SP7] Conduct Release Planning*: This process derives a release schedule that preliminarily determines when to release product increments (*e.g., deliverables*) throughout the project lifecycle. It is carried out once during the project lifecycle.

3.3.2 Sprint Lifecycle

Figure 3.20 shows the sequence of processes during the lifecycle of a Sprint. It starts with holding a Sprint Planning meeting for the current Sprint, and is followed by carrying on the following processes in sequence:

1. The current Sprint backlog setup cycle (i.e., associated with the current Sprint Planning meeting):

    - *[SP11] Create Sprint Backlog*: This process creates a backlog for the current Sprint from the highest prioritized user stories in the PPBacklog. It is carried out once per Sprint.

    - *[SP8] Approve/Estimate/Commit User Stories*: This process enables the Scrum Team to approve, estimate, and commit to the user stories in the current Sprint backlog once per Sprint.

2. The current Sprint Planning and estimation cycle (i.e., part of the current Sprint Planning meeting):

    - *[SP9] Create Tasks*: This process creates a work breakdown structure for the current Sprint by creating tasks for the user stories in the current Sprint backlog. It is carried out once per Sprint.

    - *[SP10] Estimate Tasks*: This process estimates a schedule for the current Sprint's work breakdown structure (as generated by *[SP9]*). It also allocates resources for these tasks. This process is carried out once per Sprint.

3. The current Sprint development cycle:

  - *[SP13] Conduct Daily Standup*: Throughout the Sprint's development cycle, a *daily standup meeting (DSUM)* is held every working day to discuss the Sprint's development progress while creating its planned deliverables (*e.g., 1 DSUM per day * 5 days per week * 6 weeks per Sprint = 30 DSUM per Sprint*).

  - *[SP12] Create Deliverables*: This process creates the Sprint's "planned-for" deliverables. It is carried out once per deliverable.

  - *[SP15] Convene Scrum of Scrums*: This process is used when the project is too large to be broken into multiple Scrums. It is carried out as needed.

4. The current Sprint deliverables review, ship, and implement cycle (associated with the current Sprint review meeting):

  - *[SP16] Demonstrate and Validate Sprint*: This process presents and demonstrates the current Sprint deliverables to the Product Owner, Scrum Master, and stakeholders to seek their approval before they are shipped to the customer and implemented for use. It is carried out at least once per Sprint.

  - *[SP18] Ship Deliverables*: This process ships the current Sprint-approved deliverables to the customer and implements them once per Sprint.

5. The current Sprint retrospect and updates (associated with the current Sprint Retrospective meeting):

  - *[SP17] Sprint Retrospect*: This process retrospects the current Sprint after its approved deliverables are shipped to the customer and implemented for their use. Assessing the lessons learned throughout the current Sprint's lifecycle may result in some updates on the PPBacklog, such as revising some of its user stories, reprioritizing them, and so on. It is carried out once per Sprint.

  - *[SP14] Groom Prioritized Product Backlog*: This process is used when the PPBacklog needs to be updated based on the outcomes of process *[SP17]*. It is carried out, at most, once per Sprint.

3.3.3 Scrum Project Lifecycle

Figure 3.20 shows the sequence of processes/activities during a project lifecycle. A project lifecycle starts with setting up the project, then moves on to the sequence of sprint lifecycles, and then to the project Retrospective closure stage (i.e., holding the project Retrospective meeting at the end of the project). This involves continuing the project Retrospective process (*[SP19]*).

3.4 A PROPOSED SCRUM PROCESSES/MEETINGS MODEL

The self-explanatory Figure 3.21 overviews the structure of the Scrum meetings:

1. The *initiate* phase is tied to the stakeholders meeting.

2. The *plan and estimate* phase is tied to the Sprint Planning meetings.

3. The *implement* phase is tied to the DSUMs.

4. The *review and retrospect* phase is tied to the Sprint Review and Retrospective meetings.

5. The *release* phase is tied to the project Retrospective meeting.

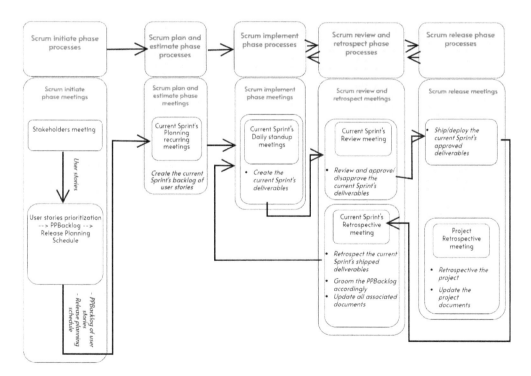

FIGURE 3.21 A proposed model for the Scrum processes and meetings

3.5 A PROPOSED SCRUM PLANNING MODEL

Tables 3.2 and 3.3 provide self-explanatory and simplified tabular identifications of the user stories and their driven requirements. This includes identifying the requirements, their dependencies, their associated risks and risk impacts, their added values to the overall software product, and their priorities (e.g., *prioritization*). The following symbols are used to compose these identifications:

- $R_{I,J}$ represents the Jth requirement of the Ith user story.
- $R_{I,J}.DP$ represents the dependencies of the Jth requirement of the Ith user story on other requirements.
- $R_{I,J}.RSK$ represents the risks associated with the Jth requirement of the Ith user story.
- $R_{I,J}.RSK.IMP$ represents the impacts of the risks associated with the Jth requirement of the Ith user story.
- $R_{I,J}.VAL$ represents the value added to the outcome software product by the Jth requirement of the Ith user story.
- $R_{I,J}.PRT$ represents the priority assigned to the Jth requirement of the Ith user story in the outcome software product.

   This prioritization is calculated using this formula: $R_{I,J}.PRT = (1 - R_{I,J}.RSK.IMP) * R_{I,J}.VAL$, given that all requirements in the $R_{I,J}.DP$ set precede the $R_{I,J}$.

Table 3.4 provides a mathematical representation of the PPBacklog of the user stories and their driven requirements as follows:

- $[US_1, US_2, …, US_U]$ represents the list of all user stories defined by the Product Owner after they meet with the project stakeholders. U represents the count of these user stories.
- $R_{I,J}$ represents the Jth requirement of the Ith user story.
- $US_I.PRT = R_{I,1}.PRT * R_{I,2}.PRT * … * R_{I,R\#}.PRT$ represents the prioritization of the Ith user story in terms of the product and the prioritization of its requirements. R# represents the number of requirements in the Ith user story.
- PPBacklog = SORTONPRTD $[(US_1, US_1.PRT), (US_2, US_2.PRT), …, (US_{U\#}, US_U.PRT)] = [SUS_1, SUS_2, …, SUS_{U\#}]$ represents the user stories' order after they were descendingly sorted based on their precalculated priorities using the SORTONPRTD sorting function. SUS_1 represents the

ith user story in the descendingly sorted list of user stories, while U# represents the number of these user stories.

Table 3.5 provides a mathematical representation of the PPBacklog of user stories and their driven requirements and deliverables as follows:

- ▩ S$_I$.Backlog represents the backlog of the Ith Sprint.
- ▩ S$_I$.Backlog.DLVS represents the Ith Sprint backlog deliverables.
- ▩ PPBacklog Deliverables $= \sum_{n=1}^{S} \left(S_n.\text{Backlog.DLVS} \right)$ represents the sum of all Sprints' backlog deliverables.

TABLE 3.2 Representations of the user stories/requirements in the proposed Scrum Planning model

	Requirement ID	Requirements of user story #1 (L requirements)
User story #1 (US$_1$)	R$_{1.1}$	Requirement #1 of user story #1
	R$_{1.2}$	Requirement #2 of user story #1
	...	...
	R$_{1.L}$	Requirement #L of user story #1
User story #2 (US$_2$)	**Requirement ID**	**Requirements of user story #2 (M requirements)**
	R$_{2.1}$	Requirement #1 of user story #2
	R$_{2.2}$	Requirement #2 of user story #2
	...	...
	R$_{2.M}$	Requirement #M of user story #2
	---------	---------
User story #U (US$_U$)	**Requirement ID**	**Requirements of user story #U (O requirements)**
	R$_{U.1}$	Requirement #1 of user story #U
	R$_{U.2}$	Requirement #2 of user story #U
	...	...
	R$_{U.O}$	Requirement #O of user story #U

TABLE 3.3 Representations of the derived requirements in the proposed Scrum Planning model

US.ID	R.ID	Dependency	Risks	Risks impact	Requirement value	Estimated priority
US$_1$	R$_{1.1}$	R$_{1.1}$.DP	R$_{1.1}$.RSK	R$_{1.1}$.RSK.IMP	R$_{1.1}$.VAL	R$_{1.1}$.PRT = (1 - R$_{1.1}$.RSK.IMP) * R$_{1.1}$.VAL MUST be preceded by all requirements in the R$_{1.1}$.DP set.
	R$_{1.2}$	R$_{1.2}$.DP	R$_{1.2}$.RSK	R$_{1.2}$.RSK.IMP	R$_{1.2}$.VAL	R$_{1.2}$.PRT = (1 - R$_{1.2}$.RSK.IMP) * R$_{1.2}$.VAL MUST be preceded by all requirements in the SPFR$_{1.2}$.DP set.
	…….	…….	…….	…….	…….	…….
	R$_{1.L}$	R$_{1.L}$.DP	R$_{1.L}$.RSK	R$_{1.L}$.RSK.IMP	R$_{1.L}$.VAL	R$_{1.L}$.PRT = (1 - R$_{1.L}$.RSK.IMP) * R$_{1.L}$.VAL MUST be preceded by all requirements in the R$_{1.L}$.DP set.
US$_2$	R$_{2.1}$	R$_{2.1}$.DP	R$_{2.1}$.RSK	R$_{2.1}$.RSK.IMP	R$_{2.1}$.VAL	R$_{2.1}$.PRT = (1 – R$_{2.1}$.RSK.IMP) * R$_{2.1}$.VAL MUST be preceded by all requirements in the R$_{2.1}$.DP set.
	R$_{2.2}$	R$_{2.2}$.DP	R$_{2.2}$.RSK	R$_{2.2}$.RSK.IMP	R$_{2.2}$.VAL	R$_{2.2}$.PRT = (1 - R$_{2.2}$.RSK.IMP) * R$_{2.2}$.VAL MUST be preceded by all requirements in the R$_{2.2}$.DP set.
	…….	…….	…….	…….	…….	…….
	R$_{2.M}$	R$_{2.M}$.DP	R$_{2.M}$.RSK	R$_{2.M}$.RSK.IMP	R$_{2.M}$.VAL	R$_{2.M}$.PRT = (1 - R$_{2.M}$.RSK.IMP) * R$_{2.M}$.VAL All requirements in the R2.M.DP set MUST precede it.
--------	------	---------	---------	---------	---------	---------

(Continued)

US.ID	R.ID	Dependency	Risks	Risks impact	Requirement value	Estimated priority
US_U	$R_{U.1}$	$R_{U.1}.DP$	$R_{U.1}.RSK$	$R_{U.1}.RSK.IMP$	$R_{U.1}.VAL$	$R_{U.1}.PRT = (1 - R_{U.1}.RSK.IMP) * R_{U.1}.VAL$ MUST be preceded by all requirements in the $R_{U.1}.DP$ set.
	$R_{U.2}$	$R_{U.2}.DP$	$R_{U.2}.RSK$	$R_{U.2}.RSK.IMP$	$R_{U.2}.VAL$	$R_{U.2}.PRT = (1 - R_{U.2}.RSK.IMP) * R_{U.2}.VAL$ MUST be preceded by all requirements in the $R_{U.2}.DP$ set.
	....	....	....	....	....	....
	$R_{U.O}$	$R_{U.O}.DP$	$R_{U.O}.RSK$	$R_{U.O}.RSK.IMP$	$R_{U.O}.VAL$	$R_{U.O}.PRT = (1 - R_{U.O}.RSK.IMP) * R_{U.O}.VAL$ MUST be preceded by all requirements in the $R_{U.O}.DP$ set.
Legend						

- US_i: The ith user story.
- $R_{i,j}$: The jth requirement of the ith user story.
- $R_{i,j}.DP$: The set of other requirements that must precede the jth requirement of the ith user story.
- $R_{i,j}.RSK$: The risks associated with the jth requirement of the ith user story.

- $R_{i,j}.RSK.IMP$: The associated set of risks impacts the jth requirement of the ith user story overall.
- $R_{i,j}.VAL$: The value (importance) of the jth requirement of the ith user story.
- $R_{i,j}.PRT$: The estimated priority of the jth requirement of the ith user story.

TABLE 3.4 Representation of the PPBacklog in the proposed Scrum Planning model

User stories	USs = $[US_1, US_2, ..., US_U]$
Requirements	Requirements in $US_1 = [R_{1.1}, R_{1.2}, ..., R_{1.L}]$ Requirements in $US_2 = [R_{2.1}, R_{2.2}, ..., R_{2.M}]$ ... Requirements in $US_U = [R_{U.1}, R_{U.2}, ..., R_{U.O}]$
User story priorities	$R_{1.1}.PRT = (1 - R_{1.1}.RSK.IMP) * R_{1.1}.VAL$ -- MUST be preceded by all requirements in the $R_{1.1}.DP$ set, $R_{1.2}.PRT = (1 - R_{1.2}.RSK.IMP) * R_{1.2}.VAL$ -- MUST be preceded by all requirements in the $SPFR_{1.2}.DP$ set, ... $R_{1.L}.PRT = (1 - R_{1.L}.RSK.IMP) * R_{1.L}.VAL$ -- MUST be preceded by all requirements in the $R_{1.L}.DP$ set] ➔ $US_1.PRT = R_{1.1}.PRT * R_{1.2}.PRT * ... * R_{1.L}.PRT$
	$[[R_{2.1}.PRT = (1 - R_{2.1}.RSK.IMP) * R_{2.1}.VAL$ -- MUST be preceded by all requirements in the $R_{2.1}.DP$ set, $R_{2.2}.PRT = (1 - R_{2.2}.RSK.IMP) * R_{2.2}.VAL$ -- MUST be preceded by all requirements in the $SPFR_{2.2}.DP$ set, ... $R_{2.M}.PRT = (1 - R_{2.M}.RSK.IMP) * R_{2.M}.VAL$ ⬅➔ MUST be preceded by all requirements in the $R_{2.1}.DP$ set] ➔ $US_2.PRT = R_{2.1}.PRT * R_{2.2}.PRT * ... * R_{2.M}.PRT$
	....
	$[R_{U.1}.PRT = (1 - R_{U.1}.RSK.IMP) * R_{U.1}.VAL$ -- MUST be preceded by all requirements in the $R_{U.1}.DP$ set, $R_{U.2}.PRT = (1 - R_{U.2}.RSK.IMP) * R_{U.2}.VAL$ -- MUST be preceded by all requirements in the $R_{U.2}.DP$ set, ... $R_{U.O}.PRT = (1 - R_{U.O}.RSK.IMP) * R_{U.O}.VAL$ -- MUST be preceded by all requirements in the $R_{U.O}.DP$ set] ➔ $US_U.PRT = R_{U.1}.PRT * R_{U.2}.PRT * ... * R_{U.O}.PRT$
PPBacklog	PPBacklog = SORTONPRTD $[(US_1, US_1.PRT), (US_2, US_2.PRT), ..., (US_U, US_U.PRT)]$

Legend	
- US_i: The ith user story. - R_{i-j}: The jth requirement of the ith user story. - $R_{i-j}.DP$: The set of other requirements that must precede the jth requirement of the ith user story. - $R_{i-j}.RSK$: The set of risks associated with the jth requirement of the ith user story.	- $R_{i-j}.RSK.IMP$: The associated set of risks overall impacts the jth requirement of the ith user story. - $R_{i-j}.VAL$: The value (importance) of the jth requirement of the ith user story. - $R_{i-j}.PRT$: The estimated priority of the jth requirement of the ith user story. - SORTONPRT: Sorts the user stories based on their priorities in descendingly order.

TABLE 3.5 Representation of the deliverables release schedule in the proposed Scrum Planning model

User stories	USs = [US$_1$, US$_2$, ..., US$_U$]	
Requirements	Requirements in US$_1$ = [R$_{1.1}$, R$_{1.2}$, ..., R$_{1.L}$]	Requirements in US$_2$ = [R$_{2.1}$, R$_{2.2}$, ..., R$_{2.M}$]
	...	Requirements in US$_U$ = [R$_{U.1}$, R$_{U.2}$, ..., R$_{U.O}$]
User story prioritization → **PPBacklog of user stories**	[R$_{1.1}$.PRT = (1 - R$_{1.1}$.RSK.IMP) * R$_{1.1}$.VAL ←→ MUST be preceded by all requirements in the R$_{1.1}$.DP set, R$_{1.2}$.PRT = (1 - R$_{1.2}$.RSK.IMP) * R$_{1.2}$.VAL ←→ MUST be preceded by all requirements in the SPFR$_{1.2}$.DP set, ... R$_{1.L}$.PRT = (1 - R$_{1.L}$.RSK.IMP) * R$_{1.L}$.VAL ←→ MUST be preceded by all requirements in the R$_{1.L}$.DP set] → US$_1$.PRT = R$_{1.1}$.PRT * R$_{1.2}$.PRT * ... * R$_{1.L}$.PRT	
	[R$_{2.1}$.PRT = (1 - R$_{2.1}$.RSK.IMP) * R$_{2.1}$.VAL ←→ MUST be preceded by all requirements in the R$_{2.1}$.DP set, R$_{2.2}$.PRT = (1 - R$_{2.2}$.RSK.IMP) * R$_{2.2}$.VAL ←→ MUST be preceded by all requirements in the SPFR$_{2.2}$.DP set, ... R$_{2.M}$.PRT = (1 - R$_{2.M}$.RSK.IMP) * R$_{2.M}$.VAL ←→ MUST be preceded by all requirements in the R$_{2.1}$.DP set] → US$_2$.PRT = R$_{2.1}$.PRT * R$_{2.2}$.PRT * ... * R$_{2.M}$.PRT	
	....	
	[R$_{U.1}$.PRT = (1 - R$_{U.1}$.RSK.IMP) * R$_{U.1}$.VAL ←→ MUST be preceded by all requirements in the R$_{U.1}$.DP set, R$_{U.2}$.PRT = (1 - R$_{U.2}$.RSK.IMP) * R$_{U.2}$.VAL ←→ MUST be preceded by all requirements in the R$_{U.2}$.DP set, ... R$_{U.O}$.PRT = (1 - R$_{U.O}$.RSK.IMP) * R$_{U.O}$.VAL ←→ MUST be preceded by all requirements in the R$_{U.O}$.DP set] → US$_U$.PRT = R$_{U.1}$.PRT * R$_{U.2}$.PRT * ... * R$_{U.O}$.PRT	
	PPBacklog = SORTONPRTD [(US$_1$, US$_1$.PRT), (US$_2$, US$_2$.PRT), ..., (US$_U$, US$_U$.PRT)] PPBacklog = [SUS$_1$, SUS$_2$, ..., SUS$_U$] ←→ Descendingly sorted user stories list.	
S-Backlogs	Sprint time-boxing = X	User story time-boxing = Y	#User stories per Sprint = Z = ROUNDDOWN (X / Y)
	#Sprints = #User stories divided by #User stories per Sprint = S = ROUNDUP (U / Z)		
	S$_1$.Backlog: Sprint#1 backlog of descendingly sorted user stories = [SUS$_1$, SUS$_2$, ..., SUS$_Z$] S$_2$.Backlog: Sprint#2 backlog of descendingly sorted user stories = [SUS$_{Z+1}$, SUS$_{Z+2}$, ..., SUS$_{2*Z}$] S$_3$.Backlog: Sprint#3 backlog of descendingly sorted user stories = [SUS$_{2*Z+1}$, SUS$_{2*Z+2}$, ..., SUS$_{3*Z}$] .... S$_S$.Backlog: Sprint#S backlog of descendingly sorted user stories = [SUS$_{(S-1)*Z+1}$, SUS$_{(S-1)*Z+2}$, ..., SUS$_{(S-1)*Z}$]		

(Continued)

PPBacklog deliverables	S_1.Backlog.DLVS: Sprint#1 deliverables = [SUS_1.DLVS, SUS_2.DLVS …, SUS_Z.DLVS] S_2.Backlog.DLVS: Sprint#2 deliverables = [SUS_{Z+1}.DLVS, SUS_{Z+2}.DLVS, …, $SUS_{2}*_Z$.DLVS] S_3.Backlog.DLVS: Sprint#3 deliverables = [SUS_2*_{Z+1}.DLVS, SUS_2*_{Z+2}.DLVS, …, SUS_3*_Z.DLVS] ……… S_S.Backlog.DLVS: Sprint#S deliverables = [$SUS_{(S-1)}*_{Z+1}$.DLVS, $SUS_{(S-1)}*_{Z+2}$.DLVS, …., $SUS_{(S-1)}*_Z$.DLVS] PPBacklog Deliverables = S_1.Backlog.DLVS + S_2.Backlog.DLVS + … + S_S.Backlog.DLVS PPBacklog Deliverables =

3.6 A SYMBOLIC SCRUM PLANNING CASE STUDY

This section illustrates the various aspects of the symbolic Scrum Planning case study, including the given artifacts, the iterative and incremental implementation of Sprints, and the calculations.

3.6.1 The Given Artifacts—Scrum Planning Symbolic Case Study

The intuitive details of the project for which we need to produce a plan are presented in Table 3.6.

TABLE 3.6 The given artifacts—Scrum Planning symbolic case study

Start date	February 1, 2025
PPBacklog	The PPBacklog contains 16 user stories (US_1 - US_{16}).
Time-boxing	- A user story can be given 1 week or less to complete all associated tasks. - A Sprint can be given up to 4 weeks to complete all tasks associated with its batch of prioritized user stories. - A Sprint Planning meeting lasts for up to 8 hours. - A Sprint Review meeting lasts for up to 4 hours. - A Sprint Retrospective meeting lasts for up to 4 hours. - A stakeholders meeting lasts as long as the Product Owner needs to identify their requirements as a list of user stories before they can prioritize them and create and populate a PPBacklog.
Prioritization of user stories	- Top-prioritized user stories: US1–US4. - 2nd batch of prioritized user stories: US5–US8. - 3rd batch of prioritized user stories: US9–US12. - 4th batch of prioritized user stories: US13–US16.
Staff	- 1 Product Owner (PO). - 1 Scrum Master (SM). - 5 Scrum Team Members (STM1 to STM5). For simplicity, all members have similar qualifications (e.g., experience, education, salaries, etc.).

(Continued)

Financials	- The monthly salary of the Product Owner is $5,000.00. - The monthly salary of the Scrum Master is $4,000.00. - The monthly salary of each team member (STM1–STM5) is $3,000.00. - Overhead (e.g., hardware, software licenses, etc.) will be approximately $30,000.00.
Acronyms	- *PPBacklog*: The PPBacklog of the entire collection of user stories, but prioritized by the predetermined user stories prioritization method. - *S-Backlog*: The current Sprint backlog contains prioritized user stories selected from the PPBacklog.

3.6.2 The Iterative and Incremental Implementation of Sprints

To simplify this case study, let's assume the following:

- Each Sprint incorporates four user stories.
- A Sprint is time-boxed for 4 weeks, and a user story takes one week to complete.
- Each user story has five tasks that should be carried out during the week of their user story.
- A task takes one business day to be carried out by any available member of the five Scrum Team members (STM_1 to STM_5).
- The final product comprises 30 deliverables (DLV_1 to DLV_{30}). These deliverables are the outcomes of the user stories and their tasks, as in the last column of the following table.

The following tables present a balanced core action plan for the project.

TABLE 3.7 Case study plan—Sprint#1 (user stories 1–4 / weeks 1–4)

S-Backlog	Tasks	Schedule	Resources	Deliverables
US_1	T_1	WK_1	STM_1	DLV_1
	T_2		STM_2	DLV_2
	T_3		STM_3	Interactive with T_1/T_2
	T_4		STM_4	DLV_3
	T_5		STM_5	Interactive with T_4
US_2	T_6	WK_2	STM_1	DLV_4
	T_7		STM_2	DLV_5
	T_8		STM_3	Interactive with T_6/T_7
	T_9		STM_4	DLV_6
	T_{10}		STM_5	Interactive with T_9

(Continued)

S-Backlog	Tasks	Schedule	Resources	Deliverables
US_3	T_{11}		STM_1	Interactive with T_{10}/T_{13}
	T_{12}		STM_2	DLV_7
	T_{13}	WK_3	STM_3	Interactive with T_{12}
	T_{14}		STM_4	DLV_8
	T_{15}		STM_5	Interactive with T_4
US_4	T_{16}		STM_1	Interactive with T_5/T_{17}
	T_{17}		STM_2	DLV_9
	T_{18}	WK_4	STM_3	Interactive with T_7
	T_{19}		STM_4	DLV_{10}
	T_{20}		STM_5	Interactive with T_9

TABLE 3.8 Case study plan—Sprint#2 (user stories 5–8 / weeks 5–8)

S-Backlog	Tasks	Schedule	Resources	Deliverables
US_5	T_{21}		STM_1	DLV_{11}
	T_{22}		STM_2	DLV_{12}
	T_{23}	WK_5	STM_3	Interactive with T_{21}/T_{22}
	T_{24}		STM_4	DLV_{13}
	T_{25}		STM_5	Interactive with T_{24}
US_6	T_{26}		STM_1	DLV_{14}
	T_{27}		STM_2	DLV_{15}
	T_{28}	WK_6	STM_3	Interactive with T_{26}/T_{27}
	T_{29}		STM_4	DLV_{16}
	T_{30}		STM_5	Interactive with T_{29}
US_7	T_{31}		STM_1	Interactive with T_{30}/T_{33}
	T_{32}		STM_2	DLV_{17}
	T_{33}	WK_7	STM_3	Interactive with T_{32}
	T_{34}		STM_4	DLV_{18}
	T_{35}		STM_5	Interactive with T_{34}
US_8	T_{36}		STM_1	Interactive with T_{35}/T_{37}
	T_{37}		STM_2	DLV_{19}
	T_{38}	WK_8	STM_3	Interactive with T_{37}
	T_{39}		STM_4	DLV_{20}
	T_{40}		STM_5	Interactive with T_{39}

TABLE 3.9 Case study plan—Sprint#3 (user stories 9–12 / weeks 9–12)

US_9	T_{41}	WK_9	STM_1	DLV_{21}
	T_{42}		STM_2	DLV_{22}
	T_{43}		STM_3	Interactive with T_{41}/T_{42}
	T_{44}		STM_4	DLV_{23}
	T_{45}		STM_5	Interactive with T_{44}
US_{10}	T_{46}	WK_{10}	STM_1	DLV_{24}
	T_{47}		STM_2	DLV_{25}
	T_{48}		STM_3	Interactive with T_{46}/T_{47}
	T_{49}		STM_4	DLV_{26}
	T_{50}		STM_5	Interactive with T_{49}
US_{11}	T_{51}	WK_{11}	STM_1	Interactive with T_{50}/T_{53}
	T_{52}		STM_2	DLV_{27}
	T_{53}		STM_3	Interactive with T_{52}
	T_{54}		STM_4	DLV_{28}
	T_{55}		STM_5	Interactive with T_{54}
US_{12}	T_{56}	WK_{12}	STM_1	Interactive with T_{55}/T_{57}
	T_{57}		STM_2	DLV_{29}
	T_{58}		STM_3	Interactive with T_{57}
	T_{59}		STM_4	DLV_{30}
	T_{60}		STM_5	Interactive with T_{59}

TABLE 3.10 Case study plan—Sprint#4 (user stories 13–16 / weeks 13–16)

US_{13}	T_{61}	WK_{13}	STM_1	DLV_{31}
	T_{62}		STM_2	DLV_{32}
	T_{63}		STM_3	Interactive with T_{61}/T_{62}
	T_{64}		STM_4	DLV_{33}
	T_{65}		STM_5	Interactive with T_{64}
US_{14}	T_{66}	WK_{14}	STM_1	DLV_{34}
	T_{67}		STM_2	DLV_{35}
	T_{68}		STM_3	Interactive with T_{66}/T_{67}
	T_{69}		STM_4	DLV_{36}
	T_{70}		STM_5	Interactive with T_{69}

(Continued)

US$_{15}$	T$_{71}$	WK$_{15}$	STM$_1$	Interactive with T$_{70}$/T$_{73}$
	T$_{72}$		STM$_2$	DLV$_{37}$
	T$_{73}$		STM$_3$	Interactive with T$_{72}$
	T$_{74}$		STM$_4$	DLV$_{38}$
	T$_{75}$		STM$_5$	Interactive with T$_{74}$
US$_{16}$	T$_{76}$	WK$_{16}$	STM$_1$	Interactive with T$_{55}$/T$_{57}$
	T$_{77}$		STM$_2$	DLV$_{29}$
	T$_{78}$		STM$_3$	Interactive with T$_{57}$
	T$_{79}$		STM$_4$	DLV$_{30}$
	T$_{80}$		STM$_5$	Interactive with T$_{59}$

3.6.3 Calculations—Scrum Planning Symbolic Case Study

Table 3.11 presents the various calculations for the case study.

TABLE 3.11 Calculations—Scrum Planning symbolic case study

Project Period	Initiation Period + Implementation Period + Project Retrospect Period
Initiation Period	?
Implementation Period	4 Sprints * 4 Weeks per Sprint
	16 Weeks
Project Retrospect Period	?
Project Base Cost	Overhead Cost + Product Owner Cost + Scrum Master Cost + Scrum Team Cost
	$30,000.00 + 4 * $5,000.00 + 4 * $4,000.00 + 5 * 4 * $3,000.00
	$126,000.00
Overall Cost	Base Cost + Risks Contingency Fund (3%)
	1.03 * Basic Cost
	$129,780.00
Price	Overall Cost + Profit (20%)
	1.2 * 129,780.00
	$155,736.00

3.7 SUMMARY

This chapter elaborated on the Scrum project management methodology, its model, and a symbolic case study as proposed by the author. The Scrum methodology (Chapter 3) and the IEEE-CS classification of software requirements (Chapter 2) form the foundation for the author's proposed RHSI methodology (Chapters 4–6).

This chapter made several contributions. Section 3.2 provided an overview of the Scrum methodology regarding the Scrum principles, aspects, and phases/processes. Section 3.3 presented the models for the interactions among the Scrum processes, the Scrum processes/meetings structure, and Scrum Planning, all as proposed by the author. Section 3.6 presented a symbolic Scrum case study to help understand Scrum Planning, as proposed by the author.

Understanding and modeling the IEEE-CS classification of software requirements and the Scrum Planning function helps readers understand the RHSI methodology, which will be proposed by the author in Chapter 4, modeled in Chapter 5, and demonstrated in a case study in Chapter 6.

4

RHSI—A New Hybrid Software Project Management Methodology

4.1 OVERVIEW

This section illustrates the purpose of this chapter, its contributions, and its organization.

4.1.1 The Purpose of This Chapter

This chapter presents the author's new hybrid software project management methodology, referred to throughout this book as RHSI (*i.e., Rationale Hybrid Scrum IEEE-CS*).

4.1.2 Acronyms

Table 4.1 presents the acronyms used throughout Chapters 4 to 6.

TABLE 4.1 Acronyms

Acronym	Description
RHSI	Rationale Hybrid Scrum IEEE-CS
IEEE	Institute of Electrical and Electronics Engineering
SPFUSs	Software product functional user stories
SPFRs	Software product functional requirements
SPNFUSs	Software product non-functional user stories
SPNFRs	Software product non-functional requirements

(Continued)

Acronym	Description
SSUSs	System and software user stories
SRSRs	System and software requirements
SPPUSs	Software project and process user stories
SPPRs	Software project and process requirements
SPTCUSs	Software product technology constraints user stories
SPTCs	Software product technology constraints
SPQSCUSs	Software product quality of service constraints user stories
SPQSCs	Software product quality of service constraints
PPBacklog	Prioritized product backlog
SPFR PPBacklog	The PPBacklog of the software product functional requirements
SPNFR PPBacklog	The PPBacklog of the software product non-functional requirements
SRSR.PPBacklog	The PPBacklog of the system and software requirements
SPPR PPBacklog	The PPBacklog of the software project and process requirements
SPTC PPBacklog	The PPBacklog of the software product technology constraints
SPQSC PPBacklog	The PPBacklog of the software product quality of service constraints
S-Backlog	A one-Sprint backlog
SPFR-S-Backlog	A one-Sprint backlog of software product functional requirements
SPNFR-S-Backlog	A one-Sprint backlog of software product non-functional requirements
SRSR-S-Backlog	A one-Sprint backlog of system and software requirements
SPPR-S-Backlog	A one-Sprint backlog of software project and process requirements
SPTC-S-Backlog	A one-Sprint backlog of software product technology constraints
SPQSC-S-Backlog	A one-Sprint backlog of software product quality of service constraints
SPFR-S-DLVS	The deliverables of a single SPFR Sprint
SPNFR-S-DLVS	The deliverables of a single SPNFR Sprint
SRSR-S-DLVS	The deliverable of a single SRSR Sprint
SPPR-S-DLVS	The deliverable of a single SPPR Sprint
SPTC-S-DLVS	The deliverable of a single SPTC Sprint
SPQSC-S-DLVS	The deliverable of a single SPQSC Sprint
I-Risks	The identified risks
M-Risks	The mitigated risks
SPFR/SPNFR/SRSR/ SPPR/SPTC/SPQSC-S-Deliverables	SPFR-S-DLVS + SPNFR-S-DLVS + SRSR-S-DLVS + SPPR-S-DLVS + SPTC-S-DLVS + SPQSC-S-DLVS
RHSI-GB-EXPERT	RHSI Guidance Body's consultants, advisors, and experts
RHSI-GB-DOCS	RHSI Guidance Body's documentation
SWOT	Strengths, weaknesses, opportunities, and threats

4.1.3 The Contributions of This Chapter

This chapter makes the following contributions:

1. Section 4.2 provides an overview of the RHSI software project management methodology and the classification of IEEE software requirements.

2. Section 4.3 provides an overview of the four RHSI batches and their associated processes, as follows:

    *   Section 4.3.1 presents the RHSI leading roles, including the Corporate Product Owner, Corporate RHSI Master, Product Owner, RHSI Team Master, RHSI Team, RHSI-GB (which stands for *RHSI Guidance Body*), Corporate Stakeholders, and stakeholders.

    *   Section 4.3.2 presents the RHSI primary documentation, including the stakeholders meeting log, lessons learned log, implementation log, Sprint Planning meetings log, Sprint Review meetings log, and Sprint Retrospective meetings log.

    *   Section 4.3.3 presents a high-level comparative view between the RHSI batch processes and the Scrum phases and processes, as shown in Table 4.4.

    *   Section 4.3.4 presents the RHSI batch #1 processes in terms of their inputs, outputs, roles, and methods. Also, it presents their interactions, as shown in Figure 4.1. These processes include *[P1] Create Project Vision, [P2] Identify RHSI Master and Shareholders, [P3] Form RHSI Team, [P4] Develop Epics, [P5] Create SPFUSs, [P6] Extract SPFRs, [P7] Create SPFR PPBacklog, [P8] Create SPNFUSs, [P9] Extract SPNFRs, [P10] Create SPNFR PPBacklog, [P11] Create SSUSs, [P12] Extract SRSRs, [P13] Create SRSR PPBacklog, [P14] Create SPPUSs, [P15] Extract SPPRs, [P16] Create SPPR PPBacklog, [P17] Create SPTCUSs, [P18] Extract SPTCs, [P19] Create SPTC PPBacklog, [P20] Create SPQSCUSs, [P21] Extract SPQSCs, [P22] Create SPQSC PPBacklog*, and *[P23] Create Overall Deliverables Release Schedule*.

    *   Section 4.4.5 presents RHSI batch #2 processes in terms of their inputs, outputs, roles, and methods. Also, it presents their interactions, as shown in Figure 4.2. These processes include *[P24] Create/Approve SPFR-S-Backlog, [P25] Create/Estimate/ Commit SPFR-S-Backlog Tasks, [P26] Create/Approve SPNFR-S-Backlog, [P27] Create/Estimate/Commit SPNFR-S-Backlog Tasks, [P28] Create/Approve SRSR-S-Backlog, [P29] Create/Estimate/Commit*

SRSR-S-Backlog Tasks, [P30] Create/ Approve SPPR-S-Backlog, [P31] Create/Estimate/Commit SPPR-S-Backlog Tasks, [P32] Create/ Approve SPTC-S-Backlog, [P33] Create/Estimate/Commit SPTC-S-Backlog, [P34] Create/Approve SPQSC-S-Backlog, and [P35] Create/ Estimate/Commit SPQSC-S-Backlog Tasks.

- Section 4.4.6 presents RHSI batch #3 processes in terms of their inputs, outputs, roles, and methods. It also presents their interactions, as shown in Figure 4.3. These processes include *[P36] Conduct SPFR-S-Backlog Daily Standup, [P37] Create SPFR--S-Backlog-DLVS, [P38] Conduct SPNFR-S-Backlog Daily Standup, [P39] Create SPNFR--S-Backlog-DLVS, [P40] Conduct SRSR-S-Backlog Daily Standup, [P41] Create SRSR--S-Backlog-DLVS, [P42] Conduct SPPR-S-Backlog Daily Standup, [P43] Create SPPR--S-Backlog-DLVS, [P44] Conduct SPTC-S-Backlog Daily Standup, [P45] Create SPTC--S-Backlog-DLVS, [P46] Conduct SPQSC-S-Backlog Daily Standup, [P47] Create SPQSC--S-Backlog-DLVS, [P48] Review/Validate/Approve SPFR/SPNFR/SRSR/SPPR/SPTC/ SPQSC-S-Deliverables, [P49] Ship Approved SPFR/SPNFR/SRSR/ SPPR/SPTC/SPQSC-S-Deliverables, [P50] Retrospect Shipped SPFR/SPNFR/SRSR/SPPR/SPTC/SPQSC-S-Deliverables, [P51] Update SPFUSs and SPFR PPBacklog, [P52] Update SPNFUS and SPNFR PPBacklog, [P53] Update SSUS and SRSR PPBacklog, [P54] Update SPPUS and SPPR PPBacklog, [P55] Update SPTCUS and SPTC PPBacklog, and [P56] Update SPQSCUS and SPQSC PPBacklog.*

- Section 4.3.7 presents the RHSI batch #4 process in terms of its inputs, outputs, roles, and methods. This process is *[P57] Project Retrospect and Closure.* Section 4.4.9 presents all the processes' overall interactions across the four batches, as shown in Figure 4.4.

3. Section 4.4 provides an overview of the RHSI meetings, including the stakeholders meeting, requirements prioritization and PPBacklogs building meeting, Sprint Planning meetings, focus groups meetings, Sprint daily standup meetings, Sprint Review meetings, Sprint Retrospective meetings, and project Retrospective meetings.

4.1.4 The Organization of This Chapter

This chapter has several sections. Section 4.1 presents the chapter's purpose, contributions, and organization; Section 4.2 provides an overview of the RHSI software project management methodology and the IEEE software requirements classification; Section 4.3 presents the RHSI batches and their associated processes; Section 4.4 presents the RHSI meetings; and Section 4.5 summarizes this chapter.

4.2   RHSI BACKGROUND

The project management methodology proposed in this chapter reformats the Scrum methodology by endorsing the IEEE-CS classification of software requirements and expanding and re-structuring the Scrum processes. The new method is called RHSI.

When we deal with software projects, it is essential that we carefully manage the software requirements. The author believes that the IEEE classification of software requirements sounds comprehensive and satisfactory for managing the requirements of any software project. Given the importance of Scrum and its commonality in the information technology and software industry, the author believes that a hybrid model can be devised and introduced by considering the IEEE-CS classification of software requirements and by restructuring and expanding the set of Scrum processes to dramatically enhance the usefulness and comprehensiveness of software projects' functions of planning, execution, and their management.

The IEEE classification of software requirements comprises the following classes:

a. *Software product functional requirements (SPFRs)*: SPFRs are the software functionalities, such as multiplying two numbers.

b. *Software product non-functional requirements (SPNFRs)*: SPNFRs are software quality requirements, including performance, maintainability, serviceability, supportability, safety, security, privacy, availability, reliability, and interoperability.

c. *System and software requirements (SRSRs)*: A system is a composition of components (e.g., hardware, software, users, operators, data and information, methods, facilities, services, etc.) used to accomplish a predefined set of objectives and functionalities.

d. *Software project and process requirements (SPPRs)*: A *project* requirement constrains the software to be developed, such as verifying that a student meets all prerequisites before being able to register for a course. A *process* requirement constrains the software development methodology, such as developing the software using a particular process.

e. *Software product technology constraints (SPTCs)*: The SPTCs, which are intricately tied to the overall system architecture and the interoperation of its components, play a crucial role in our project. For instance, "The throughput of a call center is heavily influenced by how the communication and information systems and operators interact under real circumstances."

f. *Software product quality of service constraints (SPQSCs)*: Our software requirements must be unambiguous and quantitative. For example, "The call center software must increase its throughput by 70%."

4.3   RHSI BATCHES AND PROCESSES

This section presents the primary roles in RHSI, the primary documentation in RHSI, a comparison of the RHSI batches of processes with the Scrum phases and processes, the RHSI batch #1 processes, the RHSI batch #2 processes, the RHSI batch #3 processes, the RHSI batch #4 processes, and the RHSI batches' overall process interactions.

4.3.1   The Primary Roles in RHSI

Table 4.2 presents the roles that the RHSI methodology considers. The responsibilities of these roles can be depicted in the various tables throughout this chapter (i.e., Tables 4.5 to 4.8).

TABLE 4.2 The primary roles in RHSI

The primary roles in RHSI	Description
Corporate Product Owner	This role is at the corporate/high management level and replaces the portfolio and program Product Owners in Scrum.
Corporate Master	This role also comes at the corporate/high management level. It replaces the portfolio and program Scrum Masters in Scrum.
Product Owner	This role replaces the Scrum Product Owner.
RHSI Master	This role replaces the Scrum Master in Scrum.
RHSI Team	This role replaces the Scrum Team members in Scrum.
RHSI Guidance Body	This role replaces the Scrum Guidance Body in Scrum (i.e., SGB).
Corporate Stakeholders	This role replaces the portfolio and program stakeholders in Scrum.
Stakeholders	This role replaces the stakeholders in Scrum.

4.3.2 The Primary Documentation in RHSI

Table 4.3 presents the comprehensive RHSI documentation, which meticulously records the activities, transactions, and lessons learned throughout an RHSI project, providing a complete picture of the project's journey.

TABLE 4.3 The primary documentation in RHSI

The primary documentation in RHSI	Description
Stakeholders meeting log	This document logs all activities and transactions during the stakeholders' meeting at the early stage of the project lifecycle. It also logs all recommendations and suggestions made by stakeholders during their interactions with the project team throughout the project lifecycle.
Lessons learned log	This document logs all lessons learned throughout the project lifecycle, from early planning to retrospect.
Implementation log	This document logs all activities and transactions while creating and deploying the deliverables, including the discussions and conclusions during the daily standup meetings.
Sprint Planning meetings log	This document logs all activities and transactions while planning for the project, including the creation of the following clusters: - Clusters of user stories (e.g., *SPFUSs, SPNFUSs, SSUS, SPPUS, SPTCUS,* and *SPQSCUS*) - Clusters of requirements (e.g., *SPFR, SPNFR, SRSR, SPPR, SPTC,* and *SPQSC*) - Clusters of prioritized product backlogs (e.g., *SPFR PPBacklog, SPNFR PPBacklog, SRSR PPBacklog, SPPR PPBacklog, SPTC PPBacklog,* and *SPQSC PPBacklog*) - Clusters of Sprint backlogs (e.g., *SPFR-S PPBacklog, SPNFR-S PPBacklog, SRSR-S PPBacklog, SPPR-S PPBacklog, SPTC-S PPBacklog,* and *SPQSC-S PPBacklog*). This also includes the planning activities right after the stakeholders' meeting and all activities during the Sprint Planning meetings.
Sprint Review meeting log	This document logs all activities and transactions while reviewing the shipped/deployed deliverables at the customer site (e.g., *SPFR-S PPBacklog.DLVS, SPNFR-S PPBacklog.DLVS, SRSR-S PPBacklog. DLVS, SPPR-S PPBacklog.DLVS, SPTC-S PPBacklog.DLVS,* and *SPQSC-S PPBacklog.DLVS*).
Sprints Retrospective meetings log	This document logs all activities and transactions during the retrospection of the shipped/deployed deliverables at the customer site (e.g., *SPFR-S PPBacklog.DLVS, SPNFR-S PPBacklog.DLVS, SRSR-S PPBacklog.DLVS, SPPR-S PPBacklog.DLVS, SPTC-S PPBacklog. DLVS,* and *SPQSC-S PPBacklog.DLVS*). It also includes all activities during the project's retrospection at the end.

4.3.3 RHSI Batches of Processes vs. Scrum Phases and Processes

As depicted in Table 4.4, this section provides a comparative view (i.e., at the level of phases/batches and their processes) between the Scrum project management and the author's RHSI planning model.

TABLE 4.4 RHSI batches of processes vs. Scrum phases and processes

Scrum Phases/Processes	RHSI Batches/Processes	
Scrum initiate phase	**Batch #1: Setup processes**	
[SP1] Create a Project Vision [SP2] Identify Scrum Master and Stakeholders [SP3] Form Scrum Team [SP4] Develop Epics [SP5] Create PPBacklog [SP6] Conduct Release Planning	[P1] Create Project Vision [P2] Identify the RHSI Master and Stakeholders [P3] Form RHSI Team [P4] Develop Epics [P5] Create SPFUSs [P6] Extract SPFRs [P7] Create SPFR PPBacklog [P8] Create SPNFUSs [P9] Extract SPNFRs [P10] Create SPNFR PPBacklog [P11] Create SSUSs [P12] Extract SRSRs	[P13] Create SRSR PPBacklog [P14] Create SPPUSs [P15] Extract SPPRs [P16] Create SPPR PPBacklog [P17] Create SPTCUSs [P18] Extract SPTCs [P19] Create SPTC PPBacklog [P20] Create SPQSCUSs [P21] Extract SPTCs [P22] Create SPQSC PPBacklog [P23] Create Overall Deliverables Release Schedule
Scrum plan and estimate phase	**Batch #2: Sprint Planning processes**	
[SP7] Create User Stories [SP8] Approve, Estimate, and Commit User Stories [SP9] Create Tasks [SP10] Estimate Tasks [SP11] Create Sprint Backlog	(repeated for each cluster of SPFR Sprints, SPNFR Sprints, SRSR Sprints, SPPR Sprints, SPTC Sprints, and SPQSC Sprints)	
Scrum implement phase		
[SP12] Create Deliverables [SP13] Conduct Daily Standup [SP14] Groom PPBacklog	[P24] Create/Approve SPFR-S-Backlog [P25] Create/Estimate/Commit SPFR-S-Backlog Tasks [P26] Create/Approve SPNFR-S-Backlog [P27] Create/Estimate/Commit SPNFR-S-Backlog Tasks [P28] Create/Approve SRSR-S-Backlog [P29] Create/Estimate/Commit SRSR-S-Backlog Tasks	[P30] Create/Approve SPPR-S-Backlog [P31] Create/Estimate/Commit SPPR-S-Backlog Tasks [P32] Create/Approve SPTC-S-Backlog [P33] Create/Estimate/Commit SPTC-S-Backlog Tasks [P34] Create/Approve SPQSC-S-Backlog [P35] Create/Estimate/Commit SPQSC-S-Backlog Tasks
Scrum review and retrospect phase		
[SP15] Convene Scrum of Scrums [SP16] Demonstrate and Validate Sprint [SP17] Sprint Retrospect		
Scrum release phase		
[SP18] Ship Deliverables [SP19] Retrospect Project		

Scrum Phases/Processes	RHSI Batches/Processes	
	Batch #3: Sprint execution and validation	
	(repeated for each cluster of SPFR Sprints, SPNFR Sprints, SRSR Sprints, SPPR Sprints, SPTC Sprints, and SPQSC Sprints)	
	[P36] Conduct SPFR-S-Backlog Daily Standup [P37] Create SPFR-S-Backlog Deliverables [P38] Conduct SPNFR-S-Backlog Daily Standup [P39] Create SPNFR-S-Backlog Deliverables [P40] Conduct SRSR-S-Backlog Daily Standup [P41] Create SRSR-S-Backlog Deliverables [P42] Conduct SPPR-S-Backlog Daily Standup [P43] Create SPPR-S-Backlog Deliverables [P44] Conduct SPTC-S-Backlog Daily Standup [P45] Create SPTC-S-Backlog Deliverables [P46] Conduct SPQSC-S-Backlog Daily Standup [P47] Create SPQSC-S-Backlog Deliverables	[P48] Review/Validate/Approve SPFR/SPNFR/ SRSR/SPPR/ SPTC/SPQSC-S-Deliverables [P49] Ship Approved SPFR/SPNFR/ SRSR/SPPR/SPTC/ SPQSC/-S-Deliverables [P50] Retrospect Shipped SPFR/ SPNFR/SRSR/SPPR/ SPTC/ SPQSC-S-Deliverables [P51] Update SPFUSs and SPFR PPBacklog [P52] Update SPNFUSs and SPNFR PPBacklog [P53] Update SSUS and SRSR PPBacklog [P54] Update SPPUS and SPPR PPBacklog [P55] Update SPTCUS and SPTC PPBacklog [P56] Update SPQSCUS and SPQSC PPBacklog
	Batch #4: Project retrospect and closure	
	[P57] Retrospect and Close Project	
Notes:		
PPBacklog stands for *prioritized product backlog*. S-Backlog stands for *Sprint backlog*. Each of the processes above is executed for each Sprint. The SoS has been eliminated in the RHSI planning model.		

Sections 4.3.4 through 4.3.7 provide insightful tabular views of the RHSI batches and their processes regarding their inputs, roles, methods, and outputs. They also provide graphical representations of the interactions among these processes.

Tables 4.5 through 4.61 depict the inputs, roles, methods, and outputs of the processes in the RHSI's four batches, as follows:

- Tables 4.5 through 4.27 depict the inputs, roles, methods, and outputs of batch #1 processes (*[P1] to [P23]*).
- Tables 4.28 through 4.39 depict the inputs, roles, methods, and outputs of batch #2 processes (*[P24] to [P35]*).
- Tables 4.40 through 4.60 depict the inputs, roles, methods, and outputs of batch #3 processes (*[P36] to [P56]*).
- Table 4.61 presents the inputs, roles, methods, and outputs of batch #4 processes (*[P57]*).

Figures 4.1 through 4.4 illustrate the interactions of these processes within each batch as well as across all batches, as follows:

- Figure 4.1 illustrates the interactions among the processes in batch #1 (*[P1] to [P23]*).
- Figure 4.2 illustrates the interactions among the processes in batch #2 (*[P24] to [P35]*).
- Figure 4.3 illustrates the interactions among the processes in batch #3 (*[P36] to [P56]*).
- Figure 4.4 illustrates the interactions among the processes across the four batches of the RHSI planning model.

4.3.4 Batch #1 Processes

Tables 4.5 through 4.28 depict the inputs, roles, methods, and outputs of the processes that belong to batch #1 (*[P1] to [P23]*). Toward the end of this section, Figure 4.1 illustrates the interactions between these processes.

4.3.4.1 [P1] Create Project Vision

Table 4.5 shows how the *Create Project Vision* process requires/uses/produces the following inputs/roles/methods/outputs:

- *Inputs*: Business study, proof of concept and demo prototype, vision and mission statements, and RHSI-GB documents

- *Roles*: The Corporate Product Owner, Corporate RHSI Master, Product Owner, and RHSI-GB consultants
- *Methods*: Stakeholders meetings, brainstorming meetings, SWOT analysis, gap analysis, etc.
- *Outputs*: Identified RHSI Master, vision statement, project charter, project estimated budget, identified needed resources, and selection criteria (for determining the RHSI Master, Stakeholders, and RHSI Team)

TABLE 4.5 [P1] Create Project Vision

INPUTS	ROLES	METHODS	OUTPUTS
Business case study Proof of concept and demo prototype Customer vision and mission statements RHSI-GB-DOCS	Corporate Product Owners Corporate RHSI Masters Corporate Stakeholders Product Owner RHSI-GB-EXPERT	Stakeholders meetings Brainstorming meetings SWOT analysis activities Gap analysis activities	Identified RHSI Master Vision statement Project charter Project estimated budget Selection criteria (e.g., RHSI Master, stakeholders, RHSI Team, and other roles) Identified needed resources

4.3.4.2 [P2] Identify RHSI Master and Stakeholders

Table 4.6 shows how the *Identify RHSI Master and Stakeholders* process requires/uses/produces the following inputs/roles/methods/outputs:

- *Inputs*: Vision statement, needed resources, and RHSI-GB-DOCS
- *Roles*: Corporate Product Owner, Corporate RHSI Master, Product Owner, and RHSI-GB-EXPERT
- *Methods*: Using the selection criteria, seeking advice from human resources, holding training sessions (to leverage someone's level to become an active and effective member), and conducting the costing of the identified RHSI Master and stakeholders, along with their required resources
- *Outputs*: Identified RHSI Master and stakeholders

TABLE 4.6 [P2] Identify RHSI Master and Stakeholders

INPUTS	ROLES	METHODS	OUTPUTS
- Vision statement - Needed resources (with their requirements, availability, etc.) - RHSI-GB-DOCS	- Corporate Product Owners - Corporate RHSI Masters - Corporate Stakeholders - Product Owner - RHSI-GB-EXPERT	- Using the selection criteria (to identify the RHSI Master and stakeholders) - Seeking advice from human resources - Holding training sessions - Costing for the identified RHSI Master and stakeholders, along with their required resources	- Identified RHSI Master - Identified stakeholders

4.3.4.3 [P3] Form RHSI Team

Table 4.7 shows how the *Form RHSI Team* process requires/uses/produces the following inputs/roles/methods/outputs:

- *Inputs*: Vision statement, needed resources, and RHSI-GB-DOCS
- *Roles*: Product Owner, RHSI Master, and RHSI-GB-EXPERT
- *Methods*: Applying the selection criteria (i.e., to identify the RHSI Team); seeking advice from human resources; holding training sessions to leverage someone's level to become an active and effective team member; and conducting the costing of the identified RHSI Team members along with their required resources
- *Outputs*: Identified RHSI Team, backup resources, a collaboration plan, and a team-building plan

TABLE 4.7 [P3] Form RHSI Team

INPUTS	ROLES	METHODS	OUTPUTS
- Vision statement - Needed resources - RHSI-GB-DOCS	- Product Owner - RHSI Master - RHSI-GB-EXPERT	- Applying the selection criteria - Seeking advice from human resources - Holding training sessions - Conducting the costing of the identified RHSI Team members along with their required resources	- Identified RHSI Team - Backup resources - Collaboration plan - Team building plan

4.3.4.4 [P4] Develop Epics

Table 4.8 shows how the *Develop Epics* process requires/uses/produces the following inputs/roles/methods/outputs:

- *Inputs*: Vision statement, corporate product backlogs, approved/unapproved change requests, etc.
- *Roles*: Product Owner, RHSI Master, RHSI Team, stakeholders, and RHSI-GB-EXPERT
- *Methods*: Holding focus group meetings, conducting user interviews and surveys, using RHSI-GB-EXPERT, etc.
- *Outputs*: Epics, approved/unapproved change requests, and I-Risks

TABLE 4.8 [P4] Develop Epics

INPUTS	ROLES	METHODS	OUTPUTS
- Vision statement - Corporate product backlogs - Approved/ unapproved change requests - Corporate risks - Relevant legislations - RHSI-GB-DOCS	- Product Owner - RHSI Master - RHSI Team - Stakeholders - RHSI-GB-EXPERT	- Holding focus group meetings - Conducting user interviews/surveys - Applying risk identification techniques - Using RHSI-GB-EXPERT	- Epics - Approved changes - I-Risks

4.3.4.5 [P5] Create SPFUSs

Table 4.9 shows how the *Create SPFUSs* process requires/uses/produces the following inputs/roles/methods/outputs:

- *Inputs*: Vision statement, done criteria (e.g., SPFUSs are straightforward to extract the SPFRs), epics, business requirements, relevant legislation, and RHSI-GB-DOCS
- *Roles*: Product Owner, RHSI Master, RHSI Team, stakeholders, and RHSI-GB-EXPERT
- *Methods*: Utilizing the user story writing expertise, holding focus group meetings, conducting user interviews/surveys, and using RHSI-GB-EXPERT
- *Outputs*: SPFUSs and their acceptance criteria

TABLE 4.9 [P5] Create SPFUSs

INPUTS	ROLES	METHODS	OUTPUTS
- Vision statement - Done criteria - Epics - Business requirements - Relevant legislation - RHSI-GB-DOCS	- Product Owner - RHSI Master - RHSI Team - Stakeholders - RHSI-GB-EXPERT	- Utilizing the user story writing expertise - Holding focus group meetings (e.g., SPFUSs/SPFRs focus groups) - Conducting user interviews/surveys - Using RHSI-GB-EXPERT	- SPFUSs - SPFUS acceptance criteria

4.3.4.6 [P6] Extract SPFRs

Table 4.10 shows how the *Extract SPFRs* process requires/uses/produces the following inputs/roles/methods/outputs:

- *Inputs*: Vision statement, functional user stories (SPFUSs), and RHSI-GB-DOCS
- *Roles*: Product Owner, RHSI Master, RHSI Team, stakeholders, and RHSI-GB-EXPERT
- *Methods*: Utilizing the SPFR writing expertise, holding focus group meetings to extract the SPFRs from the SPFUSs, and using RHSI-GB-EXPERT
- *Outputs*: SPFRs and their acceptance criteria

TABLE 4.10 [P6] Extract SPFRs

INPUTS	ROLES	METHODS	OUTPUTS
- Vision statement - SPFUSs - RHSI-GB-DOCS	- Product Owner - RHSI Master - RHSI Team - Stakeholders - RHSI-GB-EXPERT	- Utilizing the SPFR writing expertise - Holding focus group meetings (e.g., SPFUSs/SPFRs focus groups) - Using RHSI-GB-EXPERT	- SPFRs - SPFR acceptance criteria

4.3.4.7 [P7] Create SPFR PPBacklog

Table 4.11 shows how the *Create SPFR PPBacklog* process requires/uses/produces the following inputs/roles/methods/ outputs:

- *Inputs*: SPFRs and RHSI-GB-DOCS
- *Roles*: RHSI Master, RHSI Team, and RHSI-GB-EXPERT

🔲 *Methods*: SPFR prioritization method and RHSI-GB-EXPERT

🔲 *Outputs*: SPFR PPBacklog

TABLE 4.11 [P7] Create SPFR PPBacklog

INPUTS	ROLES	METHODS	OUTPUTS
- Software product functional requirements - RHSI-GB-DOCS	- RHSI Master - RHSI Team - RHSI-GB-EXPERT	- SPFR prioritization method - Using RHSI-GB-EXPERT	- SPFR PPBacklog

4.3.4.8 [P8] Create SPNFUSs

Table 4.12 shows how the *Create SPNFUSs* process requires/uses/produces the following inputs/roles/methods/outputs:

🔲 *Inputs*: Vision statement, done criteria (e.g., SPNFUSs are straightforward to extract the SPNFRs), epics, business requirements, relevant legislations, and RHSI-GB-DOCS

🔲 *Roles*: Product Owner, RHSI Master, RHSI Team, stakeholders, and RHSI-GB-EXPERT

🔲 *Methods*: Utilizing the user story writing expertise, holding focus group meetings, conducting user interviews and surveys, and using RHSI-GB-EXPERT

🔲 *Outputs*: SPNFUSs and their acceptance criteria

TABLE 4.12 [P8] Create SPNFUSs

INPUTS	ROLES	METHODS	OUTPUTS
- Vision statement - Done criteria - Epics - Relevant legislations - RHSI-GB-DOCS	- Product Owner - RHSI Master - RHSI Team - Stakeholders - RHSI-GB-EXPERT	- Utilizing the user story writing expertise - Holding focus group meetings (e.g., SPNFUSs/SPNFRs focus groups) - Conducting user interviews and surveys - Using RHSI-GB-EXPERT	- SPNFUSs - SPNFUS acceptance criteria

4.3.4.9 [P9] Extract SPNFRs

Table 4.13 shows how the *Extract SPNFRs* process requires/uses/produces the following inputs/roles/methods/outputs:

- *Inputs*: Vision statement, SPNFUSs, and RHSI-GB-DOCS
- *Roles*: Product Owner, RHSI Master, RHSI Team, stakeholders, and RHSI-GB-EXPERT
- *Methods*: Utilizing the SPNFR writing expertise, holding focus group meetings to extract the SPNFRs, and using RHSI-GB-EXPERT
- *Outputs*: SPNFRs and their acceptance criteria

TABLE 4.13 [P9] Extract SPNFRs

INPUTS	ROLES	METHODS	OUTPUTS
- Vision statement - SPNFUSs - RHSI-GB-DOCS	- Product Owner - RHSI Master - RHSI Team - Stakeholders - RHSI-GB-EXPERT	- Utilizing the SPNFR writing expertise - Holding focus group meetings (e.g., SPNFUSs/ SPNFRs focus groups) - Using RHSI-GB-EXPERT	- SPNFRs - SPNFR acceptance criteria

4.3.4.10 [P10] Create SPNFR PPBacklog

Table 4.14 shows how the *Create SPNFR PPBacklog* process requires/uses/produces the following inputs/roles/methods/outputs:

- *Inputs*: SPNFRs and RHSI-GB-DOCS
- *Roles*: RHSI Master, RHSI Team, and RHSI-GB-EXPERT
- *Methods*: Using the SPNFR prioritization method and RHSI-GB-EXPERT
- *Outputs*: SPNFR PPBacklog

TABLE 4.14 [P10] Create SPNFR PPBacklog

INPUTS	ROLES	METHODS	OUTPUTS
- SPNFRs - RHSI-GB-DOCS	- RHSI Master - RHSI Team - RHSI-GB-EXPERT	- SPNFR prioritization method - Using RHSI-GB-EXPERT	- SPNFR PPBacklog

4.3.4.11 [P11] Create SSUSs

Table 4.15 shows how the *Create SSUSs* process requires/uses/produces the following inputs/roles/methods/outputs:

- *Inputs*: Vision statement, done criteria (e.g., SRSRs can be extracted from the SSUSs), epics, business requirements, legislations, and RHSI-GB-DOCS
- *Roles*: Product Owner, RHSI Master, RHSI Team, stakeholders, and RHSI-GB-EXPERT
- *Methods*: Utilizing the user story writing expertise, holding focus group meetings, conducting interviews and surveys, and using RHSI-GB-EXPERT
- *Outputs*: SSUSs and their acceptance criteria

TABLE 4.15 [P11] Create SSUSs

INPUTS	ROLES	METHODS	OUTPUTS
- Vision statement - Done criteria - Epics - Business requirements - Relevant legislations - RHSI-GB-DOCS	- Product Owner - RHSI Master - RHSI Team - Stakeholders - RHSI-GB-EXPERT	- User story writing expertise - Holding focus group meetings (e.g., SSUS/SRSR focus groups) - Conducting user interviews/surveys - Using RHSI-GB-EXPERT	- SSUSs - SSUS acceptance criteria

4.3.4.12 [P12] Extract SRSRs

Table 4.16 shows how the *Extract SRSRs* process requires/uses/produces the following inputs/roles/methods/outputs:

- *Inputs*: Vision statement, SSUSs, and RHSI-GB-DOCS
- *Roles*: Product Owner, RHSI Master, RHSI Team, stakeholders, and RHSI-GB-EXPERT
- *Methods*: Utilizing the SRSR writing expertise, holding focus group meetings to extract the SRSRs, and using RHSI-GB-EXPERT
- *Outputs*: SRSRs and their acceptance criteria

TABLE 4.16 [P12] Extract SRSRs

INPUTS	ROLES	METHODS	OUTPUTS
- Vision statement - SSUSs - RHSI-GB-DOCS	- Product Owner - RHSI Master - RHSI Team - Stakeholders - RHSI-GB-EXPERT	- Utilizing the SRSR writing expertise - Holding focus group meetings (e.g., SSUSs/SRSRs focus group) - Using RHSI-GB-EXPERT	- SRSRs - SRSR acceptance criteria

4.3.4.13 [P13] Create SRSR PPBacklog

Table 4.17 shows how the *Create SRSR PPBacklog* process requires/uses/produces the following inputs/roles/methods/outputs:

- *Inputs*: SRSRs and RHSI-GB-DOCS
- *Roles*: RHSI Master, RHSI Team, and RHSI-GB-EXPERT
- *Methods*: Using the SRSR prioritization method and RHSI-GB-EXPERT
- *Outputs*: SRSR PPBacklog

TABLE 4.17 [P13] Create SRSR PPBacklog

INPUTS	ROLES	METHODS	OUTPUTS
- SRSRs - RHSI-GB-DOCS	- RHSI Master - RHSI Team - RHSI-GB-EXPERT	- SRSR prioritization method - Using RHSI-GB-EXPERT	- SRSR PPBacklog

4.3.4.14 [P14] Create SPPUSs

Table 4.18 shows how the *Create SPPUSs* process requires/uses/produces the following inputs/roles/methods/outputs:

- *Inputs*: Vision statement, done criteria (e.g., SPPUSs are clear for extracting the SPPRs later), epics, requirements, and RHSI-GB-DOCS
- *Roles*: Product Owner, RHSI Master, RHSI Team, stakeholders, and RHSI-GB-EXPERT
- *Methods*: Utilizing the user story writing expertise, holding focus group meetings to create the SPPUSs, conducting user interviews and surveys, and using RHSI-GB-EXPERT
- *Outputs*: SPPUSs and their acceptance criteria

TABLE 4.18 [P14] Create SPPUSs

INPUTS	ROLES	METHODS	OUTPUTS
– Vision statement – Done criteria – Epics – Business requirements – RHSI-GB-DOCS	– Product Owner – RHSI Master – RHSI Team – Stakeholders – RHSI-GB-EXPERT	– User story writing expertise – Holding focus group meetings (e.g., SPPUSs/SPPRs focus group) – Conducting user interviews/ surveys – Using RHSI-GB-EXPERT	– SPPUSs – SPPUS acceptance criteria

4.3.4.15 [P15] Extract SPPRs

Table 4.19 shows how the *Extract SPPRs* process requires/uses/produces the following inputs/roles/methods/outputs:

▨ *Inputs*: Vision statement, SPPUSs, and RHSI-GB-DOCS

▨ *Roles*: Product Owner, RHSI Master, RHSI Team, stakeholders, and RHSI-GB-EXPERT

▨ *Methods*: Utilizing the SPPR writing expertise, holding focus group meetings to extract the SPPRs, and using RHSI-GB-EXPERT

▨ *Outputs*: SPPRs and their acceptance criteria

TABLE 4.19 [P15] Extract SPPRs

INPUTS	ROLES	METHODS	OUTPUTS
– Vision statement – SPPUSs – RHSI-GB-DOCS	– Product Owner – RHSI Master – RHSI Team – Stakeholders – RHSI-GB-EXPERT	– Utilizing the SPPR writing expertise – Holding focus group meetings (e.g., SPPUS/SPPR focus group) – Using RHSI-GB-EXPERT	– SPPRs – SPPR acceptance criteria

4.3.4.16 [P16] Create SPPR PPBacklog

Table 4.20 shows how the *Create SPPR PPBacklog* process requires/uses/produces the following inputs/roles/methods/outputs:

▨ *Inputs*: SPPRs and RHSI-GB-DOCS

▨ *Roles*: RHSI Master, RHSI Team, and RHSI-GB-EXPERT

▨ *Methods*: Using the SPPR prioritization method and RHSI-GB-EXPERT

▨ *Outputs*: SPPR PPBacklog

TABLE 4.20 [P16] Create SPPR PPBacklog

INPUTS	ROLES	METHODS	OUTPUTS
- SPPRs - RHSI-GB-DOCS	- RHSI Master - RHSI Team - RHSI-GB-EXPERT	- SPPR prioritization method - Using RHSI-GB-EXPERT	- SPPR PPBacklog

4.3.4.17 [P17] Create SPTCUSs

Table 4.21 shows how the *Create SPTCUSs* process requires/uses/produces the following inputs/roles/methods/outputs:

- *Inputs*: Vision statement, done criteria (e.g., SPTCs can be derived from the SPTCUSs), epics, requirements, relevant legislations, and RHSI-GB-DOCS
- *Roles*: Product Owner, RHSI Master, RHSI Team, stakeholders, and RHSI-GB-EXPERT
- *Methods*: Utilizing the user story writing expertise, holding focus group meetings to create the SPTCUSs, conducting user interviews and surveys, and using RHSI-GB-EXPERT
- *Outputs*: SPTCUSs and their acceptance criteria

TABLE 4.21 [P17] Create SPTCUSs

INPUTS	ROLES	METHODS	OUTPUTS
- Vision statement - Done criteria - Epics - Business requirements - Relevant legislations - RHSI-GB-DOCS	- Product Owner - RHSI Master - RHSI Team - Stakeholders - RHSI-GB-EXPERT	- Utilizing the user story writing expertise - Holding focus group meetings (e.g., SPTCUSs/SPTCs focus group) - Conducting user interviews/surveys - Using RHSI-GB-EXPERT	- SPTCUSs - SPTCUS acceptance criteria

4.3.4.18 [P18] Extract SPTCs

Table 4.22 shows how the *Extract SPTCs* process requires/uses/produces the following inputs/roles/methods/outputs:

- *Inputs*: Vision statement, SPTCUSs, and RHSI-GB-DOCS
- *Roles*: Product Owner, RHSI Master, RHSI Team, Stakeholders, and RHSI-GB-EXPERT

▨ *Methods*: Utilizing the SPTC writing expertise, holding focus group meetings to extract the SPTCs, and using RHSI-GB-EXPERT

▨ *Outputs*: SPTCs and their acceptance criteria

TABLE 4.22 [P18] Extract SPTCs

INPUTS	ROLES	METHODS	OUTPUTS
- Vision statement - SPTCUSs - RHSI-GB-DOCS	- Product Owner - RHSI Master - RHSI Team - Stakeholders - RHSI-GB-EXPERT	- Utilizing the SPTC writing expertise - Holding focus group meetings (e.g., SPTCUSs/SPTCs focus group) - Using RHSI-GB-EXPERT	- SPTCs - SPTC acceptance criteria

4.3.4.19 [P19] Create SPTC PPBacklog

Table 4.23 shows how the *Create SPTC PPBacklog* process requires/uses/produces the following inputs/roles/methods/outputs:

▨ *Inputs*: SPTCs and RHSI-GB-DOCS

▨ *Roles*: RHSI Master, RHSI Team, and RHSI-GB-EXPERT

▨ *Methods*: Using the SPTC prioritization method and RHSI-GB-EXPERT

▨ *Outputs*: SPTC PPBacklog

TABLE 4.23 [P19] Create SPTC PPBacklog

INPUTS	ROLES	METHODS	OUTPUTS
- SPTCs - RHSI-GB-DOCS	- RHSI Master - RHSI Team - RHSI-GB-EXPERT	- SPTC prioritization method - Using RHSI-GB-EXPERT	- SPTC PPBacklog

4.3.4.20 [P20] Create SPQSCUSs

Table 4.24 shows how the *Create SPQSCUSs* process requires/uses/produces the following inputs/roles/methods/outputs:

▨ *Inputs*: Vision statement, done criteria (e.g., SPQUSs can be extracted from the SPQSCUSs), epics, requirements, legislations, and RHSI-GB-DOCS

▨ *Roles*: Product Owner, RHSI Master, RHSI Team, stakeholders, and RHSI-GB-EXPERT

▓ *Methods*: Utilizing the user story writing expertise, holding focus group meetings to create the SPQSCUSs, conducting user interviews and surveys, and using RHSI-GB-EXPERT

▓ *Outputs*: SPQSCUSs and their acceptance criteria

TABLE 4.24 [P20] Create SPQSCUSs

INPUTS	ROLES	METHODS	OUTPUTS
- Vision statement - Done criteria (e.g., SPQSCUSs are clear for extracting the SPQSCs) - Epics - Business requirements - Relevant legislations - RHSI-GB-DOCS	- Product Owner - RHSI Master - RHSI Team - Stakeholders - RHSI-GB-EXPERT	- Utilizing the user story writing expertise - Holding focus group meetings (e.g., SPQSCUSs/SPQSCs focus group) - Conducting user interviews and surveys - Using RHSI-GB-EXPERT	- SPQSCUSs - SPQSCUS acceptance criteria

4.3.4.21 [P21] Extract SPQSCs

Table 4.25 shows how the *Extract SPQSCs* process requires/uses/produces the following inputs/roles/methods/outputs:

▓ *Inputs*: Vision statement, SPQSCUSs, and RHSI-GB-DOCS

▓ *Roles*: Product Owner, RHSI Master, RHSI Team, stakeholders, and RHSI-GB-EXPERT

▓ *Methods*: Utilizing the SPQSC writing expertise, holding focus group meetings, and using RHSI-GB-EXPERT

▓ *Outputs*: SPQSCs and their acceptance criteria

TABLE 4.25 [P21] Extract SPQSCs

INPUTS	ROLES	METHODS	OUTPUTS
- Vision statement - SPQSCUS - RHSI-GB-DOCS	- Product Owner - RHSI Master - RHSI Team - Stakeholders - RHSI-GB-EXPERT	- Utilizing the SPQSC writing expertise - Holding focus group meetings (e.g., SPQSCUSs/SPQSCs focus group) - Using RHSI-GB-EXPERT	- SPQSCs - SPQSC acceptance criteria

4.3.4.22 [P22] Create SPQSC PPBacklog

Table 4.26 shows how the *Create SPQSC PPBacklog* process requires/uses/produces the following inputs/roles/methods/outputs:

◉ *Inputs*: SPQSCs and RHSI-GB-DOCS
◉ *Roles*: RHSI Master, RHSI Team, and RHSI-GB-EXPERT
◉ *Methods*: Using the SPQSC prioritization method and RHSI-GB-EXPERT
◉ *Outputs*: SPQSC PPBacklog

TABLE 4.26 [P22] Create SPQSC PPBacklog

INPUTS	ROLES	METHODS	OUTPUTS
- SPQSCs - RHSI-GB-DOCS	- RHSI Master - RHSI Team - RHSI-GB-EXPERT	- SPQSC prioritization method - Using RHSI-GB-EXPERT	- SPQSC PPBacklog

4.3.4.23 [P23] Create Overall Deliverables Release Schedule

Table 4.27 shows how the *Create Overall Deliverables Release Schedule* process requires/uses/produces the following inputs/roles/methods/outputs:

◉ *Inputs*: Vision statement, SPFR PPBacklog, SPNFR PPBacklog, SRSR PPBacklog, SPPR PPBacklog, SPTC PPBacklog, SPQSC PPBacklog, done criteria (e.g., the extracted SPTCs are clear and adequate), and RHSI-GB-DOCS
◉ *Roles*: RHSI Team, Stakeholders, Corporate Product Owner, Corporate RHSI Master, Product Owner, RHSI Master, and RHSI-GB-EXPERT
◉ *Methods*: Release planning and prioritization methods
◉ *Outputs*: Overall deliverables release schedule

TABLE 4.27 [P23] Create Overall Deliverables Release Schedule

INPUTS	ROLES	METHODS	OUTPUTS
- Vision statement - SPFR PPBacklog - SPNFR PPBacklog - SRSR PPBacklog - SPPR PPBacklog - SPTC PPBacklog - SPQSC PPBacklog - Done criteria	- RHSI Team - Stakeholders - Corporate Product Owner - Corporate RHSI Master - Product Owner - RHSI Master - RHSI-GB-EXPERT	- Release planning and prioritization methods	- Overall deliverables release schedule

4.3.4.24 Batch #1 Process Interactions

Figure 4.1 illustrates the interactions among the processes in batch #1 (*[P1]* to *[P23]*) of the author's RHSI planning model.

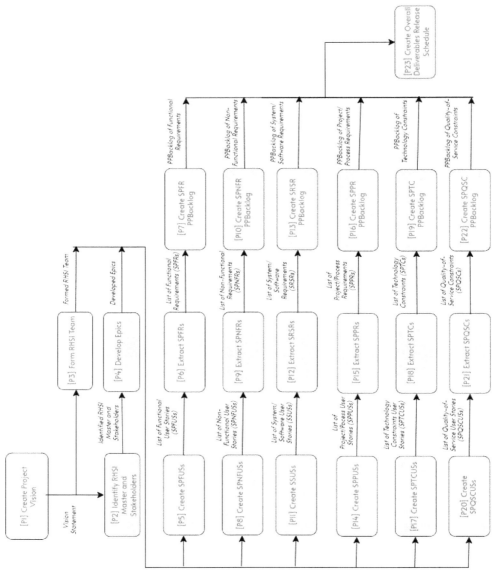

FIGURE 4.1 RHSI planning model—Batch #1 process interactions

4.3.5 Batch #2 Processes

Batch #2 processes are repeated for each cluster of SPFR Sprints, SPNFR Sprints, SRSR Sprints, SPPR Sprints, SPTC Sprints, and SPQSC Sprints. Tables 4.28 to 4.39 present the inputs/roles/methods/outputs of batch #2's processes (*[P24]* to *[P35]*). Figure 4.2 illustrates their interactions.

4.3.5.1   *[P24] Create/Approve SPFR-S-Backlog*

Table 4.28 shows how the *Create/Approve SPFR-S-Backlog* process requires/uses/produces the following inputs/roles/methods/outputs:

- *Inputs*: SPFR PPBacklog, SPFR acceptance criteria, and RHSI-GB-DOCS
- *Roles*: RHSI Master, RHSI Team, and RHSI-GB-EXPERT
- *Methods*: Conducting focus group meetings to explore how to create/approve the current SPFR-S-Backlog and using RHSI-GB-EXPERT to develop and approve it
- *Outputs*: SPFR-S-Backlog

TABLE 4.28 [P24] Create/Approve SPFR-S-Backlog

INPUTS	ROLES	METHODS	OUTPUTS
- SPFR PPBacklog - SPFR acceptance criteria - RHSI-GB-DOCS	- RHSI Team - RHSI Master - RHSI-GB-EXPERT	- Focus group meetings - RHSI-GB-EXPERT	- The current SPFR-S-Backlog

4.3.5.2   *[P25] Create/Estimate/Commit SPFR-S-Backlog Tasks*

Table 4.29 shows how the *Create/Estimate/Commit SPFR-S-Backlog Tasks* process requires/uses/produces the following inputs/roles/methods/outputs:

- *Inputs*: The current SPFR-S-Backlog, SPFR PPBacklog, SPFR-S-Backlog-Tasks estimation/commitment acceptance criteria, and RHSI-GB-DOCS
- *Roles*: RHSI Master, RHSI Team, and RHSI-GB-EXPERT
- *Methods*: Conducting focus group meetings to explore how to estimate/commit/accept tasks for the current SPFR-S-Backlog and using RHSI-GB-EXPERT
- *Outputs*: A breakdown of the estimated/committed tasks for the current SPFR-S-Backlog

TABLE 4.29 [P25] Create/Estimate/Commit SPFR-S-Backlog Tasks

INPUTS	ROLES	METHODS	OUTPUTS
- SPFR-S-Backlog - SPFR PPBacklog - SPFR-Tasks estimation/ commitment acceptance criteria - RHSI-GB-DOCS	- RHSI Team - RHSI Master - RHSI-GB-EXPERT	- Focus group meetings - RHSI-GB-EXPERT	- The breakdown of the approved estimated and committed tasks for the current SPFR-S-Backlog

4.3.5.3 [P26] Create/Approve SPNFR-S-Backlog

Table 4.30 shows how the *Create/Approve SPNFR-S-Backlog* process requires/ uses/produces the following inputs/roles/methods/ outputs:

- *Inputs*: SPNFR PPBacklog, SPNFR acceptance criteria, and RHSI-GB-DOCS
- *Roles*: RHSI Master, RHSI Team, and RHSI-GB-EXPERT
- *Methods*: Conducting focus group meetings to explore how to create/ approve the current SPNFR-S-Backlog and using RHSI-GB-EXPERT to develop/approve SPNFR-S-Backlogs
- *Outputs*: The current SPNFR-S-Backlog

TABLE 4.30 [P26] Create/Approve SPNFR-S-Backlog

INPUTS	ROLES	METHODS	OUTPUTS
- SPNFR PPBacklog - SPNFR acceptance criteria - RHSI-GB-DOCS	- RHSI Team - RHSI Master - RHSI-GB-EXPERT	- Focus group meetings - RHSI-GB-EXPERT	- The current SPNFR-S-Backlog

4.3.5.4 [P27] Create/Estimate/Commit SPNFR-S-Backlog Tasks

Table 4.31 shows how the *Create/Estimate/Commit SPNFR-S-Backlog Tasks* process requires/uses/produces the following inputs/roles/methods/ outputs:

- *Inputs*: SPNFR-S-Backlog, SPNFR PPBacklog, SPNFR-Tasks estimation/commitment acceptance criteria, and RHSI-GB-DOCS
- *Roles*: RHSI Master, RHSI Team, and RHSI-GB-EXPERT

- *Methods*: Conducting focus group meetings to explore how to estimate/commit/accept tasks for the current SPNFR-S-Backlog, and using RHSI-GB-EXPERT to estimate/commit/accept the current SPNFR-S-Backlog's tasks
- *Outputs*: A breakdown of the estimated and committed tasks for the current SPNFR-S-Backlog

TABLE 4.31 [P27] Create/Estimate/Commit SPNFR-S-Backlog Tasks

INPUTS	ROLES	METHODS	OUTPUTS
- SPNFR-S-Backlog - SPNFR PPBacklog - SPNFR-Tasks estimation/commitment acceptance criteria - RHSI-GB-DOCS	- RHSI Team - RHSI Master - RHSI-GB-EXPERT	- Focus group meetings - RHSI-GB-EXPERT	- A breakdown of the approved, estimated, and committed tasks for the current SPNFR-S-Backlog

4.3.5.5 [P28] Create/Approve SRSR-S-Backlog

Table 4.32 shows how the *Create/Approve SRSR-S-Backlog* process requires/uses/produces the following inputs/roles/methods/outputs:

- *Inputs*: SRSR PPBacklog, SRSR acceptance criteria, and RHSI-GB-DOCS
- *Roles*: RHSI Master, RHSI Team, and RHSI-GB-EXPERT
- *Methods*: Conducting focus group meetings to explore how to create and approve the current SRSR-S-Backlog and using RHSI-GB-EXPERT to develop and approve SRSR-S-Backlogs
- *Outputs*: The current SRSR-S-Backlog

TABLE 4.32 [P28] Create/Approve SRSR-S-Backlog

INPUTS	ROLES	METHODS	OUTPUTS
- SRSR PPBacklog - SRSR acceptance criteria - RHSI-GB-DOCS	- RHSI Team - RHSI Master - RHSI-GB-EXPERT	- Focus group meetings - RHSI-GB-EXPERT	- SRSR-S-Backlog

4.3.5.6 [P29] Create/Estimate/Commit SRSR-S-Backlog Tasks

Table 4.33 shows how the *Create/Estimate/Commit SRSR-S-Backlog Tasks* process requires/uses/produces the following inputs/roles/methods/outputs:

- *Inputs*: SRSR-S-Backlog, SRSR PPBacklog, SRSR Tasks estimation/ acceptance criteria, and RHSI-GB-DOCS
- *Roles*: RHSI Master, RHSI Team, and RHSI-GB-EXPERT
- *Methods*: Conducting focus group meetings to explore how to estimate/ commit/accept tasks for the current SRSR-S-Backlog, and using RHSI-GB-EXPERT to estimate/commit/accept these tasks
- *Outputs*: A breakdown of SRSR-S-Backlog's estimated and committed tasks

TABLE 4.33 [P29] Create/Estimate/Commit SRSR-S-Backlog Tasks

INPUTS	ROLES	METHODS	OUTPUTS
- SRSR-S-Backlog - SRSR PPBacklog - SRSR Tasks estimation/ commitment acceptance criteria - RHSI-GB-DOCS	- RHSI Team - RHSI Master - RHSI-GB-EXPERT	- Focus group meetings - RHSI-GB-EXPERT	- A breakdown of the approved, estimated, and committed tasks for the current SRSR-S-Backlog

4.3.5.7 [P30] Create/Approve SPPR-S-Backlog

Table 4.34 shows how the *Create/Approve SPPR-S-Backlog* process requires/ uses/produces the following inputs/roles/methods/outputs:

- *Inputs*: SPPR PPBacklog, SPPR acceptance criteria, and RHSI-GB-DOCS
- *Roles*: RHSI Master, RHSI Team, and RHSI-GB-EXPERT
- *Methods*: Conducting focus group meetings to explore how to create/ approve the current SPPR-S-Backlog and using RHSI-GB-EXPERT
- *Outputs*: The current SPPR-S-Backlog

TABLE 4.34 [P30] Create/Approve SPPR-S-Backlog

INPUTS	ROLES	METHODS	OUTPUTS
- SPPR PPBacklog - SPPR acceptance criteria - RHSI-GB-DOCS	- RHSI Team - RHSI Master - RHSI-GB-EXPERT	- Focus group meetings - RHSI-GB-EXPERT	- The current SPPR-S-Backlog

4.3.5.8 [P31] Create/Estimate/Commit SPPR-S-Backlog Tasks

Table 4.35 shows how the *Create/Estimate/Commit SPPR-S-Backlog Tasks* process requires/uses/produces the following inputs/roles/methods/outputs:

- *Inputs*: SPPR-S-Backlog, SPPR PPBacklog, SPPR-S-Backlog Tasks estimation/commitment acceptance criteria, and RHSI-GB-DOCS
- *Roles*: RHSI Master, RHSI Team, and RHSI-GB-EXPERT
- *Methods*: Conducting focus group meetings to explore how to estimate/commit/accept tasks for the current SPPR-S-Backlog, and using RHSI-GB-EXPERT to estimate/commit/accept tasks for the current SPPR-S-Backlog
- *Outputs*: A breakdown of the estimated and committed tasks of the current SPPR-S-Backlog

TABLE 4.35 [P31] Create/Estimate/Commit SPPR-S-Backlog Tasks

INPUTS	ROLES	METHODS	OUTPUTS
- SPPR-S-Backlog - SPPR PPBacklog - SPPR Tasks estimation/commitment acceptance criteria - RHSI-GB-DOCS	- RHSI Team - RHSI Master - RHSI-GB-EXPERT	- Focus group meetings - RHSI-GB-EXPERT	- A breakdown of the approved, estimated, and committed tasks for the current SPPR-S-Backlog

4.3.5.9 [P32] Create/Approve SPTC-S-Backlog

Table 4.36 shows how the *Create/Approve SPTC-S-Backlog* process requires/uses/produces the following inputs/roles/methods/ outputs:

- *Inputs*: SPTC PPBacklog, SPTC acceptance criteria, and RHSI-GB-DOCS
- *Roles*: RHSI Master, RHSI Team, and RHSI-GB-EXPERT
- *Methods*: Conducting focus group meetings to explore how to create/approve the current SPTC-S-Backlog and using RHSI-GB-EXPERT to develop/approve SPTC-S-Backlogs
- *Outputs*: The current SPTC-S-Backlog

TABLE 4.36 [P32] Create/Approve SPTC-S-Backlog

INPUTS	ROLES	METHODS	OUTPUTS
- SPTC PPBacklog - SPTC acceptance criteria - RHSI-GB-DOCS	- RHSI Team - RHSI Master - RHSI-GB-EXPERT	- Focus group meetings - RHSI-GB-EXPERT	- The current SPTC-S-Backlog

4.3.5.10 [P33] Create/Estimate/Commit SPTC-S-Backlog Tasks

Table 4.37 shows how the *Create/Estimate/Commit SPTC-S-Backlog Tasks* process requires/uses/produces the following inputs/roles/methods/outputs:

- *Inputs*: SPTC-S-Backlog, SPTC PPBacklog, SPTC-S-Backlog Tasks estimation/commitment acceptance criteria, and RHSI-GB-DOCS
- *Roles*: RHSI Master, RHSI Team, and RHSI-GB-EXPERT
- *Methods*: Conducting focus group meetings to explore how to estimate/commit/accept tasks for the current SPTC-S-Backlog, and using RHSI-GB-EXPERT to estimate/commit/accept tasks for the current SPTC-S-Backlog
- *Outputs*: A breakdown of the estimated and committed tasks for the current SPTC-S-Backlog

TABLE 4.37 [P33] Create/Estimate/Commit SPTC-S-Backlog Tasks

INPUTS	ROLES	METHODS	OUTPUTS
- SPTC-S-Backlog + SPTC PPBacklog - SPTC-Tasks estimation/ commitment acceptance criteria - RHSI-GB-DOCS	- RHSI Team - RHSI Master - RHSI-GB-EXPERT	- Focus group meetings - RHSI-GB-EXPERT	- A breakdown of the approved/estimated/ committed tasks for the current SPTC-S-Backlog

4.3.5.11 [P34] Create/Approve SPQSC-S-Backlog

Table 4.38 shows how the *Create/Approve SPQSC-S-Backlog* process requires/uses/produces the following inputs/roles/methods/ outputs:

- *Inputs*: SPQSC PPBacklog, SPQSC acceptance criteria, and RHSI-GB-DOCS
- *Roles*: RHSI Master, RHSI Team, and RHSI-GB-EXPERT

- *Methods*: Conducting focus group meetings to explore how to create/ approve the current SPQSC-S-Backlog and using RHSI-GB-EXPERT to develop and approve SPQSC-S-Backlogs
- *Outputs*: The current SPQSC-S-Backlog

TABLE 4.38 [P34] Create/Approve SPQSC-S-Backlog

INPUTS	ROLES	METHODS	OUTPUTS
- SPQSC PPBacklog - SPQSC acceptance criteria - RHSI-GB-DOCS	- RHSI Team - RHSI Master - RHSI-GB-EXPERT	- Focus group meetings - RHSI-GB-EXPERT	- The current SPQSC-S-Backlog

4.3.5.12 [P35] Create/Estimate/Commit SPQSC-S-Backlog Tasks

Table 4.39 shows that the *Create/Estimate/Commit SPQSC-S-Backlog Tasks* process requires/uses/produces the following inputs/roles/methods/ outputs:

- *Inputs*: SPQSC-S-Backlog, SPQSC PPBacklog, SPQSC Tasks estimation/ commitment acceptance criteria, and RHSI-GB-DOCS
- *Roles*: RHSI Master, RHSI Team, and RHSI-GB-EXPERT
- *Methods*: Conducting focus group meetings to explore how to estimate/commit/accept tasks for the current SPQSC-S-Backlog and using RHSI-GB-EXPERT to estimate/commit/accept tasks for the current SPQSC-S-Backlog
- *Outputs*: A breakdown of the estimated and committed tasks for the current SPQSC-S-Backlog

TABLE 4.39 [P35] Create/Estimate/Commit SPQSC-S-Backlog Tasks

INPUTS	ROLES	METHODS	OUTPUTS
- SPQSC-S-Backlog - SPQSC PPBacklog - SPQSC tasks estimation/ commitment acceptance criteria - RHSI-GB-DOCS	- RHSI Team - RHSI Master - RHSI-GB-EXPERT	- Focus group meetings - RHSI-GB-EXPERT	- A breakdown of the approved estimated/ committed tasks for the current SPQSC-S-Backlog

4.3.5.13 Batch #2 Process Interactions

Figure 4.2 illustrates the interactions among the processes in batch #2 (*[P24]* to *[P35]*) of the RHSI planning model.

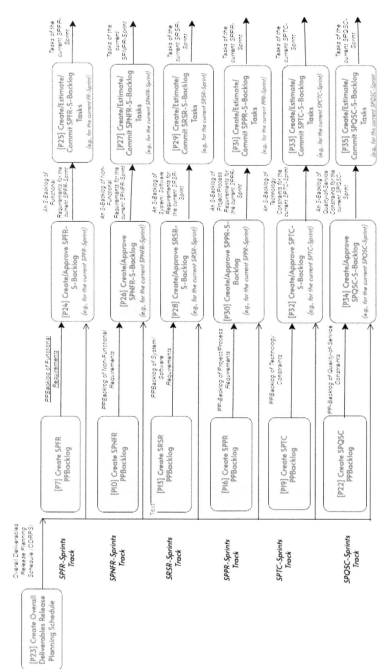

FIGURE 4.2 RHSI planning model—Batch #2 process interactions

4.3.6 Batch #3 Processes

This Sprint implementation and validation activity is repeated for each Sprint in the current SPFR Sprints, SPNFR Sprints, SRSR Sprints, SPPR Sprints, SPTC Sprints, and SPQSC Sprints clusters. Tables 4.40 through 4.61 present the inputs, roles, methods, and outputs of the processes that belong to batch #3 (*[P36] to [P56]*). Figure 4.3 illustrates the interactions among these processes.

4.3.6.1   [P36] Conduct SPFR-S-Backlog Daily Standup

Table 4.40 shows how the *Conduct SPFR-S-Backlog Daily Standup* process requires/uses/produces the following inputs/roles/methods/outputs:

- *Inputs*: RHSI burndown chart, implementation log, RHSI board, dependencies, and RHSI-GB-DOCS
- *Roles*: Product Owner, RHSI Master, RHSI Team, and RHSI-GB-EXPERT
- *Methods*: Conducting SPFR daily standup meetings, virtual meetings, and dialogues
- *Outputs*: Updated versions of the RHSI burndown chart, implementation log, RHSI board, dependencies, approved/unapproved change requests, I-Risks, and M-Risks, and a motivated RHSI Team

TABLE 4.40 [P36] Conduct SPFR-S-Backlog Daily Standup

INPUTS	ROLES	METHODS	OUTPUTS
- RHSI burndown chart - Implementation log - RHSI board - Dependencies - RHSI-GB-DOCS	- RHSI Team - RHSI Master - Product Owner - RHSI-GB-EXPERT	- SPFR daily standup meetings - Virtual meetings and dialogues	- Updated RHSI burndown chart - Updated implementation log - Updated RHSI board - Updated dependencies - Unapproved change requests - I-Risks and M-Risks - Motivated RHSI Team

4.3.6.2   [P37] Create SPFR-S-Backlog Deliverables

Table 4.41 shows how the *Create SPFR-S-Backlog Deliverables* process requires/uses/produces the following inputs/roles/methods/outputs:

▨ *Inputs*: The current SPFR-S-Backlog and its tasks, RHSI board, implementation log, overall deliverables release schedule, dependencies, and RHSI-GB-DOCS

▨ *Roles*: RHSI Master, RHSI Team, and RHSI-GB-EXPERT

▨ *Methods*: Using software development tools, and RHSI-GB-EXPERT

▨ *Outputs*: Deliverables of the current SPFR-S-Backlog, and updated versions of the implementation log, dependencies, RHSI board, approved/unapproved change requests, I-Risks, and M-Risks

TABLE 4.41 [P37] Create SPFR-S-Backlog Deliverables

INPUTS	ROLES	METHODS	OUTPUTS
- SPFR-SPFR-S-Backlog - RHSI board - Implementation log - Overall deliverables release schedule - Dependencies - RHSI-GB-DOCS	- RHSI Master - RHSI Team - RHSI-GB-EXPERT	- Using software development tools - Using RHSI-GB-EXPERT	- SPFR-S-DLVS - Updated implementation log - Updated RHSI board - Updated dependencies - Unapproved change requests - I-Risks and M-Risks

4.3.6.3   [P38] Conduct SPNFR-S-Backlog Daily Standup

Table 4.42 shows how the *Conduct SPNFR-S-Backlog Daily Standup* process requires/uses/produces the following inputs/roles/methods/outputs:

▨ *Inputs*: RHSI burndown chart, implementation log, RHSI board, dependencies, and RHSI-GB-DOCS

▨ *Roles*: Product Owner, RHSI Master, RHSI Team, and RHSI-GB-EXPERT

▨ *Methods*: SPNFR daily standup meetings, virtual meetings, and dialogues

▨ *Outputs*: Updated versions of the RHSI burndown chart, implementation log, RHSI board, dependencies, approved/unapproved change requests, I-Risks, and M-Risks; and a motivated RHSI Team

TABLE 4.42 [P38] Conduct SPNFR-S-Backlog Daily Standup

INPUTS	ROLES	METHODS	OUTPUTS
- RHSI burndown chart - Implementation log - RHSI board - Dependencies - RHSI-GB-DOCS	- RHSI Team - RHSI Master - Product Owner - RHSI-GB-EXPERT	- SPNFR daily standup meetings - Virtual meetings and dialogues	- Updated RHSI burndown chart - Updated implementation log - Updated RHSI board - Updated dependencies - Unapproved change requests - I-Risks and M-Risks - Motivated RHSI Team

4.3.6.4 [P39] Create SPNFR-S-Backlog Deliverables

Table 4.43 shows how the _Create SPNFR-S-Backlog Deliverables_ process requires/uses/produces the following inputs/roles/methods/outputs:

- _Inputs_: The current SPNFR-S-Backlog and its tasks, RHSI board, implementation log, overall deliverables release schedule, dependencies, and RHSI-GB-DOCS

- _Roles_: RHSI Master, RHSI Team, and RHSI-GB-EXPERT

- _Methods_: Using software development tools and RHSI-GB-EXPERT

- _Outputs_: Deliverables of the current SPNFR-S-Backlog and updated versions of the implementation log, dependencies, RHSI board, approved/unapproved change requests, I-Risks, and M-Risks

TABLE 4.43 [P39] Create SPNFR-S-Backlog Deliverables

INPUTS	ROLES	METHODS	OUTPUTS
- SPNFR-SPFR-S-Backlog - RHSI board - Implementation log - Overall deliverables release schedule - Dependencies - RHSI-GB-DOCS	- RHSI Master - RHSI Team - RHSI-GB-EXPERT	- Using software development tools - Using RHSI-GB-EXPERT	- SPNFR-S-DLVS - Updated implementation log - Updated RHSI board - Updated dependencies - Unapproved change requests - I-Risks and M-Risks

4.3.6.5 [P40] Conduct SRSR-S-Backlog Daily Standup

Table 4.44 shows how the *Conduct SRSR-S-Backlog Daily Standup* process requires/uses/produces the following inputs/roles/methods/outputs:

- *Inputs*: RHSI burndown chart, implementation log, RHSI board, dependencies, and RHSI-GB-DOCS
- *Roles*: Product Owner, RHSI Master, RHSI Team, and RHSI-GB-EXPERT
- *Methods*: SRSR daily standup meetings and virtual meetings
- *Outputs*: Updated versions of the RHSI burndown chart, implementation log, RHSI board, dependencies, approved/ unapproved change requests, I-Risks, M-Risks, and a motivated RHSI Team

TABLE 4.44 [P40] Conduct SRSR-S-Backlog Daily Standup

INPUTS	ROLES	METHODS	OUTPUTS
- RHSI burndown chart - Implementation log - RHSI board - Dependencies - RHSI-GB-DOCS	- RHSI Team - RHSI Master - Product Owner - RHSI-GB-EXPERT	- SRSR daily standup meetings - Virtual meetings and dialogues	- Updated RHSI burndown chart - Updated implementation log - Updated RHSI board - Updated dependencies - Unapproved change requests - I-Risks and M-Risks - Motivated RHSI Team

4.3.6.6 [P41] Create SRSR-S-Backlog Deliverables

Table 4.45 shows how the *Create SRSR-S-Backlog Deliverables* process requires/uses/produces the following inputs/roles/methods/outputs:

- *Inputs*: The current SRSR-S-Backlog and its tasks, RHSI board, implementation log, overall deliverables release schedule, dependencies, and RHSI-GB-DOCS
- *Roles*: RHSI Master, RHSI Team, and RHSI-GB-EXPERT
- *Methods*: Using software development tools and RHSI-GB-EXPERT
- *Outputs*: Deliverables of the current SRSR-S-Backlog, and updated versions of the implementation log, dependencies, RHSI board, approved/ unapproved change requests, I-Risks, and M-Risks.

TABLE 4.45 [P41] Create SRSR-S-Backlog Deliverables

INPUTS	ROLES	METHODS	OUTPUTS
- SRSR-SPFR-S-Backlog - RHSI board - Implementation log - Overall deliverables release schedule - Dependencies - RHSI-GB-DOCS	- RHSI Master - RHSI Team - RHSI-GB-EXPERT	- Using software development tools - Using RHSI-GB-EXPERT	- SRSR-Sprint functional deliverables - Updated implementation log - Updated RHSI board - Updated dependencies - Unapproved change requests - I-Risks and M-Risks

4.3.6.7 [P42] Conduct SPPR-S-Backlog Daily Standup

Table 4.46 shows how the *Conduct SPPR-S-Backlog Daily Standup* process requires/uses/produces the following inputs/roles/methods/outputs:

- *Inputs*: RHSI burndown chart, implementation log, RHSI board, dependencies, and RHSI-GB-DOCS
- *Roles*: Product Owner, RHSI Master, RHSI Team, and RHSI-GB-EXPERT
- *Methods*: Using SPPR daily standups, virtual meetings, and dialogues
- *Outputs*: Updated versions of the RHSI burndown chart, implementation log, RHSI board, dependencies, approved/ unapproved change requests, I-Risks, and M-Risks, and a motivated RHSI Team

TABLE 4.46 [P42] Conduct SPPR-S-Backlog Daily Standup

INPUTS	ROLES	METHODS	OUTPUTS
- RHSI burndown chart - Implementation log - RHSI board - Dependencies - RHSI-GB-DOCS	- RHSI Team - RHSI Master - Product Owner - RHSI-GB-EXPERT	- SPPR daily standup meetings - Virtual meetings and dialogues	- Updated RHSI burndown chart - Updated implementation log - Updated RHSI board - Updated dependencies - Unapproved change requests - I-Risks and M-Risks - Motivated RHSI Team

4.3.6.8 [P43] Create SPPR-S-Backlog Deliverables

Table 4.47 shows how the *Create SPPR-S-Backlog Deliverables* process requires/uses/produces the following inputs/roles/ methods/outputs:

- *Inputs*: The current SPPR-S-Backlog and its tasks, RHSI board, implementation log, overall deliverables release schedule, dependencies, and RHSI-GB-DOCS
- *Roles*: RHSI Master, RHSI Team, and RHSI-GB-EXPERT
- *Methods*: Using software development tools and RHSI-GB-EXPERT
- *Outputs*: Deliverables of the current SPPR-S-Backlog, and updated versions of the implementation log, dependencies, RHSI board, approved/unapproved change requests, I-Risks, and M-Risks.

TABLE 4.47 [P43] Create SPPR-S-Backlog Deliverables

INPUTS	ROLES	METHODS	OUTPUTS
- SPPR-SPFR-S-Backlog - RHSI board - Implementation log - Overall deliverables release schedule - Dependencies - RHSI-GB-DOCS	- RHSI Master - RHSI Team - RHSI-GB-EXPERT	- Using software development tools - Using RHSI-GB-EXPERT	- SPPR-Sprint functional deliverables - Updated implementation log - Updated RHSI board - Updated dependencies - Unapproved change requests - I-Risks and M-Risks

4.3.6.9 [P44] Conduct SPTC-S-Backlog Daily Standup

Table 4.48 shows how the *Conduct SPTC-S-Backlog Daily Standup* process requires/uses/produces the following inputs/roles/methods/outputs:

- *Inputs*: RHSI burndown chart, implementation log, RHSI board, dependencies, and RHSI-GB-DOCS
- *Roles*: Product Owner, RHSI Master, RHSI Team, and RHSI-GB-EXPERT
- *Methods*: Holding SPTC daily standup meetings and virtual meetings/dialogues
- *Outputs*: Updated versions of the RHSI burndown chart, implementation log, RHSI board, dependencies, approved/ unapproved change requests, I-Risks, and M-Risks, and a motivated RHSI Team

TABLE 4.48 [P44] Conduct SPTC-S-Backlog Daily Standup

INPUTS	ROLES	METHODS	OUTPUTS
- RHSI burndown chart - Implementation log - RHSI board - Dependencies - RHSI-GB-DOCS	- RHSI Team - RHSI Master - Product Owner - RHSI-GB-EXPERT	- SPTC daily standup meetings - Virtual meetings and dialogues	- Updated RHSI burndown chart - Updated implementation log - Updated RHSI board - Updated dependencies - Unapproved change requests - I-Risks and M-Risks - Motivated RHSI Team

4.3.6.10 [P45] Create SPTC-S-Backlog Deliverables

Table 4.49 shows how the *Create SPTC-S-Backlog Deliverables* process requires/uses/produces the following inputs/roles/methods/outputs:

- *Inputs*: The current SPTC-S-Backlog and its tasks, RHSI board, implementation log, overall deliverables release schedule, dependencies, and RHSI-GB-DOCS
- *Roles*: RHSI Master, RHSI Team, and RHSI-GB-EXPERT
- *Methods*: Using software development tools and RHSI-GB-EXPERT
- *Outputs*: Deliverables of the current SPTC-S-Backlog, and updated versions of the implementation log, dependencies, RHSI board, approved/unapproved change requests, I-Risks, and M-Risks

TABLE 4.49 [P45] Create SPTC-S-Backlog Deliverables

INPUTS	ROLES	METHODS	OUTPUTS
- SPTC-SPFR-S-Backlog - RHSI board - Implementation log - Overall deliverables release schedule - Dependencies - RHSI-GB-DOCS	- RHSI Master - RHSI Team - RHSI-GB-EXPERT	- Using software development tools - Using RHSI-GB-EXPERT	- SPTC Sprint-Functional Deliverables - Updated Implementation Log - Updated RHSI board - Updated Dependencies - Unapproved Change Requests - I-Risks and M-Risks

4.3.6.11 [P46] Conduct SPQSC-S-Backlog Daily Standup

Table 4.50 shows how the *Conduct SPQSC-S-Backlog Daily Standup* process requires/uses/produces the following inputs/roles/methods/outputs:

- *Inputs*: RHSI burndown chart, implementation log, RHSI board, dependencies, and RHSI-GB-DOCS
- *Roles*: Product Owner, RHSI Master, RHSI Team, and RHSI-GB-EXPERT
- *Methods*: Conducting SPQSC daily standup meetings, virtual meetings, and dialogues
- *Outputs*: Updated versions of the RHSI burndown chart, implementation log, RHSI board, dependencies, approved/unapproved change requests, I-Risks, and M-Risks, and a motivated RHSI Team

TABLE 4.50 [P46] Conduct SPQSC-S-Backlog Daily Standup

INPUTS	ROLES	METHODS	OUTPUTS
- RHSI burndown chart - Implementation log - RHSI board - Dependencies - RHSI-GB-DOCS	- RHSI Team - RHSI Master - Product Owner - RHSI-GB-EXPERT	- SPQSC daily standup meetings - Virtual meetings/dialogues	- Updated RHSI burndown chart - Updated implementation log - Updated RHSI board - Updated Dependencies - Unapproved Change Requests - I-Risks and M-Risks - Motivated RHSI Team

4.3.6.12 [P47] Create SPQSC-S-Backlog Deliverables

Table 4.51 shows how the *Create SPQSC-S-Backlog Deliverables* process requires/uses/produces the following inputs/roles/methods/outputs:

- *Inputs*: The current SPQSC-S-Backlog and its tasks, RHSI board, implementation log, overall deliverables release schedule, dependencies, and RHSI-GB-DOCS
- *Roles*: RHSI Master, RHSI Team, and RHSI-GB-EXPERT
- *Methods*: Using software development tools and RHSI-GB-EXPERT
- *Outputs*: Deliverables of the current SPQSC-S-Backlog, and updated versions of the implementation log, dependencies, RHSI board, approved/unapproved change requests, I-Risks, and M-Risks

TABLE 4.51 [P47] Create SPQSC-S-Backlog Deliverables

INPUTS	ROLES	METHODS	OUTPUTS
- SPQSC-SPFR-S-Backlog - RHSI board - Implementation log - Overall deliverables release schedule - Dependencies - RHSI-GB-DOCS	- RHSI Master - RHSI Team - RHSI-GB-EXPERT	- Using software development tools - Using RHSI-GB-EXPERT	- SPQSC-Sprint-Functional Deliverables - Updated Implementation Log - Updated RHSI board - Updated Dependencies - Unapproved Change Requests - I-Risks and M-Risks

4.3.6.13 [P48] Review/Validate/Approve SPFR/SPNFR/SRSR/SPPR/SPTC/SPQSC-S-Deliverables

Table 4.52 shows how the *Review/Validate/Approve SPFR/SPNFR/SRSR/SPPR/SPTC/SPQSC-S-Deliverables* process requires/uses/produces the following inputs/roles/methods/outputs:

- *Inputs*: Deliverables of the current cluster of SPFR Sprints, SPNFR Sprints, SRSR Sprints, SPPR Sprints, SPTC Sprints, and SPQSC Sprints; backlogs of the current cluster of sprints (i.e., SPFR-Backlog, SPNFR-Backlog, SRSR-Backlog, SPPR-Backlog, SPTC-Backlog, and SPQSC-S-Backlog); acceptance criteria for the SPFRUSs, SPNFRUSs, SSUSs, SPPRUSs, SPTCUSs, and SPQSCUSs; overall deliverables release schedule; I-Risks and M-Risks; and RHSI-GB-DOCS

- *Roles*: RHSI Master, RHSI Team, stakeholders, and RHSI-GB-EXPERT

- *Methods*: Conducting Sprint Review meetings and using RHSI-GB-EXPERT

- *Outputs*: Accepted/rejected deliverables of the current SPFR-Backlog, SPNFR-Backlog, SRSR-Backlog, SPPR-Backlog, SPTC-Backlog, and SPQSC-S-Backlog, and updated versions of the I-Risks, M-Risks, and overall deliverables release schedule

TABLE 4.52 [P48] Review/Validate/Approve SPFR/SPNFR/SRSR/SPPR/ SPTC/SPQSC-S-Deliverables

INPUTS	ROLES	METHODS	OUTPUTS
- SPFR/SPNFR/SRSR/SPPR/SPTC/SPQSC Sprints deliverables - S-Backlog (e.g., S-Backlogs of SPFR/SPNFR/SRSR/SPPR/SPTC/SPQSC requirements) - Done criteria - User story/requirement acceptance criteria - Overall deliverables release schedule - I-Risks and M-Risks - Dependencies - RHSI-GB-DOCS	- RHSI Master - RHSI Team - Stakeholders - RHSI-GB-EXPERT	- Conducting Sprint Review meetings - Using RHSI-GB-DOCS	- Accepted deliverables (e.g., SPFR/SPNFR/SRSR/SPPR/SPTC/SPQSC-S-Deliverables) - Rejected deliverables - Updated risks (i.e., I-Risks and M-Risks) - Updated overall deliverables release schedule

4.3.6.14 [P49] Ship Approved SPFR/SPNFR/SRSR/SPPR/SPTC/SPQSC-S-Deliverables

Table 4.53 shows how the *Ship Approved SPFR/SPNFR/SRSR/SPPR/SPTC/SPQSC-S-Deliverables* process requires/uses/produces the following inputs/roles/methods/outputs:

▪ *Inputs*: Accepted deliverables of the current cluster of Sprints (SPFR Sprints, SPNFR Sprints, SRSR Sprints, SPPR Sprints, SPTC Sprints, and SPQSC Sprints), release planning schedule, and RHSI-GB-DOCS

▪ *Roles*: Product Owner, RHSI Master, RHSI Team, stakeholders, and RHSI-GB-EXPERT

▪ *Methods*: Using the existing organizational deployment methods and the communication plan

▪ *Outputs*: Deployment of all accepted deliverables and recommendations for updating the set of backlogs (SPFR PPBacklog, SPNFR PPBacklog, SRSR PPBacklog, SPPR PPBacklog, SPTC PPBacklog, and SPQSC PPBacklog) according to the customer's feedback

TABLE 4.53 [P49] Ship Approved SPFR/SPNFR/SRSR/SPPR/SPTC/SPQSC- S-Deliverables

INPUTS	ROLES	METHODS	OUTPUTS
- Accepted deliverables (e.g., of the current cluster of SPFR/SPNFR/SRSR/ SPPR/SPTC/SPQSC Sprints) - Release planning schedule - RHSI-GB-DOCS	- Product Owner - RHSI Master - RHSI Team - Stakeholders - RHSI-GB-EXPERT	- Organizational deployment methods - Communication plan	- Deployment of the accepted deliverables - Proposed adjustments to the current cluster's PPBacklogs

4.3.6.15 [P50] Retrospect Shipped SPFR/SPNFR/SRSR/SPPR/SPTC/ SPQSC-S-Deliverables

Table 4.54 shows how the *Retrospect Shipped SPFR/SPNFR/SRSR/SPPR/ SPTC/SPQSC-S-Deliverables* process requires/uses/produces the following inputs/roles/methods/outputs:

- *Inputs*: The outputs of the *Review/Validate/Approve Sprint Deliverables* process, Sprint Retrospective log, lessons learned log, and RHSI-GB-DOCS
- *Roles*: Product Owner, RHSI Master, RHSI Team, and RHSI-GB-EXPERT
- *Methods*: Conducting Sprint Retrospective meetings and using RHSI-GB-DOCS
- *Outputs*: A set of endorsed recommendations for updating the backlogs (SPFR PPBacklog, SPNFR PPBacklog, SRSR PPBacklog, SPPR PPBacklog, SPTC PPBacklog, and SPQSC PPBacklog), Sprint Retrospective log, and lessons learned log according to the customer's feedback.

TABLE 4.54 [P50] Retrospect Shipped SPFR/SPNFR/SRSR/SPPR/SPTC/ SPQSC-S-Deliverables

INPUTS	ROLES	METHODS	OUTPUTS
Outputs from the *Review/Validate/ Approve Sprint Deliverables* process Sprint Retrospective log Lessons learned log RHSI-GB-DOCS	Product Owner RHSI Master RHSI Team RHSI-GB-EXPERT	Sprint Retrospective meetings Using RHSI-GB-DOCS	Proposed adjustments in the relevant PPBacklog Updated Sprint Retrospective log Updated lessons learned log

4.3.6.16 [P51] Update SPFUSs and SPFR PPBacklog

Table 4.55 shows how the *Update SPFUSs and SPFR PPBacklog* process requires/uses/produces the following inputs/roles/methods/outputs:

- *Inputs*: SPFUSs, SPFR PPBacklog, overall deliverables release schedule, RHSI burndown chart, RHSI board, and dependencies
- *Roles*: Product Owner, RHSI Master, and RHSI Team
- *Methods*: Conducting applicable PPBacklogs review and update techniques
- *Outputs*: Updated versions of the SPFUSs, SPFR PPBacklog, and overall deliverables release schedule

TABLE 4.55 [P51] Update SPFUSs and SPFR PPBacklog

INPUTS	ROLES	METHODS	OUTPUTS
- SPFUSs - SPFR PPBacklog - Overall deliverables release schedule - RHSI burndown chart - RHSI board - Dependencies	- Product Owner - RHSI Master - RHSI Team	- Conducting applicable PPBacklogs review and update techniques	- Updated SPFUSs - Updated SPFR PPBacklog - Updated overall deliverables release schedule

4.3.6.17 [P52] Update SPNFUSs and SPNFR PPBacklog

Table 4.56 shows how the *Update SPNFUSs and SPNFR PPBacklog* process requires/uses/produces the following inputs/roles/methods/outputs:

- *Inputs*: SPNFUSs, SPNFR PPBacklog, overall deliverables release schedule, RHSI burndown chart, RHSI board, and dependencies
- *Roles*: Product Owner, RHSI Master, and RHSI Team
- *Methods*: Conducting applicable PPBacklogs review and update techniques
- *Outputs*: Updated versions of the SPNFUSs, SPNFR PPBacklog, and overall deliverables release schedule

TABLE 4.56 [P52] Update SPNFUSs and SPNFR PPBacklog

INPUTS	ROLES	METHODS	OUTPUTS
- SPNFUSs - SPNFR PPBacklog - Overall deliverables release schedule - RHSI burndown chart - RHSI board - Dependencies	- Product Owner - RHSI Master - RHSI Team	- Conducting applicable PPBacklogs review/update techniques	- Updated SPNFUSs - Updated SPNFR PPBacklog - Updated overall deliverables release schedule

4.3.6.18 [P53] Update SSUSs and SRSR PPBacklog

Table 4.57 shows how the *Update SSUSs and SRSR PPBacklog* process requires/uses/produces the following inputs/roles/methods/outputs:

- *Inputs*: SSUSs, SRSR PPBacklog, overall deliverables release schedule, RHSI burndown chart, RHSI board, and dependencies
- *Roles*: Product Owner, RHSI Master, and RHSI Team
- *Methods*: Conducting applicable PPBacklogs review/update techniques
- *Outputs*: Updated versions of the SSUSs, SRSR PPBacklog, and overall deliverables release schedule

TABLE 4.57 [P53] Update SSUSs and SRSR PPBacklog

INPUTS	ROLES	METHODS	OUTPUTS
- SSUSs - SRSR PPBacklog - Overall deliverables release schedule - RHSI burndown chart - RHSI board - Dependencies	- Product Owner - RHSI Master - RHSI Team	- Conducting applicable PPBacklogs review/update techniques	- Updated SSUSs - Updated SRSR PPBacklog - Updated overall deliverables release schedule

4.3.6.19 [P54] Update SPPUSs and SPPR PPBacklog

Table 4.58 shows how the *Update SPPUSs and SPPR PPBacklog* process requires/uses/produces the following inputs/roles/methods/outputs:

- *Inputs*: SPPUSs, SPPR PPBacklog, overall deliverables release schedule, RHSI burndown chart, RHSI board, and dependencies
- *Roles*: Product Owner, RHSI Master, and RHSI Team
- *Methods*: Conducting applicable PPBacklogs review and update techniques
- *Outputs*: Updated versions of the SPPUSs, SPPR PPBacklog, and overall deliverables release schedule

TABLE 4.58 [P54] Update SPPUSs and SPPR PPBacklog

INPUTS	ROLES	METHODS	OUTPUTS
– SPPUSs – SPPR PPBacklog – Overall deliverables release schedule – RHSI burndown chart – RHSI board – Dependencies	– Product Owner – RHSI Master – RHSI Team	– Conducting applicable PPBacklogs review/ update techniques	– Updated SPPUSs – Updated SPPR PPBacklog – Updated overall deliverables release schedule

4.3.6.20 [P55] Update SPTCUSs and SPTC PPBacklog

Table 4.59 shows how the *Update SPTCUSs and SPTC PPBacklog* process requires/uses/produces the following inputs/roles/methods/outputs:

- *Inputs*: SPTCUSs, SPTC PPBacklog, overall deliverables release schedule, RHSI burndown chart, RHSI board, and dependencies
- *Roles*: Product Owner, RHSI Master, and RHSI Team
- *Methods*: Conducting applicable PPBacklogs review and update techniques
- *Outputs*: Updated versions of the SPTCUSs, SPTC PPBacklog, and overall deliverables release schedule

TABLE 4.59 [P55] Update SPTCUSs and SPTC PPBacklog

INPUTS	ROLES	METHODS	OUTPUTS
– SPTCUSs – SPTC PPBacklog – Overall deliverables release schedule – RHSI burndown chart – RHSI board – Dependencies	– Product Owner – RHSI Master – RHSI Team	– Conducting applicable PPBacklogs review/ update techniques	– Updated SPTCUSs – Updated SPTC PPBacklog – Updated overall deliverables release schedule

4.3.6.21 [P56] Update SPQSCUSs and SPQSC PPBacklog

Table 4.60 shows how the *Update SPQSCUSs and SPQSC PPBacklog* process requires/uses/produces the following inputs/roles/methods/outputs:

- *Inputs*: SPQSCUSs, SPQSC PPBacklog, overall deliverables release schedule, RHSI burndown chart, RHSI board, and dependencies
- *Roles*: Product Owner RHSI Master, and RHSI Team
- *Methods*: Conducting applicable PPBacklogs review and update techniques
- *Outputs*: Updated versions of the SPQSCUSs, SPQSC PPBacklog, and overall deliverables release schedule

TABLE 4.60 [P56] Update SPQSCUSs and SPQSC PPBacklog

INPUTS	ROLES	METHODS	OUTPUTS
- SPQSCUSs - SPQSC PPBacklog - Overall deliverables release schedule - RHSI burndown chart - RHSI board - Dependencies	- Product Owner - RHSI Master - RHSI Team	- Conducting applicable PPBacklogs review/ update techniques	- Updated SPQSCUSs - Updated SPQSC PPBacklog - Updated overall deliverables release schedule

4.3.6.22 Batch #3 Process Interactions

Figure 4.3 illustrates the interactions among the processes in batch #3 (*[P36]* to *[P56]*) of the RHSI planning model.

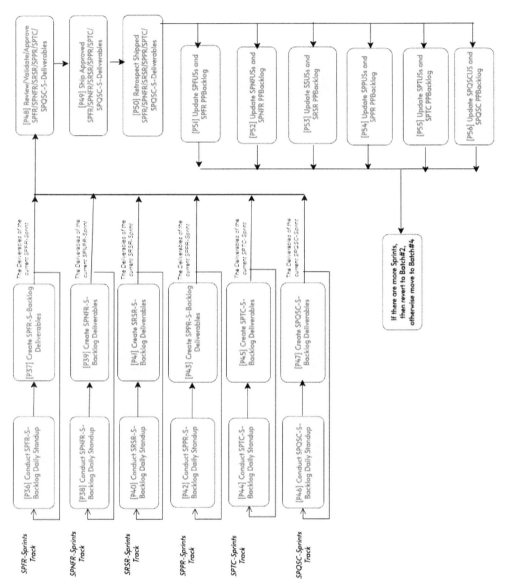

FIGURE 4.3 RHSI planning model—Batch #3 process interactions

4.3.7 Batch #4 Process

Table 4.61 presents the inputs, roles, methods, and outputs of the [P57] process that belongs to batch #4. Figure 4.4 illustrates the interactions among all processes across the four batches.

4.3.7.1 [P57] Project Retrospect and Closure

Table 4.61 shows how the *Project Retrospect and Closure* process requires/uses/produces the following inputs/roles/methods/outputs:

- *Inputs*: Sprints Retrospective log, project Retrospective log, implementation log, lessons learned log, and RHSI-GB-DOCS
- *Roles*: Product Owner, RHSI Master, RHSI Team, stakeholders, and RHSI-GB-EXPERT
- *Methods*: Conducting a project Retrospective meeting
- *Outputs*: Updated project Retrospective logs and lessons learned log

TABLE 4.61 [P57] Project Retrospect and Closure

INPUTS	ROLES	METHODS	OUTPUTS
- Sprints Retrospective log - Project Retrospective log - Implementation log - Lessons learned log - RHSI-GB-DOCS	- Product Owner - RHSI Master - RHSI Team - Stakeholders - RHSI-GB-EXPERT	- Conducting a project Retrospective meeting	- Updated project Retrospective logs - Updated lessons learned log

4.3.8 RHSI Batch Interactions

Figure 4.4 illustrates the interactions among the processes across the four batches (i.e., batch #1: *[P1]* to *[P23]*; batch #2: *[P24]* to *[P35]*; batch #3: *[P36]* to *[P56]*; and batch #4: *[P57]*) of the RHSI planning model.

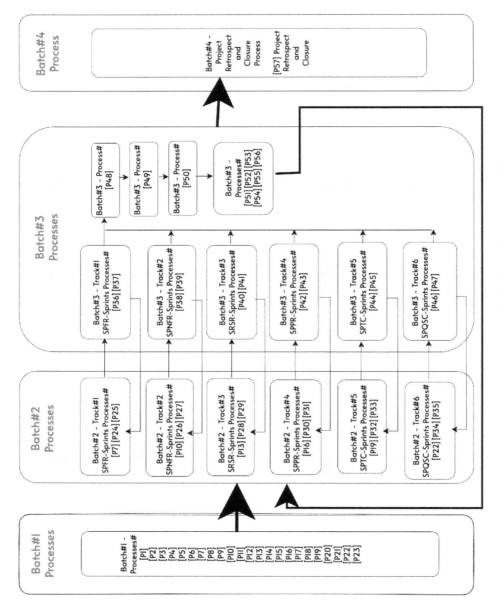

FIGURE 4.4 RHSI planning model—batches and processes overall interactions

4.4   RHSI MEETINGS

The RHSI meetings that take place throughout a project lifecycle are as follows:

- *Stakeholders meeting*: This is a lengthy meeting that takes place at the very beginning of the project. There is only one of these meetings.

- *Requirements prioritization and PPBacklogs building meeting*: This is a lengthy meeting that occurs right after the stakeholders meeting is completed. There is only one of these meetings.

- *Sprint Planning meetings*: A Sprint Planning meeting takes place at the beginning of every iteration to create a cluster of six Sprint backlogs of requirements: SPFR-S-Backlog, SPNFR-S-Backlog, SRSR-S-Backlog, SPPR-S-Backlog, SPTC-S-Backlog, and SPQSC-S-Backlog are created.

- *Focus group meetings*: A focus group meeting is held whenever needed to discuss, review, and decide on issues such as the set of SPFUSs and their SPFRs.

- *Sprint daily standup meetings*: A set of Sprint daily standup meetings (e.g., of the current cluster of sprints: SPFR Sprint, SPNFR Sprint, SRSR Sprint, SPPR Sprint, SPTC Sprint, and SPQSC Sprint) is held at the beginning of every working day to discuss the progress and status of these current Sprints.

- *Sprint Review meetings*: A Sprint Review meeting is held at the end of each cluster of Sprints. The purpose is to review and approve/disapprove the deliverables of the current cluster before the approved deliverables can be shipped/deployed at the customer site. This meeting recurs at the end of each cluster of Sprints.

- *Sprint Retrospective meetings*: A Sprint Retrospective meeting is held after deploying the approved deliverables of the current cluster of Sprints at the customer site. The purpose is to discuss and document the lessons learned throughout the journey of completing the current cluster of Sprints and the deployment of their deliverables at the customer site, and such learned lessons could then benefit the following Sprints. In addition, it is a chance to groom/update the PPBacklogs of the SPFR, SPNFR, SRSR, SPPR, SPTC, and SPQSC requirements and update the project's relevant documentation as needed. This meeting recurs at the end of each cluster of Sprints.

▨   *Project Retrospective meeting*: This is one meeting at the end of the project. The purpose is to discuss and document the lessons learned throughout the project lifecycle, which would benefit similar projects in the future.

4.4.1 Stakeholders Meeting

This meeting is held at the beginning of a project's lifecycle (i.e., occurs only once). It lasts as long as needed (its time-boxing is undefined).

The roles involved in such a meeting include, but are not limited to, the stakeholders, the RHSI Product Owner, the RHSI Master (if they are already identified), the RHSI Team (if any of the Team members are already determined), and the *RHSI Guidance Body (RHSI-GB)*.

Such a meeting is to identify and write up the user stories, and then extract the project requirements from them. The Product Owner (with the help of the RHSI Master) writes up these user stories and classifies them into six classes. Thus, the outcome of this meeting will be six groups of user stories and six groups of requirements as follows:

▨   *SPFUSs* ➜ *SPFRs*
▨   *SPNFUSs* ➜ *SPNFRs*
▨   *SSUSs* ➜ *SRSRs*
▨   *SPPUSs* ➜ *SPPRs*
▨   *SPTCUSs* ➜ *SPTCs*
▨   *SPQSCUSs* ➜ *SPQSCs*

The processes that are involved in this meeting include *Create Project Vision*, *Identify RHSI Master and Stakeholders*, *Form RHSI Team*, *Develop Epics*, *Create SPFUSs*, *Extract SPFRs*, *Create SPNFUSs*, *Extract SPNFRs*, *Create SSUSs*, *Extract SRSRs*, *Create SPPUSs*, *Extract SPPRs*, *Create SPTCUSs*, *Extract SPTCs*, *Create SPQSCUSs*, and *Extract SPTCs*.

4.4.2 PP Backlogs Building Meeting

This meeting takes place only once during the batch #1 stage of a project lifecycle and lasts for as long as needed (its time-boxing is undefined). The roles involved in this meeting include, but are not limited to, the stakeholders, Product Owner, RHSI Master, RHSI Team, and RHSI Guidance Body.

Such a meeting prioritizes the requirements in each of the six classes, then places each class of prioritized requirements in its adjacent PPBacklog of requirements. The requirements prioritization uses the following method:

$$ReqRank = ReqPriority = (1 - ReqRisksImpact) * ReqValue$$

- *ReqPriority = ReqRank*: The requirement's priority (rank) *(0 <= ReqRank)*
- *ReqRisksImpact = RRI*: The impact of the requirement risks *(0% <= RRI <= 100%)*
- *ReqValue*: The estimated value added by the requirement *(0 <= ReqValue)*

Where:

- *ReRank*: The priority/ranking of the concerned requirement
- *ReqRisksImpact*: The impact of the risks of the concerned requirement
- *ReqValue*: The value/importance of the concerned requirement

Thus, this meeting will result in six PPBacklogs of requirements: SPFR PPBacklog, SPNFR PPBacklog, SRSR PPBacklog, SPPR PPBacklog, SPTC PPBacklog, and SPQSC PPBacklog.

This meeting involves the processes of *Create SPFR PPBacklog, Create SPNFR PPBacklog, Create SRSR PPBacklog, Create SPPR PPBacklog, Create SPTC PPBacklog, Create SPQSC PPBacklog,* and *Create Overall Deliverables Release Schedule.*

4.4.3 Sprint Planning Meetings

This meeting occurs at the beginning of batch #2 and recurs every time batch #2 is iterated (its time-boxing is undefined). The roles involved in such a meeting include, but are not limited to, the RHSI Master, RHSI Team, and RHSI Guidance Body.

Such a meeting is to plan for the current cluster of Sprints: current Sprint of software product functional requirements (SPFR Sprint), current Sprint of software product non-functional requirements (SPNFR Sprint), current sprint of system and software requirements (SRSR Sprint), current Sprint of software project/process (SPPR Sprint), current Sprint of software product technology constraints (SPTC Sprint), and current Sprint of software product quality of services constraints (SPQSC Sprint).

Thus, the outcomes at every recurrence of this meeting will be the current SPFR Sprint's SPFR-S-Backlog, the current SPNFR Sprint's SPNFR-S-Backlog, the current SRSR Sprint's SRSR-S-Backlog, the current SPPR Sprint's SPPR-S-Backlog, the current SPTC Sprint's SPTC-S-Backlog, and the current SPQSC-S-Backlog.

The processes that are involved in this meeting include the following: *Create/Approve SPFR-S-Backlog, Create/Estimate/Commit SPFR-S-Backlog Tasks, Create/Approve SPNFR-S-Backlog, Create/Estimate/Commit SPNFR-S-Backlog Tasks, Create/Approve SRSR-S-Backlog, Create/Estimate/Commit SRSR-S-Backlog Tasks, Create/Approve SPPR-S-Backlog, Create/Estimate/Commit SPPR-S-Backlog Tasks, Create/Approve SPTC-S-Backlog, Create/Estimate/Commit SPTC-S-Backlog Tasks, Create/Approve SPQSC-S-Backlog,* and *Create/Estimate/Commit SPQSC-S-Backlog Tasks.*

4.4.4 Focus Group Meetings

These meetings take place whenever needed. The primary focus groups include, but are not limited to, the following: SPFUSs/SPFRs focus group, SPNFUSs/SPNFRs focus group, SSUSs/SRSRs focus group, SPPUSs/SPPRs focus group, SPTCUSs/SPTCs focus group, and SPQSCUSs/SPQSCs focus group.

4.4.5 Sprint Daily Standup Meetings

These are daily meetings (i.e., daily standup meetings of the current cluster of Sprints: SPFR Sprint, SPNFR Sprint, SRSR Sprint, SPPR Sprint, SPTC Sprint, and SPQSC Sprint). These meetings are held at the beginning of every working day during batch #3. The time-box of each is about 15 minutes. The roles involved in such meetings include, but are not limited to, the RHSI Master, RHSI Team, and RHSI Guidance Body. Such a meeting enables the RHSI Team to quickly exchange information, expertise, lessons learned, issues, and so on.

The daily standup meetings are associated with the following processes of batch #3: *Conduct SPFR-S-Backlog Daily Standup, Create SPFR-S-Backlog Deliverables, Conduct SPNFR-S-Backlog Daily Standup, Create SPNFR-S-Backlog Deliverables, Conduct SRSR-S-Backlog Daily Standup, Create SRSR-S-Backlog Deliverables, Conduct SPPR-S-Backlog Daily Standup, Create SPPR-S-Backlog Deliverables, Conduct SPTC-S-Backlog Daily*

Standup, Create SPTC-S-Backlog Deliverables, Conduct SPQSC-S-Backlog Daily Standup, and *Create SPQSC-S-Backlog Deliverables.*

4.4.6 Sprint Review Meetings

These meetings are held at the end of each cluster of Sprints (their time-box is about 4 hours). The roles involved in such meetings include, but are not limited to, the Product Owner, RHSI Master, RHSI Team, and RHSI Guidance Body.

Such meetings are to review and approve or disapprove the deliverables of the current cluster of Sprints (e.g., SPFR Sprint, SPNFR Sprint, SRSRP Sprint, SPPR Sprint, SPTC Sprint, and SPQSC Sprint). Thus, the outcome of every recurrence of these meetings will be the deliverables of the current SPFR Sprint, the current SPNFR Sprint, the current SRSR Sprint, the current SPPR Sprint, the current SPTC Sprint, and the current SPQSC Sprint. The processes involved in this meeting include the following: *Review/Validate/Approve SPFR/SPNFR/SRSR/SPPR/SPTC/SPQSC-S-Deliverables*, and *Ship Approved SPFR/SPNFR/SRSR/SPPR/SPTC/SPQSC-S-Deliverables.*

4.4.7 Sprint Retrospective Meetings

These meetings are held at the end of each cluster of Sprints after shipping and implementing the deliverables of that cluster of Sprints at the customer site (their time-box is about 4 hours). The roles involved in such meetings include, but are not limited to, the Product Owner, RHSI Master, RHSI Team, and RHSI Guidance Body.

Such meetings are to discuss the feedback from the customer and the lessons learned by the RHSI Team while planning for the current cluster of Sprints (SPFR Sprint, SPNFR Sprint, SRSRP Sprint, SPPR Sprint, SPTC Sprint, and SPQSC Sprint), implementing them, creating their deliverables, and shipping and implementing these deliverables to the customer site. Thus, the outcome at every recurrence of these meetings will be updated versions of the PPBacklogs (i.e., none, some, or all of the SPFR PPBacklog, SPNFR PPBacklog, SRSR PPBacklog, SPPR PPBacklog, SPTC PPBacklog, and SPQSC PPBacklog), and updated versions of the project documents.

The processes involved in these meetings include *Retrospect Shipped SPFR/SPNFR/SRSR/SPPR/SPTC/SPQSC-S-Deliverables, Update SPFUSs and SPFR PPBacklog, Update SPNFUSs and SPNFR PPBacklog, Update SSUS and SRSR PPBacklog, Update SPPUS and SPPR PPBacklog, Update SPTCUS and SPTC PPBacklog*, and *Update SPQSCUS and SPQSC PPBacklog*.

4.4.8 Project Retrospective Meeting

This meeting occurs at the end of the project (its time-boxing is undefined). The roles involved in such a meeting include, but are not limited to, the Product Owner, RHSI Master, RHSI Team, stakeholders, and RHSI Guidance Body. Such a meeting aims to discuss the project insightfully regarding its lessons learned, challenges, threats, risks, etc. Thus, the outcome at every recurring meeting will be updated versions of the project documents. The process involved in this meeting is *Retrospect and Close Project*.

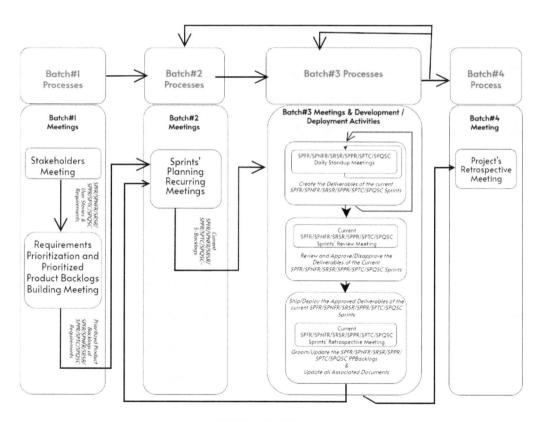

FIGURE 4.5 RHSI planning model

4.5 SUMMARY

This chapter introduced the RHSI methodology as proposed by the author. RHSI is a new software project management approach designed to address the gaps in Scrum and traditional project management approaches by hybridizing Scrum and IEEE-CS approaches. Chapter 5 will provide its modeling as proposed by the author, and Chapter 6 will provide its symbolic case study.

This chapter provided several contributions, including the following:

- An overview of the RHSI methodology and its alignment with the IEEE-CS software requirements classification, as in Section 4.2
- A detailed description of RHSI batches and processes, as in Section 4.3, including a comparative analysis of RHSI processes versus Scrum phases, as in Section 4.3.3

This chapter also provided a robust framework for understanding the structure, roles, and deliverables of the RHSI methodology, setting the stage for its detailed modeling, application, and analysis in Chapters 5 and 6.

5

A *Proposed* RHSI *Planning* Model

5.1 OVERVIEW

This section illustrates the purpose of this chapter, its contributions, and its organization.

5.1.1 The Purpose of This Chapter

This chapter presents the proposed RHSI planning model based on the RHSI software project management methodology explained in Chapter 4.

5.1.2 The Contributions of This Chapter

This chapter presents the proposed RHSI planning model in Section 5.2, including the user stories and requirements identifications, the representation of the derived software product functional requirements, the representation of the derived software product non-functional requirements, the representation of the derived system and software requirements, the representation of the derived software project and process requirements, the representation of the derived software product technology constraints, the representation of the derived software product quality of service constraints, the representation of the derived prioritized product backlogs, and the representation of the derived overall deliverables release schedule.

5.1.3 The Organization of This Chapter

This chapter has three sections, as follows:

- Section 5.1 depicts the purpose of this chapter, its contributions, and its organization.
- Section 5.2 presents the various representations of the proposed RHSI planning model, including the representation of user stories and the derived *software product functional requirements (SPFRs), software product non-functional requirements (SPNFRs), system requirements and software requirements (SRSRs), software project and process requirements (SPPRs), software product technology constraints (SPTCs), software product quality of service constraints (SPQSCs), prioritized product backlogs (PPBacklogs)*, and the overall deliverables release schedule.
- Section 5.3 summarizes this chapter.

5.2 THE PROPOSED RHSI PLANNING MODEL

This section provides the details of the proposed RHSI planning model in terms of its user stories and requirements identification, and its representations of the derived software product functional requirements, non-functional requirements, system and software requirements, project and process requirements, technology constraints, quality of service constraints, prioritized product backlogs, and overall deliverables release schedule.

5.2.1 The User Stories and Requirements Identification

The RHSI planning model proposed here is a dramatically revised and enhanced version of the Scrum project management methodology.

Table 5.1 provides self-explanatory and simplified tabular identifications of the user stories associated with their driven requirements. This includes identifying the requirements, their dependencies, their associated risks and risk impacts, their added value to the overall software product, and their priorities (i.e., prioritization).

In Table 5.1, the following symbols are used to identify the SPFRs and their dependencies, associated risks and risk impacts, added values to the overall software product, and priorities following the IEEE-CS software requirements classification as presented at the beginning of Chapter 4:

- $SPFR_{I,J}$ represents the Jth SPFR of the Ith SPFUS.
- $SPNFR_{I,J}$ represents the Jth SPNFR of the Ith SPNFUS.

- $\text{SRSR}_{I,J}$ represents the Jth SRSR of the Ith SSUS.
- $\text{SPPR}_{I,J}$ represents the Jth SPPR of the Ith SPPUS.
- $\text{SPTC}_{I,J}$ represents the Jth SPTC of the Ith SPTCUS.
- $\text{SPQSC}_{I,J}$ represents the Jth SPQSC of the Ith SPQSCUS.

TABLE 5.1 The user stories and requirements identification in the proposed RHSI planning model

User stories classification	SPFR.ID	The derived SPFRs (#SPFRs contain L requirements)	
Software product functional user stories (SPFUSs)	SPFR_1	Software product functional requirement #1	SPFR.ID: A functional requirement identification. SPFRs include the functionality of the targeted software solution.
	SPFR_2	Software product functional requirement #2	
	...	...	
	SPFR_L	Software product functional requirement #L	
	SPNFR.ID	**The derived SPNFRs (#SPNFRs contain M requirements)**	
Software product non-functional user stories (SPNFUSs)	SPNFR_1	Software product non-functional requirement #1	SPNFR.ID: A non-functional requirement identification. Software product non-functional requirements include the quality factors (*e.g., performance, privacy, security, safety, scalability, maintainability, serviceability, supportability, availability, interoperability, and reliability*) associated with their quality metrics to assess and evaluate the solution.
	SPNFR_2	Software product non-functional requirement #2	
	...	...	
	SPNFR_M	Software product non-functional requirement #M	
	SRSR.ID	**The derived SRSRs (#SRSRs contain N requirements)**	
System and software user stories (SSUSs)	SRSR_1	System and software requirement #1	SRSR.ID: A system and software requirement identification.
	SRSR_2	System and software requirement #2	
	...	...	
	SRSR_N	System and software requirement #N	
	SPPR.ID	**The derived SPPRs (#SPPRs contain O requirements)**	
Software project and process user stories (SPPUSs)	SPPR_1	Software project and process requirement #1	SPPR.ID: A project/process requirement identification.
	SPPR_2	Software project and process requirement #2	
	...	...	
	SPPR_O	Software project and process requirement #O	

(Continued)

	SPTC.ID	The derived SPTCs (#SPTCs contain P requirements)	
Software product technology constraints user stories (SPTCUSs)	SPTC$_1$	Software product technology constraint #1	SPTC.ID: A software product technology constraints requirement identification. SPTCs are ones that a single system component cannot address; rather, they depend on how the software components interoperate.
	SPTC$_2$	Software product technology constraint #2	
	...	...	
	SPTC$_P$	Software product technology constraint #P	
	SPQSC.ID	**The derived SPQSCs (#SPQSCs contain Q requirements)**	
Software product quality of service constraints user stories (SPQSCUSs)	SPQSC$_1$	Software product quality of service constraint #1	SPQSC.ID: A quantifiable requirement identification. SPQSCs refer to the SPNFRs that should be precise, verified, clear, unambiguous, qualitative, and quantitative.
	SPQSC$_2$	Software product quality of service constraint #2	
	...	...	
	SPQSC$_Q$	Software product quality of service constraint #Q	

5.2.2 The Representation of the Derived Software Product Functional Requirements

In Table 5.2, the SPFRs are derived from the SPFUSs by the RHSI Product Owner. The following symbols are used to identify the SPFRs and their dependencies, associated risks and risk impacts, added values to the overall software product, and priorities:

- SPFR$_{I,J}$ represents the Jth SPFR of the Ith SPFUS.

- SPFR$_{I,J}$.DP represents the dependencies of the Jth SPFR of the Ith SPFUS on other requirements.

- SPFR$_{I,J}$.RSK represents the risks associated with the Jth SPFR of the Ith SPFUS.

- SPFR$_{I,J}$.RSK.IMP represents the impacts of the risks associated with the Jth SPFR of the Ith SPFUS.

- SPFR$_{I,J}$.VAL represents the value added to the outcome software product by the Jth SPFR of the Ith SPFUS.

- SPFR$_{I,J}$.PRT represents the priority assigned to the Jth SPFR of the Ith SPFUS in the outcome software product. This prioritization is calculated using this formula: $SPFR_{I,J}.PRT = (1 - SPFR_{I,J}.RSK.IMP) * SPFR_{I,J}.VAL$ given that all requirements in the SPFR$_{I,J}$.DP set precede the SPFR$_{I,J}$.

5.2.3 The Representation of the Derived Software Product Non-Functional Requirements

In Table 5.3, the SPNFRs are derived from the SPNFUSs by the RHSI Product Owner. The following symbols are used to identify the SPNFRs and their dependencies, associated risks and risk impacts, added values to the overall software product, and priorities:

- $SPNFR_{I.J}$ represents the Jth SPNFR of the Ith SPNFUS.
- $SPNFR_{I.J}.DP$ represents the dependencies of the Jth SPNFR of the Ith SPNFUS on other requirements.
- $SPNFR_{I.J}.RSK$ represents the risks associated with the Jth SPNFR of the Ith SPNFUS.
- $SPNFR_{I.J}.RSK.IMP$ represents the impacts of the risks associated with the Jth SPNFR of the Ith SPNFUS.
- $SPNFR_{I.J}.VAL$ represents the value added to the outcome software product by the Jth SPNFR of the Ith SPNFUS.
- $SPNFR_{I.J}.PRT$ represents the priority assigned to the Jth SPNFR of the Ith SPNFUS in the outcome software product. This prioritization is calculated using this formula: $SPNFR_{I.J}.PRT = (1 - SPNFR_{I.J}.RSK.IMP) * SPNFR_{I.J}.VAL$ given that all requirements in the $SPNFR_{I.J}.DP$ set precede the $SPNFR_{I.J}$.

5.2.4 The Representation of the Derived System and Software Requirements

In Table 5.4, the Product Owner derives the SRSRs from the SSUSs. The following symbols are used to identify the SRSRs and their dependencies, associated risks and risk impacts, added values to the overall software product, and priorities:

- $SRSR_{I.J}$ represents the Jth SRSR of the Ith SSUS.
- $SRSR_{I.J}.DP$ represents the dependencies of the Jth SRSR of the Ith SSUS on other requirements.
- $SRSR_{I.J}.RSK$ represents the risks associated with the Jth SRSR of the Ith SSUS.
- $SRSR_{I.J}.RSK.IMP$ represents the impacts of the risks associated with the Jth SRSR of the Ith SSUS.
- $SRSR_{I.J}.VAL$ represents the value added to the outcome software product by the Jth SRSR of the Ith SSUS.

- $SRSR_{I.J}.PRT$ represents the priority assigned to the Jth SRSR of the Ith SSUS in the outcome software product. This prioritization is calculated using this formula: $SRSR_{I.J}.PRT = (1 - SRSR_{I.J}.RSK.IMP) * SRSR_{I.J}.VAL$ given that all requirements in the $SRSR_{I.J}.DP$ set precede the $SRSR_{I.J}$.

5.2.5 The Representation of the Derived Software Project and Process Requirements

In Table 5.5, the RHSI Product Owner derives the SPPRs from the SPPUSs. The following symbols are used to identify the SPPRs and their dependencies, associated risks and risk impacts, added values to the overall software product, and priorities:

- $SPPR_{I.J}$ represents the Jth SPPR of the Ith SPPUS.
- $SPPR_{I.J}.DP$ represents the dependencies of the Jth SPPR of the Ith SPPUS on other requirements.
- $SPPR_{I.J}.RSK$ represents the risks associated with the Jth SPPR of the Ith SPPUS.
- $SPPR_{I.J}.RSK.IMP$ represents the impacts of the risks associated with the Jth SPPR of the Ith SPPUS.
- $SPPR_{I.J}.VAL$ represents the value added to the outcome software product by the Jth SPPR of the Ith SPPUS.
- $SPPR_{I.J}.PRT$ represents the priority assigned to the Jth SPPR of the Ith SPPUS in the outcome software product. This prioritization is calculated using this formula: $SPPR_{I.J}.PRT = (1 - SPPR_{I.J}.RSK.IMP) * SPPR_{I.J}.VAL$ given that all requirements in the $SPPR_{I.J}.DP$ set precede the $SPPR_{I.J}$.

5.2.6 The Representation of the Derived Software Product Technology Constraints

In Table 5.6, the SPTCs are derived from the SPTCUSs by the RHSI Product Owner. The following symbols are used to identify the SPTCs and their dependencies, associated risks and risk impacts, added values to the overall software product, and priorities:

- $SPTC_{I.J}$ represents the Jth SPTC of the Ith SPTCUS.
- $SPTC_{I.J}.DP$ represents the dependencies of the Jth SPTC of the Ith SPTCUS on other constraints.
- $SPTC_{I.J}.RSK$ represents the risks associated with the Jth SPTCS of the Ith SPTCUS.

- $SPTC_{I.J}.RSK.IMP$ represents the impacts of the risks associated with the Jth SPTC of the Ith SPTCUS.

- $SPTC_{I.J}.VAL$ represents the value added to the outcome software product by the Jth SPTC of the Ith SPTCUS.

- $SPTC_{I.J}.PRT$ represents the priority assigned to the Jth SPTC of the Ith SPTCUS in the outcome software product. This prioritization is calculated using this formula: $SPTC_{I.J}.PRT = (1 - SPTC_{I.J}.RSK.IMP) * SPTC_{I.J}.VAL$ given that all constraints in the $SPTC_{I.J}.DP$ set precede the $SPTC_{I.J}$.

5.2.7 The Representation of the Derived Software Product Quality of Service Constraints

In Table 5.7, the SPQSCs are derived from the SPQSCUSs by the RHSI Product Owner. The following symbols are used to identify the SPQSCs and their dependencies, associated risks and risk impacts, added values to the overall software product, and priorities:

- $SPQSC_I$ represents the ith SPQSC .

- $SPQSC_I.DP$ represents the dependencies of the Ith SPQSC.

- $SPQSC_I.RSK$ represents the risks associated with the Ith SPQSC.

- $SPQSC_I.RSK.IMP$ represents the impacts of the risks associated with the Ith SPQSC.

- $SPQSC_I.VAL$ represents the value added to the outcome software product by the Ith SPQSC.

- $SPQSC_I.PRT$ represents the priority assigned to the Ith SPQSC . This prioritization is calculated using this formula: $SPQSC_I.PRT = (1 - SPQSC_I.RSK.IMP) * SPQSC_I.VAL$ given that all constraints in the $SPQSC_I.DP$ set precede the $SPQSC_I$.

TABLE 5.2 The representation of the derived software product functional requirements in the proposed RHSI planning model

SPFR.ID	Dependency	Risks	Risk impact (0-100% of the requirement value)	Requirement value	Priority
$SPFR_1$	$SPFR_1.DP$	$SPFR_1.RSK$	$SPFR_1.RSK.IMP$	$SPFR_1.VAL$	$SPFR_1.PRT = (1 - SPFR_1.RSK.IMP) * SPFR_1.VAL$ All requirements MUST observe their dependencies.
$SPFR_2$	$SPFR_2.DP$	$SPFR_2.RSK$	$SPFR_2.RSK.IMP$	$SPFR_2.VAL$	$SPFR_2.PRT = (1 - SPFR_2.RSK.IMP) * SPFR_2.VAL$ All requirements MUST observe their dependencies.

(Continued)

SPFR.ID	Dependency	Risks	Risk impact (0-100% of the requirement value)	Requirement value	Priority
....	....	....	....	....	....
$SPFR_L$	$SPFR_L.DP$	$SPFR_L.RSK$	$SPFR_L.RSK.IMP$	$SPFR_L.VAL$	$SPFR_L.1.PRT = (1 - SPFR_L.RSK.IMP) * SPFR_L.VAL$ All requirements MUST observe their dependencies.
Legend					

- SPFR: Software product functional requirement.
- L: Number of SPFRs.
- $SPFR_I$: The Ith functional requirement.
- $SPFR_I.RSK$: The set of risks associated with the Ith functional requirement.
- $SPFR_I.RSK.IMP$: The overall impact of the risks associated with the Ith functional requirement.

- $SPFR_I.VAL$: The added value (importance) added by the Ith functional requirement.
- $SPFR_I.PRT$: The calculated priority of the Ith functional requirement. The Ith functional requirement is placed in the SPFR PPBacklog in ascending order according to its priority.

TABLE 5.3 The representation of the software product non-functional requirements in the proposed RHSI planning model

SPNFR.ID	Dependency	Risks	Risk impact (0-100% of the requirement value)	Requirement value	Priority
$SPNFR_1$	$SPNFR_1.DP$	$SPNFR_1.RSK$	$SPNFR_1.RSK.IMP$	$SPNFR_1.VAL$	$SPNFR_1.PRT = (1 - SPNFR_1.RSK.IMP) * SPNFR_1.VAL$ All requirement MUST observe their dependencies.
$SPNFR_2$	$SPNFR_2.DP$	$SPNFR_2.RSK$	$SPNFR_2.RSK.IMP$	$SPNFR_2.VAL$	$SPNFR_2.PRT = (1 - SPNFR_2.RSK.IMP) * SPNFR_2.VAL$ All requirements MUST observe their dependencies.
....	....	....	....	....	....
$SPNFR_M$	$SPNFR_M.DP$	$SPNFR_M.RSK$	$SPNFR_M.RSK.IMP$	$SPNFR_M.VAL$	$SPNFR_M.PRT = (1 - SPNFR_M.RSK.IMP) * SPNFR_M.VAL$ All requirements MUST observe their dependencies.

(Continued)

Legend	
<ul><li>SPNFR: Software product non-functional requirement.</li><li>M: Number of SPNFRs.</li><li>$SPNFR_I$: The Ith non-functional requirement.</li><li>$SPNFR_I$.RSK: The set of risks associated with the Ith non-functional requirement.</li><li>$SPNFR_I$.RSK.IMP: The overall impact of the risks associated with the Ith non-functional requirement.</li></ul>	<ul><li>$SPNFR_I$.VAL: The added value (importance) added by the Ith non-functional requirement.</li><li>$SPNFR_I$.PRT: The calculated priority of the Ith non-functional requirement. The Ith non-functional requirement is placed in ascending order in the SPNFR PPBacklog according to its priority.</li></ul>

TABLE 5.4 The representation of the derived system and software requirements in the proposed RHSI planning model

SRSR.ID	Dependency	Risks	Risk impact (0-100% of the requirement value)	Requirement value	Priority
$SRSR_1$	$SRSR_1$.DP	$SRSR_1$.RSK	$SRSR_1$.RSK.IMP	$SRSR_1$.VAL	$SRSR_1$.PRT = (1 - $SRSR_1$.RSK.IMP) * $SRSR_1$.VAL All requirements MUST observe their dependencies.
$SRSR_2$	$SRSR_2$.DP	$SRSR_2$.RSK	$SRSR_2$.RSK.IMP	$SRSR_2$.VAL	$SRSR_2$.PRT = (1 - $SRSR_2$.RSK.IMP) * $SRSR_2$.VAL All requirements MUST observe their dependencies.
…….	…….	…….	…….	…….	…….
$SRSR_N$	$SRSR_N$.DP	$SRSR_N$.RSK	$SRSR_N$.RSK.IMP	$SRSR_N$.VAL	$SRSR_N$.PRT = (1 - $SRSR_N$.RSK.IMP) * $SRSR_N$.VAL All requirements MUST observe their dependencies.
Legend					
<ul><li>SRSR: Software/system requirement.</li><li>N: Number of SRSRs.</li><li>$SRSR_I$: The Ith software/system requirement.</li><li>$SRSR_I$.RSK: The risks associated with the Ith software/system requirement.</li><li>$SRSR_I$.RSK.IMP: The overall impact of the risks associated with the Ith software/system requirement.</li></ul>			<ul><li>$SRSR_I$.VAL: The added value (importance) the Ith software/system requirement adds.</li><li>$SRSR_I$.PRT: The calculated priority of the Ith software/system requirement. The Ith software/system sequirement is placed in the SRSR PPBacklog in ascending order according to its priority.</li></ul>		

TABLE 5.5 The representation of the derived software product and process requirements in the proposed RHSI planning model

SPPR.ID	Dependency	Risks	Risk impact (0-100% of the requirement value)	Requirement value	Priority
$SPPR_1$	$SPPR_1.DP$	$SPPR_1.RSK$	$SPPR_1.RSK.IMP$	$SPPR_1.VAL$	$SPPR_1.PRT = (1 - SPPR_1.RSK.IMP) * SPPR_1.VAL$ All requirements MUST observe their dependencies.
$SPPR_2$	$SPPR_2.DP$	$SPPR_2.RSK$	$SPPR_2.RSK.IMP$	$SPPR_2.VAL$	$SPPR_2.PRT = (1 - SPPR_2.RSK.IMP) * SPPR_2.VAL$ All requirements MUST observe their dependencies.
…….	…….	…….	…….	…….	…….
$SPPR_O$	$SPPR_O.DP$	$SPPR_O.RSK$	$SPPR_O.RSK.IMP$	$SPPR_O.VAL$	$SPPR_O.PRT = (1 - SPPR_O.RSK.IMP) * SPPR_O.VAL$ All requirements MUST observe their dependencies.
Legend					
- SPPR: Software project/process requirement. - O: Number of SPPRs. - $SPPR_I$: The Ith software project/process requirement. - $SPPR_I.RSK$: The risks associated with the Ith software project/process requirement. - $SPPR_I.RSK.IMP$: The overall impact of the Ith software project/process requirement risks.			- $SPPR_I.VAL$: The added value (importance) added by the Ith software project/process requirement. - $SPPR_I.PRT$: The calculated priority of the Ith software project/process requirement. The Ith software project/process requirement is placed in the SPPR PPBacklog in ascending order according to its priority.		

TABLE 5.6 The representation of the derived software product technology constraints in the proposed RHSI planning model

SPTC.ID	Dependency	Risks	Risk impact (0-100% of the requirement value)	Requirement value	Priority
$SPTC_1$	$SPTC_1.DP$	$SPTC_1.RSK$	$SPTC_1.RSK.IMP$	$SPTC_1.VAL$	$SPTC_1.PRT = (1 - SPTC_1.RSK.IMP) * SPTC_1.VAL$ All requirements MUST observe their dependencies.
$SPTC_2$	$SPTC_2.DP$	$SPTC_2.RSK$	$SPTC_2.RSK.IMP$	$SPTC_2.VAL$	$SPTC_2.PRT = (1 - SPTC_2.RSK.IMP) * SPTC_2.VAL$ All requirements MUST observe their dependencies.
…….	…….	…….	…….	…….	…….
$SPTC_P$	$SPTC_P.DP$	$SPTC_P.RSK$	$SPTC_P.RSK.IMP$	$SPTC_P.VAL$	$SPTC_P.PRT = (1 - SPTC_P.RSK.IMP) * SPTC_P.VAL$ All requirements MUST observe their dependencies.

(Continued)

Legend	
- SPTC: Software product technology constraint. - P: Number of SPTCs. - $SPTC_I$: The Ith software product technology constraint requirement. - $SPTC_I.RSK$: The risks associated with the Ith software product technology constraint requirement. - $SPTC_I.RSK.IMP$: The overall impact of the risks associated with the Ith software product technology constraint requirement.	- $SPTC_I.VAL$: The added value (importance) the Ith software product technology constraint requirement adds. - $SPTC_I.PRT$: The calculated priority of the Ith software product technology constraint requirement. It is placed in the SPTC PPBacklog in ascending order according to its priority.

TABLE 5.7 The representation of the derived software product quality of service constraints in the proposed RHSI planning model

SPQSC.ID	Dependency	Risks	Risk impact (0-100% of the requirement value)	Requirement value	Priority
$SPQSC_1$	$SPQSC_1.DP$	$SPQSC_1.RSK$	$SPQSC_1.RSK.IMP$	$SPQSC_1.VAL$	$SPQSC_1.PRT =$ $(1 - SPQSC_1.RSK.IMP)*$ $SPQSC_1.VAL$ All requirements MUST observe their dependencies.
$SPQSC_2$	$SPQSC_2.DP$	$SPQSC_2.RSK$	$SPQSC_2.RSK.IMP$	$SPQSC_2.VAL$	$SPQSC_2.PRT =$ $(1 - SPQSC_2.RSK.IMP)*$ $SPQSC_2.VAL$ All requirements MUST observe their dependencies.
……..	……..	……..	……..	……..	……..
$SPQSC_Q$	$SPQSC_Q.DP$	$SPQSC_Q.RSK$	$SPQSC_Q.RSK.IMP$	$SPQSC_Q.VAL$	$SPQSC_Q.PRT =$ $(1 - SPQSC_Q.RSK.IMP)*$ $SPQSC_Q.VAL$ All requirements MUST observe their dependencies.
Legend					
- SPQSC: Software product quality of services constraint. - Q: Number of SPQSCs. - $SPQSC_I$: The Ith software product quality of services constraint requirement. - $SPQSC_I.RSK$: The set of risks associated with the Ith software product quality of services constraint requirement. - $SPQSC_I.RSK.IMP$: The overall impact of the risks associated with the Ith software product quality of services constraint requirement.			- $SPQSC_I.VAL$: The Ith software product quality of services constraint requirement's added value (importance). - $SPQSC_I.PRT$: The calculated priority of the Ith software product quality of services constraint requirement. The Ith software product quality of services constraint requirement is placed in the SPQSC PPBacklog in ascending order according to its priority.		

5.2.8 The Representation of the Derived Prioritized Product Backlogs

Table 5.8 presents the representations of the various PPBacklogs of requirements as follows:

- The RHSI Product Owner derives the *software product functional requirements backlog* (*SPFR-PPBacklog*) from the SPFRs.

- The RHSI Product Owner derives the *software product non-functional requirements backlog* (*SPNFR-PPBacklog*) from the SPNFRs.

- The RHSI Product Owner derives the *system and software requirements backlog* (*SRSR-PPBacklog*) from the SRSRs.

- The RHSI Product Owner derives the *software project and process requirements backlog* (*SPPR-PPBacklog*) from the SPPRs.

- The RHSI Product Owner derives the *software product technology constraints backlog* (*SPTC-PPBacklog*) from the SPTCs.

- The RHSI Product Owner derives the *software product quality of services constraints* (*SPQSC-PPBacklog*) from the SPQSCs.

TABLE 5.8 The representations of the various prioritized product backlogs of requirements

Software product functional requirements (SPFRs)	List of SPFRs	$SPFRs = [SPFR_1, SPFR_2, ..., SPFR_L]$
	List of SPFR priorities	$SPFR.PR = [SPFR_1.PRT, SPFR_2.PRT, ..., SPFR_L.PRT]$
	SPFR PPBacklog	$Sorted\text{-}SPFRs = SORTONPRT((SPFR_1, SPFR_1.PRT), (SPFR_2, SPFR_2.PRT), ..., (SPFR_L, SPFR_L.PRT))$
Software product non-functional requirements (SPNFRs)	List of SPNFRs	$SPNFRs = [SPNFR_1, SPNFR_2, ..., SPNFR_M]$
	List of SPNFR priorities	$SPNFR.PR = [SPNFR_1.PRT, SPNFR_2.PRT, ..., SPNFR_M.PRT]$
	SPNFR PPBacklog	$Sorted\text{-}SPNFRs = SORTONPRT((SPNFR_1, SPNFR_1.PRT), (SPNFR_2, SPNFR_2.PRT), ..., (SPNFR_L, SPNFR_M.PRT))$
System and software requirements (SRSRs)	List of SRSRs	$SRSRs = [SRSR_1, SRSR_2, ..., SRSR_N]$
	List of SRSR priorities	$SRSR.PR = [SRSR_1.PRT, SRSR_2.PRT, ..., SRSR_N.PRT]$
	SRSR PPBacklog	$Sorted\text{-}SRSRs = SORTONPRT((SRSR_1, SRSR_1.PRT), (SRSR_2, SRSR_2.PRT), ..., (SRSR_N, SRSR_N.PRT))$
Software project and process requirements (SPPRs)	List of SPPRs	$SPPRs = [SPPR_1, SPPR_2, ..., SPPR_O]$
	List of SPPR priorities	$SPPR.PR = [SPPR_1.PRT, SPPR_2.PRT, ..., SRSR_O.PRT]$
	SPPR PPBacklog	$Sorted\text{-}SPPRs = SORTONPRT((SPPR_1, SPPR_1.PRT), (SPPR_2, SPPR_2.PRT), ..., (SPPR_O, SPPR_O.PRT))$

(Continued)

Software product technology constraints (SPTCs)	List of SPTCs	SPTCs = [SPTC$_1$, SPTC$_2$, ..., SPTC$_P$]
	List of SPTC priorities	SPTC.PR = [SPTC$_1$.PRT, SPTC$_2$.PRT, ..., SPTC$_P$.PRT]
	SPTC PPBacklog	Sorted-SPTCs = SORTONPRT((SPTC$_1$, SPTC$_1$.PRT), (SPTC$_2$, SPTC$_2$.PRT), ..., (SPTC$_P$, SPTC$_P$.PRT))
Software product quality of service constraints (SPQSCs)	List of SPQSCs	SPQSCs = [SPQSC$_1$, SPQSC$_2$, ..., SPQSC$_Q$]
	List of SPQSC priorities	SPQSC.PR = [SPQSC$_1$.PRT, SPQSC$_2$.PRT, ..., SPQSC$_Q$.PRT]
	SPQSC PPBacklog	Sorted-SPQSCs = SORTONPRT((SPQSC$_1$, SPQSC$_1$.PRT), (SPQSC$_2$, SPQSC$_2$.PRT), ..., (SPQSC$_Q$, SPQSC$_Q$.PRT))

Legend			
SPFRs: Software product functional requirements SPNFRs: Software product non-functional requirements SRSRs: Software/system requirements SPPRs: Software project/process requirements SPTCs: Software product technology constraints SPQSCs: Software product quality of service constraints	L: Number of SPFRs M: Number of SPNFRs N: Number of SRSRs O: Number of SPPRs P: Number of SPTCs Q: Number of SPQSCs	SPFR$_I$: The Ith SPFR SPNFR$_I$: The Ith SPNFR SRSR$_I$: The Ith SRSR SPPR$_I$: The Ith SPPR SPTC$_I$: The Ith SPTC requirement SPQSC$_I$: The Ith SPQSC requirement	PRT: Priority SORTONPRT(): Sort the given requirements based on their priorities in descending order.

5.2.9 The Representation of the Derived Deliverables Release Schedule

By recalling Figure 4.4, we can depict the following:

- The lifecycle of each cluster of Sprints repetitively spans batch #2 (i.e., Sprint Planning) and batch #3 (i.e., Sprint execution: deliverables' creation, reviewing, deployment, and Retrospection).

- The sets of tasks in the current cluster of Sprint backlogs (i.e., current SPFR-S-Backlog tasks, SPNFR-S-Backlog tasks, SRSR-S-Backlog tasks, SPPR-S-Backlog tasks, SPTC-S-Backlog tasks, and SPQSC-S-Backlog tasks) are executed concurrently, but each in its own tasks' sequencing.

- The sets of deliverables of each Sprint in the current Sprints cluster (i.e., SPFR-S-Backlog deliverables, SPNFR-S-Backlog deliverables, SRSR-S-Backlog deliverables, SPPR-S-Backlog deliverables, SPTC-S-Backlog deliverables, and SPQSC-S-Backlog deliverables) are handled (i.e., created, reviewed, deployed, and retrospected) concurrently, but each in its own deliverables' sequencing.

   ▪   The time-boxing for each cluster of Sprints (i.e., current SPFR Sprint, SPNFR Sprint, SRSR Sprint, SPPR Sprint, SPTC Sprint, and SPQSC Sprint) would be the same as in Scrum's 1–6 weeks, but typically would be 4 weeks.

Table 5.9 provides the representation of the release planning schedule.

TABLE 5.9 The representation of the deliverables release schedule

Software product functional requirements (SPFRs)	List of SPFRs	SPFRs = [SPFR$_1$, SPFR$_2$, …, SPFR$_L$]
	List of SPFR priorities	SPFR.PRT = [SPFR$_1$.PRT, SPFR$_2$.PRT, …, SPFR$_L$.PRT]
	SPFR PPBacklog	Sorted-SPFRs = SORTONPRT((SPFR$_1$, SPFR$_1$.PRT), (SPFR$_2$, SPFR$_2$.PRT), …, (SPFR$_L$, SPFR$_L$.PRT))
	List of SPFR-S-Backlogs	SPFR-S-Backlogs = [SPFR-S-Backlog of Sprint#1, SPFR-S-Backlog of Sprint#2, …..] such that: SPFR-S-Backlog of Sprint#1 includes the highest-priority software product functional requirements SPFR-S-Backlog of the last includes the lowest-priority software product functional requirements
	SPFR-S-Backlogs' deliverables	SPFR.DLVS = {[Deliverables of SPFR-S-Backlog of Sprint#1], [Deliverables of SPFR-S-Backlog of Sprint#2], …..}
Software product non-functional requirements (SPNFRs)	List of SPNFRs	SPNFRs = [SPNFR$_1$, SPNFR$_2$, …, SPNFR$_M$]
	List of SPNFR priorities	SPNFR.PRT = [SPNFR$_1$.PRT, SPNFR$_2$.PRT, …, SPNFR$_M$.PRT]
	SPNFR PPBacklog	Sorted-SPNFRs = SORTONPRT((SPNFR$_1$, SPNFR$_1$.PRT), (SPNFR$_2$, SPNFR$_2$.PRT), …, (SPNFR$_M$, SPNFR$_M$.PRT))
	List of SPNFR-S-Backlogs	SPNFR-S-Backlogs = [SPNFR-S-Backlog of Sprint#1, SPNFR-S-Backlog of Sprint#2, …..] such that: SPNFR-S-Backlog of Sprint#1 includes the highest-priority software product non-functional requirements SPNFR-S-Backlog of the last includes the lowest-priority software product non-functional requirements
	SPNFR-S-Backlogs' deliverables	SPNFR.DLVS = {[Deliverables of SPNFR-S-Backlog of Sprint#1], [Deliverables of SPNFR-S-Backlog of Sprint#2], …..}
System and software requirements (SRSRs)	List of SRSRs	SRSRs = [SRSR$_1$, SRSR$_2$, …, SRSR$_N$]
	List of SRSR priorities	SRSR.PRT = [SRSR$_1$.PRT, SRSR$_2$.PRT, …, SRSR$_N$.PRT]
	SRSR PPBacklog	Sorted-SRSRs = SORTONPRT((SRSR$_1$, SRSR$_1$.PRT), (SRSR$_2$, SRSR$_2$.PRT), …, (SRSR$_N$, SRSR$_N$.PRT))
	List of SRSR-S-Backlogs	SRSR-S-Backlogs = [SRSR-S-Backlog of Sprint#1, SRSR-S-Backlog of Sprint#2, …..] such that: SRSR-S-Backlog of Sprint#1 includes the highest-priority software/system requirements SRSR-S-Backlog of the last includes the lowest-priority software/system requirements
	SRSR-S-Backlogs' deliverables	SRSR.DLVS = {[Deliverables of SRSR-S-Backlog of Sprint#1], [Deliverables of SRSR-S-Backlog of Sprint#2], …..}

(Continued)

Software project and process requirements (SPPRs)	List of SPPRs	$SPPRs = [SPPR_1, SPPR_2, ..., SPPR_O]$
	List of SPPR priorities	$SPPR.PRT = [SPPR_1.PRT, SPPR_2.PRT, ..., SPPR_O.PRT]$
	SPPR PPBacklog	$Sorted\text{-}SPPRs = SORTONPRT((SPPR_1, SPPR_1.PRT), (SPPR_2, SPPR_2.PRT), ..., (SPPR_O, SPPR_O.PRT))$
	List of SPPR-S-Backlogs	SPPR-S-Backlogs = [SPPR-S-Backlog of Sprint#1, SPPR-S-Backlog of Sprint#2, ...] such that: SPPR-S-Backlog of Sprint#1 includes the highest-priority software project/process requirements SPPR-S-Backlog of the last includes the lowest-priority software project/process requirements
	SPPR-S-Backlogs' deliverables	$SPPR.DLVS = \{[\text{Deliverables of SPPR-S-Backlog of Sprint\#1}], [\text{Deliverables of SPPR-S-Backlog of Sprint\#2}], ...\}$
Software product technology constraints (SPTCs)	List of SPTC	$SPTCs = [SPTC_1, SPTC_2, ..., SPTC_P]$
	List of SPTC priorities	$SPTC.PRT = [SPTC_1.PRT, SPTC_2.PRT, ..., SPTC_P.PRT]$
	SPTC PPBacklog	$Sorted\text{-}SPTCs = SORTONPRT((SPTC_1, SPTC_1.PRT), (SPTC_2, SPTC_2.PRT), ..., (SPTC_P, SPTC_P.PRT))$
	List of SPTC-S-Backlogs	SPTC-S-Backlogs = [SPTC-S-Backlog of Sprint#1, SPTC-S-Backlog of Sprint#2, ...] such that: SPTC-S-Backlog of Sprint#1 includes the highest-priority software product technology constraints SPTC-S-Backlog of the last includes the lowest-priority software product technology constraints
	SPTC-S-Backlogs' deliverables	$SPTC.DLVS = \{[\text{Deliverables of SPTC-S-Backlog of Sprint\#1}], [\text{Deliverables of SPTC-S-Backlog of Sprint\#2}], ...\}$
Software product quality of service constraints (SPQSCs)	List of SPQSC	$SPQSCs = [SPQSC_1, SPQSC_2, ..., SPQSC_Q]$
	List of SPQSC priorities	$SPQSC.PRT = [SPQSC_1.PRT, SPQSC_2.PRT, ..., SPQSC_Q.PRT]$
	SPQSC PPBacklog	$Sorted\text{-}SPQSCs = SORTONPRT((SPQSC_1, SPQSC_1.PRT), (SPQSC_2, SPQSC_2.PRT), ..., (SPQSC_Q, SPQSC_Q.PRT))$
	List of SPQSC-S-Backlogs	SPQSC-S-Backlogs = [SPQSC-S-Backlog of Sprint#1, SPQSC-S-Backlog of Sprint#2, ...] such that: SPQSC-S-Backlog of Sprint#1 includes the highest-priority software product quality of service constraints SPQSC-S-Backlog of the last includes the lowest-priority software product quality of service constraints
	SPQSC-S-Backlogs' deliverables	$SPQSC.DLVS = \{[\text{Deliverables of SPQSC-S-Backlog of Sprint\#1}], [\text{Deliverables of SPQSC-S-Backlog of Sprint\#2}], ...\}$

(Continued)

Legend			
SPFRs: Software product functional requirements SPNFRs: Software product non-functional requirements SRSRs: Software/system requirements SPPRs: Software project/process requirements SPTCs: Software product technology constraints SPQSCs: Software product quality of service constraints	L: Number of SPFRs M: Number of SPNFRs N: Number of SRSRs O: Number of SPPRs P: Number of SPTCs Q: Number of SPQSCs	$SPFR_I$: The Ith SPFR $SPNFR_I$: The Ith SPNFR $SRSR_I$: The Ith SRSR $SPPR_I$: The Ith SPPR $SPTC_I$: The Ith SPTC requirement $SPQSC_I$: The Ith SPQSC requirement	PRT: Priority SORTONPRT(): Sort the given requirements based on their priorities in descending order.

5.3 SUMMARY

This chapter presented the proposed RHSI planning model, which builds upon the Scrum principles discussed earlier and provides a structured approach to planning and managing requirements.

This chapter's main contribution was a detailed RHSI planning model that outlined the identification of user stories and requirements (Section 5.2) and their derivation into various categories such as functional requirements, non-functional requirements, system and software requirements, project and process requirements, technology constraints, and quality of service constraints (Sections 5.2.1–5.2.9). The importance of the model is the fact that project management and information technology professionals can use it as the foundation for new RHSI-based software project management tools.

6

A SYMBOLIC RHSI CASE STUDY

6.1 OVERVIEW

This section illustrates the purpose of this chapter, its contributions, and its organization.

6.1.1 The Purpose of This Chapter

This chapter presents a case study to help readers understand the planning function using the RHSI software project management methodology presented and modeled in Chapters 4 and 5.

6.1.2 The Contributions of This Chapter

This chapter provides a case study to help understand the planning function with the RHSI software project management methodology.

6.1.3 The Organization of This Chapter

This chapter comes in three sections: Section 6.1 describes the purpose of this chapter, its contributions, and its organization. Section 6.2 provides the artifacts of the symbolic case study that this chapter is concerned with. Section 6.3 presents the implementation of the case study in terms of its derived clusters, Sprints, etc. Section 6.4 summarizes this chapter.

6.2 THE GIVEN CASE STUDY ARTIFACTS

This section presents the artifacts of the symbolic RHSI case study that this chapter is concerned with. This includes the given user stories and requirements and their prioritization, the given time-boxes, the given staffing, the given financial aspects, the given requirement prioritization into product prioritized backlogs, and the given Sprint backlogs of requirements.

6.2.1 The Given User Stories, Requirements, and Prioritization

The details of the given user stories and their associated requirements are presented in Table 6.1, which indicates that the intended symbolic case study involves the following user stories and requirements:

- A set of six *software product functional user stories* (*SPFUSs*), each generating five *software product functional requirements* (*SPFRs*) (i.e., $SPFUS_1$ ➔ $SPFR_1$ to $SPFR_5$), for a total of thirty requirements (i.e., $SPFUS_1$ ➔ $SPFR_1$–$SPFR_5$; $SPFUS_2$ ➔ $SPFR_6$–$SPFR_{10}$; $SPFUS_3$ ➔ $SPFR_{11}$–$SPFR_{15}$; $SPFUS_4$ ➔ $SPFR_{16}$–$SPFR_{20}$; $SPFUS_5$ ➔ $SPFR_{21}$–$SPFR_{25}$; and $SPFUS_6$ ➔ $SPFR_{26}$–$SPFR_{30}$)

- A set of four *software product non-functional user stories* (*SPNFUSs*), each of which generates five *software product non-functional requirements* (*SPNFRs*), for a total of twenty requirements (i.e., $SPNFUS_1$ ➔ $SPNFR_1$–$SPNFR_5$; $SPNFUS_2$ ➔ $SPNFR_6$–$SPNFR_{10}$; $SPNFUS_3$ ➔ $SPNFR_{11}$–$SPNFR_{15}$; and $SPNFUS_4$ ➔ $SPNFR_{16}$–$SPNFR_{20}$)

- A set of two *system and software user stories* (*SSUSs*), each generating five *system and software requirements* (*SRSRs*), for a total of ten requirements (i.e., $SRUS_1$ ➔ $SRSR_1$ to $SRSR_5$, and $SRUS_2$ ➔ $SRSR_6$ to $SRSR_{10}$)

- A set of two *software project and process user stories* (*SPPUSs*), each of which generates five *software project and process requirements* (*SPPRs*), for a total of ten requirements (i.e., $SPPUS_1$ ➔ $SPPR_1$ to $SPPR_5$, and $SPPUS_2$ ➔ $SPPR_6$ to $SPPR_{10}$)

- One *software product technology constraints user story* (*SPTCUS*), which generates five *software product technology constraints* (*SPTCs*), for a total of five constraints (i.e., $SPTCUS_1$ ➔ $SPTC_1$ to $SPTC_5$)

- One *software product quality of service constraints user story* (*SPQSCUS*), which generates five *software product quality of service constraints* (*SPQSCs*), for a total of five constraints (i.e., $SPQSCUS_1$ ➔ $SPQSC_1$ to $SPQSC_5$)

6.2.2 The Given Time-Boxes

The time-boxes are as follows:

- *User story time-box*: A user story can be given up to one week to complete all its associated requirements' tasks (i.e., one user story, five requirements, twenty-five tasks, five tasks per working day).

- *Sprint time-box*: A Sprint can last up to six weeks, during which time, all tasks associated with its set of prioritized requirements can be completed.

- *Sprint Planning meeting time-box*: A Sprint Planning meeting can last up to eight hours.

- *Sprint Review meeting time-box*: A Sprint Review meeting can last up to four hours.

- *Sprint Retrospective meeting time-box*: A Sprint Retrospective meeting can last up to four hours.

- *Stakeholders meeting time-box*: The stakeholders meeting can last for as long as the Product Owner needs to identify their requirements through a list of user stories. Then, the Product Owner can prioritize these user stories and create and populate a PPBacklog accordingly.

TABLE 6.1 The given user stories, requirements, and their prioritization

Categories of user stories	# of user stories	User stories	User stories' requirements	Backlogs of requirements
Software product functional user stories (SPFUSs)	6 SPFUSs	$SPFUS_1$	$SPFR_1$–$SPFR_5$	PPBacklog of software product functional requirements (SPFR PPBacklog)
		$SPFUS_2$	$SPFR_6$–$SPFR_{10}$	
		$SPFUS_3$	$SPFR_{11}$–$SPFR_{15}$	
		$SPFUS_4$	$SPFR_{16}$–$SPFR_{20}$	
		$SPFUS_5$	$SPFR_{21}$–$SPFR_{25}$	
		$SPFUS_6$	$SPFR_{26}$–$SPFR_{30}$	
Software product non-functional user stories (SPNFUSs)	4 SPNFUSs	$SPNFUS_1$	$SPNFR_1$–$SPNFR_5$	PPBacklog of software product non-functional requirements (SPNFR PPBacklog)
		$SPNFUS_2$	$SPNFR_6$–$SPNFR_{10}$	
		$SPNFUS_3$	$SPNFR_{11}$–$SPNFR_{15}$	
		$SPNFUS_4$	$SPNFR_{16}$–$SPNFR_{20}$	
System and software user stories (SSUSs)	2 SSUSs	$SSUS_1$	$SRSR_1$–$SRSR_5$	PPBacklog of system and software requirements (SRSR PPBacklog)
		$SSUS_2$	$SRSR_6$–$SRSR_{10}$	

(Continued)

Categories of user stories	# of user stories	User stories	User stories' requirements	Backlogs of requirements
Project and process user stories (SPPUSs)	2 SPPUSs	$SPPUS_1$	$SPPR_1$–$SPPR_5$	PPBacklog of software project and process requirements (SPPR PPBacklog)
		$SPPUS_2$	$SPPR_6$–$SPPR_{10}$	
Software product technology constraints user stories (SPTCUSs)	1 SPTCUS	$SPTCUS_1$	$SPTC_1$–$SPTC_5$	PPBacklog of software product technology constraints (SPTC PPBacklog)
Software product quality of service constraints user stories (SPQSCUSs)	1 SPQSCUS	$SPQSCUS_1$	$SPQSC_1$–$SPQSC_5$	PPBacklog of software product quality of service constraints (SPQSC PPBacklog)

6.2.3 The Given Staffing

The staff that can be involved in this symbolic case study include the following:

- One *RHSI Product Owner (RPO)*
- One *RHSI Master (RSM)*
- Five *RHSI Team members (RTM_1 to RTM_5)*

For simplicity, let's assume that all RHSI Team members have similar qualifications (i.e., experience, education, salaries, etc.).

6.2.4 The Given Financial Aspects

The financial perspective of this symbolic case study is as follows:

- *RHSI Product Owner*: The monthly salary of the Product Owner is $5,000.00 ($1,153.85 weekly).
- *RHSI RHSI Master*: The monthly salary of the RHSI Master is $4,000.00 ($923.08 weekly).
- *RHSI Team*: The monthly salary of each RHSI Team member (i.e., $RTM_1...RTM_5$) is $3,000.00 ($692.31 weekly).
- *Overhead*: The overhead (i.e., hardware, software licenses, etc.) will be approximately $30,000.00.

6.2.5 The Given Requirements' Prioritization into PPBacklogs

Table 6.2 indicates the prioritization of the various sets of requirements of this symbolic case study as follows:

- The thirty functional requirements of software products (i.e., $SPFR_1$ to $SPFR_{30}$) are prioritized in five levels. The $SPFR\text{-}Level_1$ requirements have the highest priority and are placed at the top of the SPFR PPBacklog, while the $SPFR\text{-}Level_5$ requirements have the lowest priority and are placed at the bottom.

- The twenty software product non-functional requirements (i.e., $SPNFR_1$ to $SPNFR_{20}$) are also prioritized in five levels. The $SPNFR\text{-}Level_1$ requirements have the highest priority and are placed at the top of the SPNFR PPBacklog, while the $SPNFR\text{-}Level_5$ requirements have the lowest priority and are placed at the bottom.

- The ten system and software requirements (i,e., $SRSR_1$ to $SRSR_{10}$) are also prioritized in five levels. The $SRSR\text{-}Level_1$ requirements have the highest priority and are placed at the top of the SRSR PPBacklog, while the $SRSR\text{-}Level_5$ requirements have the lowest priority and are placed at the bottom.

- The ten project and process requirements (i.e., $SPPR_1$ to $SPPR_{10}$) are also prioritized in five levels. The $SPPR\text{-}Level_1$ requirements have the highest priority and are placed at the top of the SPPR PPBacklog, while the $SPPR\text{-}Level_5$ requirements have the lowest priority and are placed at the bottom.

- The five software product technology constraints (i.e., $SPTC_1$ to $SPTC_5$) are also prioritized in five levels. The $SPTC\text{-}Level_1$ requirements have the highest priority and are placed at the top of the SPTC PPBacklog, while the $SPTC\text{-}Level_5$ requirements have the lowest priority and are placed at the bottom.

- The five software product quality service constraints (i.e., $SPQSC_1$ to $SPQSC_5$) are also prioritized in five levels. The $SPQSC\text{-}Level_1$ requirements have the highest priority and are placed at the top of the SPQSC PPBacklog, while the $SPQSC\text{-}Level_5$ requirements have the lowest priority and are placed at the bottom.

TABLE 6.2 The given requirements' prioritization into backlogs

Backlogs of requirements	Requirements' prioritization	
SPFR PPBacklog	SPFR-Level$_1$ priority (highest): [SPFR$_1$, SPFR$_6$, SPFR$_{11}$, SPFR$_{16}$, SPFR$_{21}$, SPFR$_{26}$]	
	SPFR-Level$_2$ priority: [SPFR$_2$, SPFR$_7$, SPFR$_{12}$, SPFR$_{17}$, SPFR$_{22}$, SPFR$_{27}$]	
	SPFR-Level$_3$ priority: [SPFR$_3$, SPFR$_8$, SPFR$_{13}$, SPFR$_{18}$, SPFR$_{23}$, SPFR$_{28}$]	
	SPFR-Level$_4$ priority: [SPFR$_4$, SPFR$_9$, SPFR$_{14}$, SPFR$_{19}$, SPFR$_{24}$, SPFR$_{29}$]	
	SPFR-Level$_5$ priority (lowest): [SPFR$_5$, SPFR$_{10}$, SPFR$_{15}$, SPFR$_{20}$, SPFR$_{25}$, SPFR$_{30}$]	
SPNFR PPBacklog	SPNFR-Level$_1$ priority (highest): [SPNFR1, SPNFR6, SPNFR11, SPNFR16]	
	SPNFR-Level$_2$ priority: [SPNFR$_2$, SPNFR$_7$, SPNFR$_{12}$, SPNFR$_{17}$]	
	SPNFR-Level$_3$ priority: [SPNFR$_3$, SPNFR$_8$, SPNFR$_{14}$, SPNFR$_{18}$]	
	SPNFR-Level$_4$ priority: [SPNFR$_4$, SPNFR$_9$, SPNFR$_{14}$, SPNFR$_{19}$]	
	SPNFR-Level$_5$ priority (lowest): [SPNFR$_5$, SPNFR$_{10}$, SPNFR$_{15}$, SPNFR$_{20}$]	
SRSR PPBacklog	SRSR-Level$_1$ priority (highest): [SRSR$_1$, SRSR$_6$]	SRSR-Level$_4$ priority: [SRSR$_4$, SRSR$_9$]
	SRSR-Level$_2$ priority: [SRSR$_2$, SRSR$_7$]	SRSR-Level$_5$ priority (lowest): [SRSR$_5$, SRSR$_{10}$]
	SRSR-Level$_3$ priority: [SRSR$_3$, SRSR$_8$]	
SPPR PPBacklog	SPPR-Level$_1$ priority (highest): [SPPR$_1$, SPPR$_6$]	SPPR-Level$_4$ priority: [SPPR$_4$, SPPR$_9$]
	SPPR-Level$_2$ priority: [SPPR$_2$, SPPR$_7$]	SPPR-Level$_5$ priority (lowest): [SPPR$_5$, SPPR$_{10}$]
	SPPR-Level$_3$ priority: [SPPR$_3$, SPPR$_8$]	
SPTC PPBacklog	SPTC-Level$_1$ priority (highest): [SPTC$_1$]	SPTC-Level$_4$ priority: [SPTC$_4$]
	SPTC-Level$_2$ priority: [SPTC$_2$]	SPTC-Level$_5$ priority (lowest): [SPTC$_5$]
	SPTC-Level$_3$ priority: [SPTC$_3$]	
SPQSC PPBacklog	SPQSC-Level$_1$ priority (highest): [SPQSC$_1$]	SPQSC-Level$_4$ priority: [SPQSC$_4$]
	SPQSC-Level$_2$ priority: [SPQSC$_2$]	SPQSC-Level$_5$ priority (lowest): [SPQSC$_5$]
	SPQSC-Level$_3$ priority: [SPQSC$_3$]	

6.2.6 The Given Sprint Backlogs of Requirements

Table 6.3 indicates the Sprint backlogs obtained from each of the requirements-specific backlogs as follows:

▪ The thirty software product functional requirements (i.e., SPFR$_1$ to SPFR$_{30}$) of the SPFR PPBacklog serve six SPFR Sprints (i.e., SPFR Sprint$_1$ to SPFR Sprint$_6$), and each Sprint comprises five of the thirty SPFRs, but in a predefined order.

- The twenty software product non-functional requirements (i.e., $SPNFR_1$ to $SPNFR_{20}$) of the SPNFR PPBacklog serve four SPNFR Sprints (i.e., SPNFR Sprint$_1$ to SPNFR Sprint$_4$), and each Sprint comprises five of the twenty SPNFRs, but in a predefined order.

- The ten system and software requirements (i.e., $SRSR_1$ to $SRSR_{10}$) of the SRSR PPBacklog serve two SRSR Sprints (i.e., SRSR Sprint$_1$ to SRSR Sprint$_2$), and each Sprint comprises five of the ten SRSRs, but in a predefined order.

- The ten project and process requirements (i.e., $SPPR_1$ to $SPPR_{10}$) of the SPPR PPBacklog serve two SPPR Sprints (i.e., SPPR Sprint$_1$ to SPPR Sprint$_2$), and each Sprint comprises five of the ten SPPRs, but in a predefined order.

- The five software product technology constraints/requirements (i.e., $SPTC_1$ to $SPTC_{10}$) of the SPTC PPBacklog serve one SPTC Sprint (i.e., SPTC Sprint$_1$), and that Sprint comprises the five SPTCs, but in a predefined order.

- The five software product quality of service constraints/requirements (i.e., $SPQSC_1$ to $SPQSC_{10}$) of the SPQSC PPBacklog serve one SPQSC Sprint (i.e., SPQSC Sprint$_1$), and that Sprint comprises the five SPQSCs, but in a predefined order.

TABLE 6.3 The given Sprint backlogs of requirements

Backlogs of requirements	#of Sprints	Sprints	Sprint backlogs
SPFR PPBacklog	6 SPFR Sprints	SPFR Sprint$_1$	SPFR-S-Backlog$_1$: [$SPFR_1$, $SPFR_6$, $SPFR_{11}$, $SPFR_{16}$, $SPFR_{21}$]
		SPFR Sprint$_2$	SPFR-S-Backlog$_2$: [$SPFR_{26}$, $SPFR_2$, $SPFR_7$, $SPFR_{12}$, $SPFR_{17}$]
		SPFR Sprint$_3$	SPFR-S-Backlog$_3$: [$SPFR_{22}$, $SPFR_{27}$, $SPFR_3$, $SPFR_8$, $SPFR_{13}$]
		SPFR Sprint$_4$	SPFR-S-Backlog$_4$: [$SPFR_{18}$, $SPFR_{23}$, $SPFR_{28}$, $SPFR_4$, $SPFR_9$]
		SPFR Sprint$_5$	SPFR-S-Backlog$_5$: [$SPFR_{14}$, $SPFR_{19}$, $SPFR_{24}$, $SPFR_{29}$, $SPFR_5$]
		SPFR Sprint$_6$	SPFR-S-Backlog$_6$: [$SPFR_{10}$, $SPFR_{15}$, $SPFR_{20}$, $SPFR_{25}$, $SPFR_{30}$]

(Continued)

Backlogs of requirements	#of Sprints	Sprints	Sprint backlogs
SPNFR PPBacklog	4 SPNFR Sprints	SPNFR Sprint$_1$	SPNFR-S-Backlog$_1$: [SPNFR$_1$, SPNFR$_6$, SPNFR$_{11}$, SPNFR$_{16}$, SPNFR$_2$]
		SPNFR Sprint$_2$	SPNFR-S-Backlog$_2$: [SPNFR$_7$, SPNFR$_{12}$, SPNFR$_{17}$, SPNFR$_3$, SPNFR$_8$]
		SPNFR Sprint$_3$	SPNFR-S-Backlog$_3$: [SPNFR$_{14}$, SPNFR$_{18}$, SPNFR$_4$, SPNFR$_9$, SPNFR$_{14}$]
		SPNFR Sprint$_4$	SPNFR-S-Backlog$_4$: [SPNFR$_{19}$, SPNFR$_5$, SPNFR$_{10}$, SPNFR$_{15}$, SPNFR$_{20}$]
SRSR PPBacklog	2 SRSR Sprints	SRSR Sprint$_1$	SRSR-S-Backlog$_1$: [SRSR$_1$, SRSR$_6$, SRSR$_2$, SRSR$_7$, SRSR$_3$]
		SRSR Sprint$_2$	SRSR-S-Backlog$_2$: [SRSR$_8$, SRSR$_4$, SRSR$_9$, SRSR$_5$, SRSR$_{10}$]
SPPR PPBacklog	2 SPPR Sprints	SPPR Sprint$_1$	SPPR-S-Backlog$_1$: [SPPR$_1$, SPPR$_6$, SPPR$_2$, SPPR$_7$, SPPR$_3$]
		SPPR Sprint$_2$	SPPR-S-Backlog$_2$: [SPPR$_8$, SPPR$_4$, SPPR$_9$, SPPR$_5$, SPPR$_{10}$]
SPTC PPBacklog	1 SPTC Sprint	SPTC Sprint$_1$	SPTC-Backlog$_1$: [SPTC$_1$, SPTC$_2$, SPTC$_3$, SPTC$_4$, SPTC$_5$]
SPQSC PPBacklog	1 SPQSC Sprint	SPQSC Sprint$_1$	SPQSC-Backlog$_1$: [SPQSC$_1$, SPQSC$_2$, SPQSC$_3$, SPQSC$_4$, SPQSC$_5$]

6.3 THE DERIVED CLUSTERS OF SPRINT BACKLOGS

Table 6.4 indicates the clusters of the Sprint backlogs, in which the Sprint backlogs in the same cluster are carried out in parallel, similar to the multi-Scrum and SoS structure in the Scrum project management for large projects (refer to Chapter 3 in this book). These clusters of Sprint backlogs are as follows:

- The first cluster (Cluster$_1$) comprises six Sprint backlogs covering the six categories of software requirements (SPFR-S-Backlog$_1$, SPNFR-S-Backlog$_1$, SRSR-S-Backlog$_1$, SPPR-S-Backlog$_1$, SPTC-S-Backlog$_1$, and SPQSC-S-Backlog$_1$).

- The second cluster (Cluster$_2$) comprises four Sprint backlogs covering four of the six software requirements categories (SPFR-S-Backlog$_2$, SPNFR-S-Backlog$_2$, SRSR-S-Backlog$_2$, and SPPR-S-Backlog$_2$).

- The third cluster (Cluster$_3$) comprises two Sprint backlogs covering two of the six software requirements categories (SPFR-S-Backlog$_3$ and SPNFR-S-Backlog$_3$).

- The fourth cluster (Cluster$_4$) comprises two Sprint backlogs covering two of the six categories of software requirements (SPFR-S-Backlog$_4$ and SPNFR-S-Backlog$_4$).

- The fifth cluster (Cluster$_5$) comprises one Sprint backlog covering one of the six categories of software requirements (SPFR-S-Backlog$_5$).

- The sixth cluster (Cluster$_6$) comprises one Sprint backlog covering one of the six categories of software requirements (SPFR-S-Backlog$_6$).

The tasks of these clusters and their breakdown structures are provided in the following six sections: *6.3.1 through 6.3.6.*

TABLE 6.4 The derived clusters of Sprint backlogs of requirements

Cluster	Included Sprint backlogs of requirements	Included requirements				
Cluster$_1$	SPFR-S-Backlog$_1$	SPFR$_1$	SPFR$_6$	SPFR$_{11}$	SPFR$_{16}$	SPFR$_{21}$
	SPNFR-S-Backlog$_1$	SPNFR$_1$	SPNFR$_6$	SPNFR$_{11}$	SPNFR$_{16}$	SPNFR$_2$
	SRSR-S-Backlog$_1$	SRSR$_1$	SRSR$_6$	SRSR$_2$	SRSR$_7$	SRSR$_3$
	SPPR-S-Backlog$_1$	SPPR$_1$	SPPR$_6$	SPPR$_2$	SPPR$_7$	SPPR$_3$
	SPTC-S-Backlog$_1$	SPTC$_1$	SPTC$_2$	SPTC$_3$	SPTC$_4$	SPTC$_5$
	SPQSC-S-Backlog$_1$	SPQSC$_1$	SPQSC$_2$	SPQSC$_3$	SPQSC$_4$	SPQSC$_5$
Cluster$_2$	SPFR-S-Backlog$_2$	SPFR$_{26}$	SPFR$_2$	SPFR$_7$	SPFR$_{12}$	SPFR$_{17}$
	SPNFR-S-Backlog$_2$	SPNFR$_7$	SPNFR$_{12}$	SPNFR$_{17}$	SPNFR$_3$	SPNFR$_8$
	SRSR-S-Backlog$_2$	SRSR$_8$	SRSR$_4$	SRSR$_9$	SRSR$_5$	SRSR$_{10}$
	SPPR-S-Backlog$_2$	SPPR$_8$	SPPR$_4$	SPPR$_9$	SPPR$_5$	SPPR$_{10}$
Cluster$_3$	SPFR-S-Backlog$_3$	SPFR$_{22}$	SPFR$_{27}$	SPFR$_3$	SPFR$_8$	SPFR$_{13}$
	SPNFR-S-Backlog$_3$	SPNFR$_{14}$	SPNFR$_{18}$	SPNFR$_4$	SPNFR$_3$	SPNFR$_{14}$
Cluster$_4$	SPFR-S-Backlog$_4$	SPFR$_{18}$	SPFR$_{23}$	SPFR$_{28}$	SPFR$_4$	SPFR$_9$
	SPNFR-S-Backlog$_4$	SPNFR$_{19}$	SPNFR$_5$	SPNFR$_{10}$	SPNFR$_{15}$	SPNFR$_{20}$
Cluster$_5$	SPFR-S-Backlog$_5$	SPFR$_{14}$	SPFR$_{19}$	SPFR$_{24}$	SPFR$_{29}$	SPFR$_5$
Cluster$_6$	SPFR-S-Backlog$_6$	SPFR$_{10}$	SPFR$_{15}$	SPFR$_{20}$	SPFR$_{25}$	SPFR$_{30}$

6.3.1 The First Cluster of Sprints' Backlogs of Requirements

In reference to Tables 6.1–6.4, Tables 6.5.1–6.5.6 present the breakdown structures, schedules, resource allocations, deliverables, Review schedules, ship and deploy schedules, and Retrospective schedules for the backlogs of the first cluster's Sprints as follows:

- Sub-Table 6.5.1 presents the plan for carrying on the first set of software product functional requirements (i.e., SPFR first Sprint backlog:

SPFR-S-Backlog$_1$, including five SPFRs: SPFR$_1$, SPFR$_6$, SPFR$_{11}$, SPFR$_{16}$, and SPFR$_{21}$). It presents the tasks needed to carry out these requirements (i.e., SPFR$_1$.T$_1$–T$_5$, SPFR$_6$.T$_1$–T$_5$, SPFR$_{11}$.T$_1$–T$_5$, SPFR$_{16}$.T$_1$–T$_5$, and SPFR$_{21}$.T$_1$–T$_5$), their schedules (i.e., week number and day number), their allocated resources (i.e., of RTM$_1$ through RTM$_5$), their anticipated deliverables (i.e., SPFR.DLV$_1$ through SPFR.DLV$_5$), their anticipated Review dates (i.e., *week number and day number, WK$_\#$.D$_\#$*), their anticipated ship and deploy dates (i.e., *week number and day number, WK$_\#$.D$_\#$*), and their anticipated Retrospective dates (i.e., *week number and day number, WK$_\#$.D$_\#$*).

▨ Sub-Table 6.5.2 presents the plan for carrying on the first set of software product non-functional requirements (i.e., SPNFR first Sprint backlog: SPNFR-S-Backlog$_1$, including five SPNFRs: SPNFR$_1$, SPNFR$_6$, SPNFR$_{11}$, SPNFR$_{16}$, and SPNFR$_2$). It presents the tasks needed to carry out these requirements (i.e., SPNFR$_1$.T$_1$–T$_5$, SPNFR$_6$.T$_1$–T$_5$, SPNFR$_{11}$.T$_1$–T$_5$, SPNFR$_{16}$.T$_1$–T$_5$, and SPNFR$_2$.T$_1$–T$_5$), their schedules (i.e., week number and day number), their allocated resources (i.e., of RTM$_1$ through RTM$_5$), their anticipated deliverables (i.e., SPNFR.DLV$_1$ through SPNFR.DLV$_5$), their anticipated Review dates (i.e., week number and day number, WK$_\#$.D$_\#$), their anticipated ship and deploy dates (i.e., week number and day number, WK$_\#$.D$_\#$), and their anticipated Retrospective dates (i.e., week number and day number, WK$_\#$.D$_\#$).

▨ Sub-Table 6.5.3 presents the plan for carrying on the first set of system and software requirements (i.e., SRSR first Sprint backlog: SRSR-S-Backlog$_1$, including five SRSRs: SRSR$_1$, SRSR$_6$, SRSR$_2$, SRSR$_7$, and SRSR$_3$). It presents the tasks needed to carry out these requirements (i.e., SRSR$_1$.T$_1$–T$_5$, SRSR$_6$.T$_1$–T$_5$, SRSR$_2$.T$_1$–T$_5$, SRSR$_7$.T$_1$–T$_5$, and SRSR$_3$.T$_1$–T$_5$), their schedules (i.e., week number and day number), their allocated resources (i.e., of RTM$_1$ through RTM$_5$), their anticipated deliverables (i.e., SRSR.DLV$_1$ through SRSR.DLV$_5$), their anticipated Review dates (i.e., week number and day number, WK$_\#$.D$_\#$), their anticipated ship and deploy dates (i.e., week number and day number, WK$_\#$.D$_\#$), and their anticipated Retrospective dates (i.e., week number and day number, WK$_\#$.D$_\#$).

▨ Sub-Table 6.5.4 presents the plan for carrying on the first set of software project and process requirements (i.e., SPPR first Sprint backlog: SPPR-S-Backlog$_1$, including five SPPRs: SPPR$_1$, SPPR$_6$, SPPR$_2$, SPPR$_7$, and SPPR$_3$). It presents the tasks needed to carry out these requirements (i.e., SPPR$_1$.T$_1$–T$_5$, SPPR$_6$.T$_1$–T$_5$, SPPR$_2$.T$_1$–T$_5$, SPPR$_7$.T$_1$–T$_5$, and SPPR$_3$.

T_1–T_5), their schedules (i.e., week number and day number), their allocated resources (i.e., of RTM_1 through RTM_5), their anticipated deliverables (i.e., $SPPR.DLV_1$ through $SPPR.DLV_5$), their anticipated Review dates (i.e., week number and day number, $WK_{\#}.D_{\#}$), their anticipated ship and deploy dates (i.e., week number and day number, $WK_{\#}.D_{\#}$), and their anticipated Retrospectives dates (i.e., week number and day number, $WK_{\#}.D_{\#}$).

▪ Sub-Table 6.5.5 presents the plan for carrying on the first set of software product technology constraints (i.e., SPTC first Sprint backlog: SPTC-S-Backlog$_1$, including five SPTC requirements: $SPTC_1$, $SPTC_2$, $SPTC_3$, $SPTC_4$, and $SPTC_5$). It presents the tasks needed to carry out these requirements (i.e., $SPTC_1.T_1$–T_5, $SPTC_2.T_1$–T_5, $SPTC_3.T_1$–T_5, $SPTC_4.T_1$–T_5, and $SPTC_5.T_1$–T_5), their schedules (i.e., week number and day number), their allocated resources (i.e., of RTM_1 through RTM_5), their anticipated deliverables (i.e., $SPTC.DLV_1$ through $SPTC.DLV_5$), their anticipated Review dates (i.e., week number and day number, $WK_{\#}.D_{\#}$), their anticipated ship and deploy dates (i.e., week number and day number, $WK_{\#}.D_{\#}$), and their anticipated Retrospective dates (i.e., week number and day number, $WK_{\#}.D_{\#}$).

▪ Sub-Table 6.5.6 presents the plan for carrying on the first set of software product quality of service constraints (i.e., SPQSC first Sprint backlog: SPQSC-S-Backlog$_1$, including five SPQSC requirements: $SPQSC_1$, $SPQSC_2$, $SPQSC_3$, $SPQSC_4$, and $SPQSC_5$). It presents the tasks needed to carry out these requirements (i.e., $SPQSC_1.T_1$–T_5, $SPQSC_2.T_1$–T_5, $SPQSC_3.T_1$–T_5, $SPQSC_4.T_1$–T_5, and $SQSTC_5.T_1$–T_5), their schedules (i.e., week number and day number), their allocated resources (i.e., of RTM_1 through RTM_5), their anticipated deliverables (i.e., $SPQSC.DLV_1$ through $SPQSC.DLV_5$), their anticipated Review dates (i.e., week number and day number, $WK_{\#}.D_{\#}$), their anticipated ship and deploy dates (i.e., week number and day number, $WK_{\#}.D_{\#}$), and their anticipated Retrospective dates (i.e., week number and day number, $WK_{\#}.D_{\#}$).

TABLE 6.5 Cluster$_1$ of Sprint backlogs of requirements

SPFR-S-Backlog$_1$	[SPFR$_1$, SPFR$_6$, SPFR$_{11}$, SPFR$_{16}$, SPFR$_{21}$]
SPNFR-S-Backlog$_1$	[SPNFR$_1$, SPNFR$_6$, SPNFR$_{11}$, SPNFR$_{16}$, SPNFR$_2$]
SRSR-S-Backlog$_1$	[SRSR$_1$, SRSR$_6$, SRSR$_2$, SRSR$_7$, SRSR$_3$]
SPPR-S-Backlog$_1$	[SPPR$_1$, SPPR$_6$, SPPR$_2$, SPPR$_7$, SPPR$_3$]
SPTC-S-Backlog$_1$	[SPTC$_1$, SPTC$_2$, SPTC$_3$, SPTC$_4$, SPTC$_5$]
SPQSC-S-Backlog$_1$	[SPQSC$_1$, SPQSC$_2$, SPQSC$_3$, SPQSC$_4$, SPQSC$_5$]

SUB-TABLE 6.5.1 SPFR Sprint1 - SPFR-S-Backlog$_1$

Requirements	Tasks	Schedule WK	Schedule D	Resource	Deliverable	Review	Ship/ Deploy	Retrospective
SPFR$_1$	SPFR$_1$.T$_1$	1	1	RTM$_1$	SPFR.DLV$_1$	WK$_7$.D$_1$	WK$_7$.D$_1$	WK$_7$-D$_5$
	SPFR$_1$.T$_2$	1	2	RTM$_1$				
	SPFR$_1$.T$_3$	1	3	RTM$_1$				
	SPFR$_1$.T$_4$	1	4	RTM$_1$				
	SPFR$_1$.T$_5$	1	5	RTM$_1$				
SPFR$_6$	SPFR$_6$.T$_1$	1	1	RTM$_2$	SPFR.DLV$_2$	WK$_7$.D$_1$	WK$_7$.D$_1$	WK$_7$.D$_5$
	SPFR$_6$.T$_2$	1	2	RTM$_2$				
	SPFR$_6$.T$_3$	1	3	RTM$_2$				
	SPFR$_6$.T$_4$	1	4	RTM$_2$				
	SPFR$_6$.T$_5$	1	5	RTM$_2$				
SPFR$_{11}$	SPFR$_{11}$.T$_1$	1	1	RTM$_3$	SPFR.DLV$_3$	WK$_7$.D$_1$	WK$_7$.D$_1$	WK$_7$.D$_5$
	SPFR$_{11}$.T$_2$	1	2	RTM$_3$				
	SPFR$_{11}$.T$_3$	1	3	RTM$_3$				
	SPFR$_{11}$.T$_4$	1	4	RTM$_3$				
	SPFR$_{11}$.T$_5$	1	5	RTM$_3$				
SPFR$_{16}$	SPFR$_{16}$.T$_1$	1	1	RTM$_4$	SPFR.DLV$_4$	WK$_7$.D$_1$	WK$_7$.D$_1$	WK$_7$.D$_5$
	SPFR$_{16}$.T$_2$	1	2	RTM$_4$				
	SPFR$_{16}$.T$_3$	1	3	RTM$_4$				
	SPFR$_{16}$.T$_4$	1	4	RTM$_4$				
	SPFR$_{16}$.T$_5$	1	5	RTM$_4$				
SPFR$_{21}$	SPFR$_{21}$.T$_1$	1	1	RTM$_5$	SPFR.DLV$_5$	WK$_7$.D$_1$	WK$_7$.D$_1$	WK$_7$.D$_5$
	SPFR$_{21}$.T$_2$	1	2	RTM$_5$				
	SPFR$_{21}$.T$_3$	1	3	RTM$_5$				
	SPFR$_{21}$.T$_4$	1	4	RTM$_5$				
	SPFR$_{21}$.T$_5$	1	5	RTM$_5$				

SUB-TABLE 6.5.2 SPNFR Sprint$_1$ - SPNFR-S-Backlog$_1$

| Requirements | Tasks | Schedule | | Resource | Deliverable | Review | Ship/Deploy | Retrospective |
		WK	D					
SPNFR$_1$	SPNFR$_1$.T$_1$	2	1	RTM$_1$	SPNFR.DLV$_1$	WK7.D$_1$	WK$_7$.D$_2$	WK$_7$.D$_5$
	SPNFR$_1$.T$_2$	2	2	RTM$_1$				
	SPNFR$_1$.T$_3$	2	3	RTM$_1$				
	SPNFR$_1$.T$_4$	2	4	RTM$_1$				
	SPNFR$_1$.T$_5$	2	5	RTM$_1$				
SPNFR$_6$	SPNFR$_6$.T$_1$	2	1	RTM$_2$	SPNFR.DLV$_2$	WK7.D$_1$	WK$_7$.D$_2$	WK$_7$.D$_5$
	SPNFR$_6$.T$_2$	2	2	RTM$_2$				
	SPNFR$_6$.T$_3$	2	3	RTM$_2$				
	SPNFR$_6$.T$_4$	2	4	RTM$_2$				
	SPNFR$_6$.T$_5$	2	5	RTM$_2$				
SPNFR$_{11}$	SPNFR$_{11}$.T$_1$	2	1	RTM$_3$	SPNFR.DLV$_3$	WK$_7$.D$_1$	WK$_7$.D$_2$	WK$_7$.D$_5$
	SPNFR$_{11}$.T$_2$	2	2	RTM$_3$				
	SPNFR$_{11}$.T$_3$	2	3	RTM$_3$				
	SPNFR$_{11}$.T$_4$	2	4	RTM$_3$				
	SPNFR$_{11}$.T$_5$	2	5	RTM$_3$				
SPNFR$_{16}$	SPNFR$_{16}$.T$_1$	2	1	RTM$_4$	SPNFR.DLV$_4$	WK$_7$.D$_1$	WK$_7$.D$_2$	WK$_7$.D$_5$
	SPNFR$_{16}$.T$_2$	2	2	RTM$_4$				
	SPNFR$_{16}$.T$_3$	2	3	RTM$_4$				
	SPNFR$_{16}$.T$_4$	2	4	RTM$_4$				
	SPNFR$_{16}$.T$_5$	2	5	RTM$_4$				
SPNFR$_2$	SPNFR$_2$.T$_1$	2	1	RTM$_5$	SPNFR.DLV$_5$	WK$_7$.D$_1$	WK$_7$.D$_2$	WK$_7$.D$_5$
	SPNFR$_2$.T$_2$	2	2	RTM$_5$				
	SPNFR$_2$.T$_3$	2	3	RTM$_5$				
	SPNFR$_2$.T$_4$	2	4	RTM$_5$				
	SPNFR$_2$.T$_5$	2	5	RTM$_5$				

SUB-TABLE 6.5.3 SRSR Sprint$_1$ - SRSR-S-Backlog$_1$

Requirements	Tasks	Schedule WK	Schedule D	Resource	Deliverable	Review	Ship/ Deploy	Retrospective
SRSR$_1$	SRSR$_1$.T$_1$	3	1	RTM$_1$	SRSR.DLV$_1$	WK$_7$.D$_1$	WK$_7$.D$_3$	WK$_7$.D$_5$
	SRSR$_1$.T$_2$	3	2	RTM$_1$				
	SRSR$_1$.T$_3$	3	3	RTM$_1$				
	SRSR$_1$.T$_4$	3	4	RTM$_1$				
	SRSR$_1$.T$_5$	3	5	RTM$_1$				
SRSR$_6$	SRSR$_6$.T$_1$	3	1	RTM$_2$	SRSR.DLV$_2$	WK$_7$.D$_1$	WK$_7$.D$_3$	WK$_7$.D$_5$
	SRSR$_6$.T$_2$	3	2	RTM$_2$				
	SRSR$_6$.T$_3$	3	3	RTM$_2$				
	SRSR$_6$.T$_4$	3	4	RTM$_2$				
	SRSR$_6$.T$_5$	3	5	RTM$_2$				
SRSR$_2$	SRSR$_2$.T$_1$	3	1	RTM$_3$	SRSR.DLV$_3$	WK$_7$.D$_1$	WK$_7$.D$_3$	WK$_7$.D$_5$
	SRSR$_2$.T$_2$	3	2	RTM$_3$				
	SRSR$_2$.T$_3$	3	3	RTM$_3$				
	SRSR$_2$.T$_4$	3	4	RTM$_3$				
	SRSR$_2$.T$_5$	3	5	RTM$_3$				
SRSR$_7$	SRSR$_7$.T$_1$	3	1	RTM$_4$	SRSR.DLV$_4$	WK$_7$.D$_1$	WK$_7$.D$_3$	WK$_7$.D$_5$
	SRSR$_7$.T$_2$	3	2	RTM$_4$				
	SRSR$_7$.T$_3$	3	3	RTM$_4$				
	SRSR$_7$.T$_4$	3	4	RTM$_4$				
	SRSR$_7$.T$_5$	3	5	RTM$_4$				
SRSR$_3$	SRSR$_3$.T$_1$	3	1	RTM$_5$	SRSR.DLV$_5$	WK$_7$.D$_1$	WK$_7$.D$_3$	WK$_7$.D$_5$
	SRSR$_3$.T$_2$	3	2	RTM$_5$				
	SRSR$_3$.T$_3$	3	3	RTM$_5$				
	SRSR$_3$.T$_4$	3	4	RTM$_5$				
	SRSR$_3$.T$_5$	3	5	RTM$_5$				

SUB-TABLE 6.5.4 SPPR Sprint$_1$ - SPPR-S-Backlog$_1$

Requirements	Tasks	Schedule WK	Schedule D	Resource	Deliverable	Review	Ship/ Deploy	Retrospective
SPPR$_1$	SPPR$_1$.T$_1$	4	1	RTM$_1$	SPPR.DLV$_1$	WK$_7$.D$_1$	WK$_7$.D$_4$	WK$_7$.D$_5$
	SPPR$_1$.T$_2$	4	2	RTM$_1$				
	SPPR$_1$.T$_3$	4	3	RTM$_1$				
	SPPR$_1$.T$_4$	4	4	RTM$_1$				
	SPPR$_1$.T$_5$	4	5	RTM$_1$				
SPPR$_6$	SPPR$_6$.T$_1$	4	1	RTM$_2$	SPPR.DLV$_2$	WK$_7$.D$_1$	WK$_7$.D$_4$	WK$_7$.D$_5$
	SPPR$_6$.T$_2$	4	2	RTM$_2$				
	SPPR$_6$.T$_3$	4	3	RTM$_2$				
	SPPR$_6$.T$_4$	4	4	RTM$_2$				
	SPPR$_6$.T$_5$	4	5	RTM$_2$				
SPPR$_2$	SPPR$_2$.T$_1$	4	1	RTM$_3$	SPPR.DLV$_3$	WK$_7$.D$_1$	WK$_7$.D$_4$	WK$_7$.D$_5$
	SPPR$_2$.T$_2$	4	2	RTM$_3$				
	SPPR$_2$.T$_3$	4	3	RTM$_3$				
	SPPR$_2$.T$_4$	4	4	RTM$_3$				
	SPPR$_2$.T$_5$	4	5	RTM$_3$				
SPPR$_7$	SPPR$_7$.T$_1$	4	1	RTM$_4$	SPPR.DLV$_4$	WK$_7$.D$_1$	WK$_7$.D$_4$	WK$_7$.D$_5$
	SPPR$_7$.T$_2$	4	2	RTM$_4$				
	SPPR$_7$.T$_3$	4	3	RTM$_4$				
	SPPR$_7$.T$_4$	4	4	RTM$_4$				
	SPPR$_7$.T$_5$	4	5	RTM$_4$				
SPPR$_3$	SPPR$_3$.T$_1$	4	1	RTM$_5$	SPPR.DLV$_5$	WK$_7$.D$_1$	WK$_7$.D$_4$	WK$_7$.D$_5$
	SPPR$_3$.T$_2$	4	2	RTM$_5$				
	SPPR$_3$.T$_3$	4	3	RTM$_5$				
	SPPR$_3$.T$_4$	4	4	RTM$_5$				
	SPPR$_3$.T$_5$	4	5	RTM$_5$				

SUB-TABLE 6.5.5 SPTC Sprint$_1$ - SPTC-S-Backlog$_1$

Requirements	Tasks	Schedule		Resource	Deliverable	Review	Ship/ Deploy	Retrospective
		WK	D					
SPTC$_1$	SPTC$_1$.T$_1$	5	1	RTM$_1$	SPTC.DLV$_1$	WK$_7$.D$_1$	WK$_7$.D$_5$	WK$_7$.D$_5$
	SPTC$_1$.T$_2$	5	2	RTM$_1$				
	SPTC$_1$.T$_3$	5	3	RTM$_1$				
	SPTC$_1$.T$_4$	5	4	RTM$_1$				
	SPTC$_1$.T$_5$	5	5	RTM$_1$				
SPTC$_2$	SPTC$_2$.T$_1$	5	1	RTM$_2$	SPTC.DLV$_2$	WK$_7$.D$_1$	WK$_7$.D$_5$	WK$_7$.D$_5$
	SPTC$_2$.T$_2$	5	2	RTM$_2$				
	SPTC$_2$.T$_3$	5	3	RTM$_2$				
	SPTC$_2$.T$_4$	5	4	RTM$_2$				
	SPTC$_2$.T$_5$	5	5	RTM$_2$				
SPTC$_3$	SPTC$_3$.T$_1$	5	1	RTM$_3$	SPTC.DLV$_3$	WK$_7$.D$_1$	WK$_7$.D$_5$	WK$_7$.D$_5$
	SPTC$_3$.T$_2$	5	2	RTM$_3$				
	SPTC$_3$.T$_3$	5	3	RTM$_3$				
	SPTC$_3$.T$_4$	5	4	RTM$_3$				
	SPTC$_3$.T$_5$	5	5	RTM$_3$				
SPTC$_4$	SPTC$_4$.T$_1$	5	1	RTM$_4$	SPTC.DLV$_4$	WK$_7$.D$_1$	WK$_7$.D$_5$	WK$_7$.D$_5$
	SPTC$_4$.T$_2$	5	2	RTM$_4$				
	SPTC$_4$.T$_3$	5	3	RTM$_4$				
	SPTC$_4$.T$_4$	5	4	RTM$_4$				
	SPTC$_4$.T$_5$	5	5	RTM$_4$				
SPTC$_5$	SPTC$_5$.T$_1$	5	1	RTM$_5$	SPTC.DLV$_5$	WK$_7$.D$_1$	WK$_7$.D$_5$	WK$_7$.D$_5$
	SPTC$_5$.T$_2$	5	2	RTM$_5$				
	SPTC$_5$.T$_3$	5	3	RTM$_5$				
	SPTC$_5$.T$_4$	5	4	RTM$_5$				
	SPTC$_5$.T$_5$	5	5	RTM$_5$				

SUB-TABLE 6.5.6 SPQSC Sprint$_1$ - SPQSC-S-Backlog$_1$

Requirements	Tasks	Schedule		Resource	Deliverable	Review	Ship/ Deploy	Retrospective
		WK	**D**					
SPQSC$_1$	SPQSC$_1$.T$_1$	6	1	RTM$_1$	SPQSC.DLV$_1$	WK$_7$.D$_1$	WK$_7$.D$_5$	WK$_7$.D$_5$
	SPQSC$_1$.T$_2$	6	2	RTM$_1$				
	SPQSC$_1$.T$_3$	6	3	RTM$_1$				
	SPQSC$_1$.T$_4$	6	4	RTM$_1$				
	SPQSC$_1$.T$_5$	6	5	RTM$_1$				
SPQSC$_2$	SPQSC$_2$.T$_1$	6	1	RTM$_2$	SPQSC.DLV$_2$	WK$_7$.D$_1$	WK$_7$.D$_5$	WK$_7$.D$_5$
	SPQSC$_2$.T$_2$	6	2	RTM$_2$				
	SPQSC$_2$.T$_3$	6	3	RTM$_2$				
	SPQSC$_2$.T$_4$	6	4	RTM$_2$				
	SPQSC$_2$.T$_5$	6	5	RTM$_2$				
SPQSC$_3$	SPQSC$_3$.T$_1$	6	1	RTM$_3$	SPQSC.DLV$_3$	WK$_7$.D$_1$	WK$_7$.D$_5$	WK$_7$.D$_5$
	SPQSC$_3$.T$_2$	6	2	RTM$_3$				
	SPQSC$_3$.T$_3$	6	3	RTM$_3$				
	SPQSC$_3$.T$_4$	6	4	RTM$_3$				
	SPQSC$_3$.T$_5$	6	5	RTM$_3$				
SPQSC$_4$	SPQSC$_4$.T$_1$	6	1	RTM$_4$	SPQSC.DLV$_4$	WK$_7$.D$_1$	WK$_7$.D$_5$	WK$_7$.D$_5$
	SPQSC$_4$.T$_2$	6	2	RTM$_4$				
	SPQSC$_4$.T$_3$	6	3	RTM$_4$				
	SPQSC$_4$.T$_4$	6	4	RTM$_4$				
	SPQSC$_4$.T$_5$	6	5	RTM$_4$				
SPQSC$_5$	SPQSC$_5$.T$_1$	6	1	RTM$_5$	SPQSC.DLV$_5$	WK$_7$.D$_1$	WK$_7$.D$_5$	WK$_7$.D$_5$
	SPQSC$_5$.T$_2$	6	2	RTM$_5$				
	SPQSC$_5$.T$_3$	6	3	RTM$_5$				
	SPQSC$_5$.T$_4$	6	4	RTM$_5$				
	SPQSC$_5$.T$_5$	6	5	RTM$_5$				

6.3.2 The Second Cluster of Sprints' Backlogs of Requirements

In reference to Tables 6.1 to 6.4, Tables 6.6.1 to 6.6.4 present the breakdown structures, schedules, resource allocations, deliverables, Review schedules, ship and deploy schedules, and Retrospective schedules for the backlogs of the second cluster's Sprints as follows:

- Sub-Table 6.6.1 presents the plan for carrying on the second set of software product functional requirements (i.e., SPFR second Sprint backlog: SPFR-S-Backlog$_2$, including five SPFRs: SPFR$_{26}$, SPFR$_2$, SPFR$_7$, SPFR$_{12}$, and SPFR$_{17}$). It presents the tasks needed to carry out these requirements (i.e., SPFR$_{26}$.T$_1$–T$_5$, SPFR$_2$.T$_1$–T$_5$, SPFR$_7$.T$_1$–T$_5$, SPFR$_{12}$.T$_1$–T$_5$, and SPFR$_{17}$.T$_1$–T$_5$), their schedules (i.e., week number and day number), their allocated resources (i.e., of RTM$_1$ through RTM$_5$), their anticipated deliverables (i.e., SPFR.DLV$_6$ through SPFR.DLV$_{10}$), their anticipated Review dates (i.e., week number and day number, WK$_\#$.D$_\#$), their anticipated ship and deploy dates (i.e., week number and day number, WK$_\#$.D$_\#$), and their anticipated Retrospective dates (i.e., week number and day number, WK$_\#$.D$_\#$).

- Sub-Table 6.6.2 presents the plan for carrying on the second set of software product non-functional requirements (i.e., SPNFR second Sprint backlog: SPNFR-S-Backlog$_2$, including five SPNFRs: SPNFR$_7$, SPNFR$_{12}$, SPNFR$_{17}$, SPNFR$_3$, and SPNFR$_8$). It presents the tasks needed to carry out these requirements (i.e., SPNFR$_7$.T$_1$–T$_5$, SPNFR$_{12}$.T$_1$–T$_5$, SPNFR$_{17}$.T$_1$–T$_5$, SPNFR$_3$.T$_1$–T$_5$, and SPNFR$_8$.T$_1$–T$_5$), their schedules (i.e., week number and day number), their allocated resources (i.e., of RTM$_1$ through RTM$_5$), their anticipated deliverables (i.e., SPNFR.DLV$_6$ through SPNFR.DLV$_{10}$), their anticipated Review dates (i.e., week number and day number, WK$_\#$.D$_\#$), their anticipated ship and deploy dates (i.e., week number and day number, WK$_\#$.D$_\#$), and their anticipated Retrospective dates (i.e., week number and day number, WK$_\#$.D$_\#$).

- Sub-Table 6.6.3 presents the plan for carrying on the second set of system and software requirements (i.e., SRSR second Sprint backlog: SRSR-S-Backlog$_2$, including five SRSRs: SRSR$_8$, SRSR$_4$, SRSR$_9$, SRSR$_5$, and SRSR$_{10}$). It presents the tasks needed to carry out these requirements (i.e., SRSR$_8$.T$_1$–T$_5$, SRSR$_4$.T$_1$–T$_5$, SRSR$_9$.T$_1$–T$_5$, SRSR$_5$.T$_1$–T$_5$, and SRSR$_{10}$.T$_1$–T$_5$), their schedules (i.e., week number and day number), their allocated resources (i.e., of RTM$_1$ through RTM$_5$), their anticipated deliverables (i.e., SRSR.DLV$_6$ through SRSR.DLV$_{10}$), their anticipated Review dates (i.e., week number and day number, WK$_\#$.D$_\#$), their anticipated ship and deploy dates (i.e., week number and day number, WK$_\#$.D$_\#$), and their anticipated Retrospective dates (i.e., week number and day number, $WK_\#.D_\#$).

 ▪ Sub-Table 6.6.4 presents the plan for carrying on the second set of software project and process requirements (i.e., SPPR first Sprint backlog: SPPR-S-Backlog$_2$, including five SPPRs: SPPR$_8$, SPPR$_4$, SPPR$_9$, SPPR$_5$, and SPPR$_{10}$). It presents the tasks needed to carry out these requirements (i.e., SPPR$_8$.T$_1$–T$_5$, SPPR$_4$.T$_1$–T$_5$, SPPR$_9$.T$_1$–T$_5$, SPPR$_5$.T$_1$–T$_5$, and SPPR$_{10}$.T$_1$–T$_5$), their schedules (i.e., week number and day number), their allocated resources (i.e., of RTM$_1$ through RTM$_5$), their anticipated deliverables (i.e., SPPR.DLV$_6$ through SPPR.DLV$_{10}$), their anticipated Review dates (i.e., week number and day number, $WK_\#.D_\#$), their anticipated ship and deploy dates (i.e., week number and day number, $WK_\#.D_\#$), and their anticipated Retrospective dates (i.e., week number and day number, $WK_\#.D_\#$).

TABLE 6.6 Cluster$_2$ of Sprints' backlogs of requirements

SPFR-S-Backlog$_2$	[SPFR$_{26}$, SPFR$_2$, SPFR$_7$, SPFR$_{12}$, SPFR$_{17}$]
SPNFR-S-Backlog$_2$	[SPNFR$_7$, SPNFR$_{12}$, SPNFR$_{17}$, SPNFR$_3$, SPNFR$_8$]
SRSR-S-Backlog$_2$	[SRSR$_8$, SRSR$_4$, SRSR$_9$, SRSR$_5$, SRSR$_{10}$]
SPPR-S-Backlog$_2$	[SPPR$_8$, SPPR$_4$, SPPR$_9$, SPPR$_5$, SPPR$_{10}$]

SUB-TABLE 6.6.1 SPFR Sprint$_2$ - SPFR-S-Backlog$_2$

Requirements	Tasks	Schedule WK	Schedule D	Resource	Deliverable	Review	Ship/ Deploy	Retrospective
SPFR$_{26}$	SPFR$_{26}$.T$_1$	8	1	RTM$_1$	SPFR.DLV$_6$	$WK_{12}.D_1$	$WK_{12}.D_1$	$WK_{12}.D_5$
	SPFR$_{26}$.T$_2$	8	2	RTM$_1$				
	SPFR$_{26}$.T$_3$	8	3	RTM$_1$				
	SPFR$_{26}$.T$_4$	8	4	RTM$_1$				
	SPFR$_{26}$.T$_5$	8	5	RTM$_1$				
SPFR$_2$	SPFR$_2$.T$_1$	8	1	RTM$_2$	SPFR.DLV$_7$	$WK_{12}.D_1$	$WK_{12}.D_1$	$WK_{12}.D_5$
	SPFR$_2$.T$_2$	8	2	RTM$_2$				
	SPFR$_2$.T$_3$	8	3	RTM$_2$				
	SPFR$_2$.T$_4$	8	4	RTM$_2$				
	SPFR$_2$.T$_5$	8	5	RTM$_2$				
SPFR$_7$	SPFR$_7$.T$_1$	8	1	RTM$_3$	SPFR.DLV$_8$	$WK_{12}.D_1$	$WK_{12}.D_1$	$WK_{12}.D_5$
	SPFR$_7$.T$_2$	8	2	RTM$_3$				
	SPFR$_7$.T$_3$	8	3	RTM$_3$				
	SPFR$_7$.T$_4$	8	4	RTM$_3$				
	SPFR$_7$.T$_5$	8	5	RTM$_3$				

(Continued)

Requirements	Tasks	Schedule		Resource	Deliverable	Review	Ship/ Deploy	Retrospective
		WK	D					
SPFR$_{12}$	SPFR$_{12}$.T$_1$	8	1	RTM$_4$	SPFR.DLV$_9$	WK$_{12}$.D$_1$	WK$_{12}$.D$_1$	WK$_{12}$.D$_5$
	SPFR$_{12}$.T$_2$	8	2	RTM$_4$				
	SPFR$_{12}$.T$_3$	8	3	RTM$_4$				
	SPFR$_{12}$.T$_4$	8	4	RTM$_4$				
	SPFR$_{12}$.T$_5$	8	5	RTM$_4$				
SPFR$_{17}$	SPFR$_{17}$.T$_1$	8	1	RTM$_5$	SPFR.DLV$_{10}$	WK$_{12}$.D$_1$	WK$_{12}$.D$_1$	WK$_{12}$.D$_5$
	SPFR$_{17}$.T$_2$	8	2	RTM$_5$				
	SPFR$_{17}$.T$_3$	8	3	RTM$_5$				
	SPFR$_{17}$.T$_4$	8	4	RTM$_5$				
	SPFR$_{17}$.T$_5$	8	5	RTM$_5$				

SUB-TABLE 6.6.2 SPNFR Sprint$_2$ - SPNFR-S-Backlog$_2$

Requirements	Tasks	Schedule		Resource	Deliverable	Review	Ship/Deploy	Retrospective
		WK	D					
SPNFR$_7$	SPNFR$_7$.T$_1$	9	1	RTM$_1$	SPNFR.DLV$_6$	WK$_{12}$.D$_1$	WK$_{12}$.D$_2$	WK$_{12}$.D$_5$
	SPNFR$_7$.T$_2$	9	2	RTM$_1$				
	SPNFR$_7$.T$_3$	9	3	RTM$_1$				
	SPNFR$_7$.T$_4$	9	4	RTM$_1$				
	SPNFR$_7$.T$_5$	9	5	RTM$_1$				
SPNFR$_{12}$	SPNFR$_{12}$.T$_1$	9	1	RTM$_2$	SPNFR.DLV$_7$	WK$_{12}$.D$_1$	WK$_{12}$.D$_2$	WK$_{12}$.D$_5$
	SPNFR$_{12}$.T$_2$	9	2	RTM$_2$				
	SPNFR$_{12}$.T$_3$	9	3	RTM$_2$				
	SPNFR$_{12}$.T$_4$	9	4	RTM$_2$				
	SPNFR$_{12}$.T$_5$	9	5	RTM$_2$				
SPNFR$_{17}$	SPNFR$_{17}$.T$_1$	9	1	RTM$_3$	SPNFR.DLV$_8$	WK$_{12}$.D$_1$	WK$_{12}$.D$_2$	WK$_{12}$.D$_5$
	SPNFR$_{17}$.T$_2$	9	2	RTM$_3$				
	SPNFR$_{17}$.T$_3$	9	3	RTM$_3$				
	SPNFR$_{17}$.T$_4$	9	4	RTM$_3$				
	SPNFR$_{17}$.T$_5$	9	5	RTM$_3$				
SPNFR$_3$	SPNFR$_3$.T$_1$	9	1	RTM$_4$	SPNFR.DLV$_9$	WK$_{12}$.D$_1$	WK$_{12}$.D$_2$	WK$_{12}$.D$_5$
	SPNFR$_3$.T$_2$	9	2	RTM$_4$				
	SPNFR$_3$.T$_3$	9	3	RTM$_4$				
	SPNFR$_3$.T$_4$	9	4	RTM$_4$				
	SPNFR$_3$.T$_5$	9	5	RTM$_4$				

(Continued)

Requirements	Tasks	Schedule		Resource	Deliverable	Review	Ship/Deploy	Retrospective
		WK	D					
SPNFR$_8$	SPNFR$_8$.T$_1$	9	1	RTM$_5$	SPNFR. DLV$_{10}$	WK$_{12}$.D$_1$	WK$_{12}$.D$_2$	WK$_{12}$.D$_5$
	SPNFR$_8$.T$_2$	9	2	RTM$_5$				
	SPNFR$_8$.T$_3$	9	3	RTM$_5$				
	SPNFR$_8$.T$_4$	9	4	RTM$_5$				
	SPNFR$_8$.T$_5$	9	5	RTM$_5$				

SUB-TABLE 6.6.3 SRSR Sprint$_2$ - SRSR-S-Backlog$_2$

Requirements	Tasks	Schedule		Resource	Deliverable	Review	Ship/ Deploy	Retrospective
		WK	D					
SRSR$_8$	SRSR$_8$.T$_1$	10	1	RTM$_1$	SRSR.DLV$_6$	WK$_{12}$.D$_1$	WK$_{12}$.D$_3$	WK$_{12}$.D$_5$
	SRSR$_8$.T$_2$	10	2	RTM$_1$				
	SRSR$_8$.T$_3$	10	3	RTM$_1$				
	SRSR$_8$.T$_4$	10	4	RTM$_1$				
	SRSR$_8$.T$_5$	10	5	RTM$_1$				
SRSR$_4$	SRSR$_4$.T$_1$	10	1	RTM$_2$	SRSR.DLV$_7$	WK$_{12}$.D$_1$	WK$_{12}$.D$_3$	WK$_{12}$.D$_5$
	SRSR$_4$.T$_2$	10	2	RTM$_2$				
	SRSR$_4$.T$_3$	10	3	RTM$_2$				
	SRSR$_4$.T$_4$	10	4	RTM$_2$				
	SRSR$_4$.T$_5$	10	5	RTM$_2$				
SRSR$_9$	SRSR$_9$.T$_1$	10	1	RTM$_3$	SRSR.DLV$_8$	WK$_{12}$.D$_1$	WK$_{12}$.D$_3$	WK$_{12}$.D$_5$
	SRSR$_9$.T$_2$	10	2	RTM$_3$				
	SRSR$_9$.T$_3$	10	3	RTM$_3$				
	SRSR$_9$.T$_4$	10	4	RTM$_3$				
	SRSR$_9$.T$_5$	10	5	RTM$_3$				
SRSR$_5$	SRSR$_5$.T$_1$	10	1	RTM$_4$	SRSR.DLV$_9$	WK$_{12}$.D$_1$	WK$_{12}$.D$_3$	WK$_{12}$.D$_5$
	SRSR$_5$.T$_2$	10	2	RTM$_4$				
	SRSR$_5$.T$_3$	10	3	RTM$_4$				
	SRSR$_5$.T$_4$	10	4	RTM$_4$				
	SRSR$_5$.T$_5$	10	5	RTM$_4$				
SRSR$_{10}$	SRSR$_{10}$.T$_1$	10	1	RTM$_5$	SRSR.DLV$_{10}$	WK$_{12}$.D$_1$	WK$_{12}$.D$_3$	WK$_{12}$.D$_5$
	SRSR$_{10}$.T$_2$	10	2	RTM$_5$				
	SRSR$_{10}$.T$_3$	10	3	RTM$_5$				
	SRSR$_{10}$.T$_4$	10	4	RTM$_5$				
	SRSR$_{10}$.T$_5$	10	5	RTM$_5$				

(Continued)

SUB-TABLE 6.6.4 SPPR Sprint$_2$ - SPPR-S-Backlog$_2$

Requirements	Tasks	Schedule		Resource	Deliverable	Review	Ship/ Deploy	Retrospective
		WK	D					
SPPR$_8$	SPPR$_8$.T$_1$	11	1	RTM$_1$	SPPR.DLV$_6$	WK$_{12}$.D$_1$	WK$_{12}$.D$_4$	WK$_{12}$.D$_5$
	SPPR$_8$.T$_2$	11	2	RTM$_1$				
	SPPR$_8$.T$_3$	11	3	RTM$_1$				
	SPPR$_8$.T$_4$	11	4	RTM$_1$				
	SPPR$_8$.T$_5$	11	5	RTM$_1$				
SPPR$_4$	SPPR$_4$.T$_1$	11	1	RTM$_2$	SPPR.DLV$_7$	WK$_{12}$.D$_1$	WK$_{12}$.D$_4$	WK$_{12}$.D$_5$
	SPPR$_4$.T$_2$	11	2	RTM$_2$				
	SPPR$_4$.T$_3$	11	3	RTM$_2$				
	SPPR$_4$.T$_4$	11	4	RTM$_2$				
	SPPR$_4$.T$_5$	11	5	RTM$_2$				
SPPR$_9$	SPPR$_9$.T$_1$	11	1	RTM$_3$	SPPR.DLV$_8$	WK$_{12}$.D$_1$	WK$_{12}$.D$_4$	WK$_{12}$.D$_5$
	SPPR$_9$.T$_2$	11	2	RTM$_3$				
	SPPR$_9$.T$_3$	11	3	RTM$_3$				
	SPPR$_9$.T$_4$	11	4	RTM$_3$				
	SPPR$_9$.T$_5$	11	5	RTM$_3$				
SPPR$_5$	SPPR$_5$.T$_1$	11	1	RTM$_4$	SPPR.DLV$_9$	WK$_{12}$.D$_1$	WK$_{12}$.D$_4$	WK$_{12}$.D$_5$
	SPPR$_5$.T$_2$	11	2	RTM$_4$				
	SPPR$_5$.T$_3$	11	3	RTM$_4$				
	SPPR$_5$.T$_4$	11	4	RTM$_4$				
	SPPR$_5$.T$_5$	11	5	RTM$_4$				
SPPR$_{10}$	SPPR$_{10}$.T$_1$	11	1	RTM$_5$	SPPR.DLV$_{10}$	WK$_{12}$.D$_1$	WK$_{12}$.D$_4$	WK$_{12}$.D$_5$
	SPPR$_{10}$.T$_2$	11	2	RTM$_5$				
	SPPR$_{10}$.T$_3$	11	3	RTM$_5$				
	SPPR$_{10}$.T$_4$	11	4	RTM$_5$				
	SPPR$_{10}$.T$_5$	11	5	RTM$_5$				

6.3.3 The Third Cluster of Sprints' Backlogs of Requirements

In reference to Tables 6.1-6.4, Tables 6.7.1 and 6.7.2 present the breakdown structures, schedules, resource allocations, deliverables, Review schedules, ship and deploy schedules, and Retrospective schedules for the backlogs of the third cluster's Sprints as follows:

- Sub-Table 6.7.1 presents the plan for carrying on the third set of software product functional requirements (i.e., SPFR third Sprint backlog: SPFR-S-Backlog$_3$, including five SPFRs: SPFR$_{22}$, SPFR$_{27}$, SPFR$_3$, SPFR$_8$, and SPFR$_{13}$). It presents the tasks needed to carry out these requirements (i.e., SPFR$_{22}$.T$_1$–T$_5$, SPFR$_{27}$.T$_1$–T$_5$, SPFR$_3$.T$_1$–T$_5$, SPFR$_8$.T$_1$–T$_5$, and SPFR$_{13}$. T$_1$–T$_5$), their schedules (i.e., week number and day number), their allocated resources (i.e., of RTM$_1$ through RTM$_5$), their anticipated deliverables (i.e., SPFR.DLV$_{11}$ through SPFR.DLV$_{15}$), their anticipated Review dates (i.e., week number and day number, WK$_\#$.D$_\#$), their anticipated ship and deploy dates (i.e., week number and day number, WK$_\#$.D$_\#$), and their anticipated Retrospective dates (i.e., week number and day number, WK$_\#$.D$_\#$).

- Sub-Table 6.7.2 presents the plan for carrying on the third set of software product non-functional requirements (i.e., SPNFR third Sprint backlog: SPNFR-S-Backlog$_3$, including five SPNFRs: SPNFR$_7$, SPNFR$_{12}$, SPNFR$_{17}$, SPNFR$_3$, and SPNFR$_8$). It presents the tasks needed to carry out these requirements (i.e., SPNFR$_7$.T$_1$–T$_5$, SPNFR$_{12}$.T$_1$–T$_5$, SPNFR$_{17}$. T$_1$–T$_5$, SPNFR$_3$.T$_1$–T$_5$, and SPNFR$_8$.T$_1$–T$_5$), their schedules (i.e., week number and day number), their allocated resources (i.e., of RTM$_1$ through RTM$_5$), their anticipated deliverables (i.e., SPNFR.DLV$_{11}$ through SPNFR.DLV$_{15}$), their anticipated Review dates (i.e., week number and day number, WK$_\#$.D$_\#$), their anticipated ship and deploy dates (i.e., week number and day number, WK$_\#$.D$_\#$), and their anticipated Retrospective dates (i.e., week number and day number, WK$_\#$.D$_\#$).

TABLE 6.7 Cluster$_3$ of Sprints' backlogs of requirements

SPFR-S-Backlog$_3$	[SPFR$_{22}$, SPFR$_{27}$, SPFR$_3$, SPFR$_8$, SPFR$_{13}$]
SPNFR-S-Backlog$_3$	[SPNFR$_7$, SPNFR$_{12}$, SPNFR$_{17}$, SPNFR$_3$, SPNFR$_8$]

SUB-TABLE 6.7.1 SPFR Sprint$_3$ - SPFR-S-Backlog$_3$

Requirements	Tasks	Schedule		Resource	Deliverable	Review	Ship/ Deploy	Retrospective
		WK	D					
SPFR$_{22}$	SPFR$_{22}$.T$_1$	13	1	RTM$_1$	SPFR.DLV$_{11}$	WK$_{15}$.D$_1$	WK$_{15}$.D$_1$	WK$_{15}$.D$_5$
	SPFR$_{22}$.T$_2$	13	2	RTM$_1$				
	SPFR$_{22}$.T$_3$	13	3	RTM$_1$				
	SPFR$_{22}$.T$_4$	13	4	RTM$_1$				
	SPFR$_{22}$.T$_5$	13	5	RTM$_1$				
SPFR$_{27}$	SPFR$_{27}$.T$_1$	13	1	RTM$_2$	SPFR.DLV$_{12}$	WK$_{15}$.D$_1$	WK$_{15}$.D$_1$	WK$_{15}$.D$_5$
	SPFR$_{27}$.T$_2$	13	2	RTM$_2$				
	SPFR$_{27}$.T$_3$	13	3	RTM$_2$				
	SPFR$_{27}$.T$_4$	13	4	RTM$_2$				
	SPFR$_{27}$.T$_5$	13	5	RTM$_2$				
SPFR$_3$	SPFR$_3$.T$_1$	13	1	RTM$_3$	SPFR.DLV$_{13}$	WK$_{15}$.D$_1$	WK$_{15}$.D$_1$	WK$_{15}$.D$_5$
	SPFR$_3$.T$_2$	13	2	RTM$_3$				
	SPFR$_3$.T$_3$	13	3	RTM$_3$				
	SPFR$_3$.T$_4$	13	4	RTM$_3$				
	SPFR$_3$.T$_5$	13	5	RTM$_3$				
SPFR$_8$	SPFR$_8$.T$_1$	13	1	RTM$_4$	SPFR.DLV$_{14}$	WK$_{15}$.D$_1$	WK$_{15}$.D$_1$	WK$_{15}$.D$_5$
	SPFR$_8$.T$_2$	13	2	RTM$_4$				
	SPFR$_8$.T$_3$	13	3	RTM$_4$				
	SPFR$_8$.T$_4$	13	4	RTM$_4$				
	SPFR$_8$.T$_5$	13	5	RTM$_4$				
SPFR$_{13}$	SPFR$_{13}$.T$_1$	13	1	RTM$_5$	SPFR.DLV$_{15}$	WK$_{15}$.D$_1$	WK$_{15}$.D$_1$	WK$_{15}$.D$_5$
	SPFR$_{13}$.T$_2$	13	2	RTM$_5$				
	SPFR$_{13}$.T$_3$	13	3	RTM$_5$				
	SPFR$_{13}$.T$_4$	13	4	RTM$_5$				
	SPFR$_{13}$.T$_5$	13	5	RTM$_5$				

SUB-TABLE 6.7.2 SPNFR Sprint$_3$ - SPNFR-S-Backlog$_3$

Requirements	Tasks	Schedule WK	Schedule D	Resource	Deliverable	Review	Ship/ Deploy	Retrospective
SPNFR$_7$	SPNFR$_7$.T$_1$	14	1	RTM$_1$	SPNFR.DLV$_{11}$	WK$_{15}$.D$_1$	WK$_{15}$.D$_2$	WK$_{15}$.D$_5$
	SPNFR$_7$.T$_2$	14	2	RTM$_1$				
	SPNFR$_7$.T$_3$	14	3	RTM$_1$				
	SPNFR$_7$.T$_4$	14	4	RTM$_1$				
	SPNFR$_7$.T$_5$	14	5	RTM$_1$				
SPNFR$_{12}$	SPNFR$_{12}$.T$_1$	14	1	RTM$_2$	SPNFR.DLV$_{12}$	WK$_{15}$.D$_1$	WK$_{15}$.D$_2$	WK$_{15}$.D$_5$
	SPNFR$_{12}$.T$_2$	14	2	RTM$_2$				
	SPNFR$_{12}$.T$_3$	14	3	RTM$_2$				
	SPNFR$_{12}$.T$_4$	14	4	RTM$_2$				
	SPNFR$_{12}$.T$_5$	14	5	RTM$_2$				
SPNFR$_{17}$	SPNFR$_{17}$.T$_1$	14	1	RTM$_3$	SPNFR.DLV$_{13}$	WK$_{15}$.D$_1$	WK$_{15}$.D$_2$	WK$_{15}$.D$_5$
	SPNFR$_{17}$.T$_2$	14	2	RTM$_3$				
	SPNFR$_{17}$.T$_3$	14	3	RTM$_3$				
	SPNFR$_{17}$.T$_4$	14	4	RTM$_3$				
	SPNFR$_{17}$.T$_5$	14	5	RTM$_3$				
SPNFR$_3$	SPNFR$_3$.T$_1$	14	1	RTM$_4$	SPNFR.DLV$_{14}$	WK$_{15}$.D$_1$	WK$_{15}$.D$_2$	WK$_{15}$.D$_5$
	SPNFR$_3$.T$_2$	14	2	RTM$_4$				
	SPNFR$_3$.T$_3$	14	3	RTM$_4$				
	SPNFR$_3$.T$_4$	14	4	RTM$_4$				
	SPNFR$_3$.T$_5$	14	5	RTM$_4$				
SPNFR$_8$	SPNFR$_8$.T$_1$	14	1	RTM$_5$	SPNFR.DLV$_{15}$	WK$_{15}$.D$_1$	WK$_{15}$.D$_2$	WK$_{15}$.D$_5$
	SPNFR$_8$.T$_2$	14	2	RTM$_5$				
	SPNFR$_8$.T$_3$	14	3	RTM$_5$				
	SPNFR$_8$.T$_4$	14	4	RTM$_5$				
	SPNFR$_8$.T$_5$	14	5	RTM$_5$				

6.3.4 The Fourth Cluster of Sprints' Backlogs of Requirements

In reference to Tables 6.1–6.4, Tables 6.8.1 and 6.8.2 present the breakdown structures, schedules, resource allocations, deliverables, Review schedules, ship and deploy schedules, and Retrospective schedules for the backlogs of the fourth cluster's Sprints as follows:

▪ Sub-Table 6.8.1 presents the plan for carrying on the fourth set of software product functional requirements (i.e., SPFR fourth Sprint backlog: SPFR-S-Backlog$_4$, including five SPFRs: SPFR$_{18}$, SPFR$_{23}$, SPFR$_{28}$,

SPFR$_4$, and SPFR$_9$). It presents the tasks needed to carry out these requirements (i.e., SPFR$_{18}$.T$_1$–T$_5$, SPFR$_{23}$.T$_1$–T$_5$, SPFR$_{28}$.T$_1$–T$_5$, SPFR$_4$. T$_1$–T$_5$, and SPFR$_9$.T$_1$–T$_5$), their schedules (i.e., week number and day number), their allocated resources (i.e., of RTM$_1$ through RTM$_5$), their anticipated deliverables (i.e., SPFR.DLV$_{16}$ through SPFR.DLV$_{20}$), their anticipated Review dates (i.e., week number and day number, WK$_\#$.D$_\#$), their anticipated ship and deploy dates (i.e., week number and day number, WK$_\#$.D$_\#$), and their anticipated Retrospective dates (i.e., week number and day number, WK$_\#$.D$_\#$).

- Sub-Table 6.8.2 presents the plan for carrying on the fourth set of software product non-functional requirements (i.e., SPNFR fourth Sprint backlog: SPNFR-S-Backlog$_4$, including five SPNFRs: SPNFR$_{19}$, SPNFR$_5$, SPNFR$_{10}$, SPNFR$_{15}$, and SPNFR$_{20}$). It presents the tasks needed to carry out these requirements (i.e., SPNFR$_{19}$.T$_1$–T$_5$, SPNFR$_5$.T$_1$–T$_5$, SPNFR$_{10}$. T$_1$–T$_5$, SPNFR$_{15}$.T$_1$–T$_5$, and SPNFR$_{20}$.T$_1$–T$_5$), their schedules (i.e., week number and day number), their allocated resources (i.e., of RTM$_1$ through RTM$_5$), their anticipated deliverables (i.e., SPNFR.DLV$_{16}$ through SPNFR.DLV$_{20}$), their anticipated Review dates (i.e., week number and day number, WK$_\#$.D$_\#$), their anticipated ship and deploy dates (i.e., week number and day number, WK$_\#$.D$_\#$), and their anticipated Retrospective dates (i.e., week number and day number, WK$_\#$.D$_\#$).

TABLE 6.8 Cluster$_4$ of Sprints' backlogs of requirements

SPFR-S-Backlog$_4$	[SPFR$_{18}$, SPFR$_{23}$, SPFR$_{28}$, SPFR$_4$, SPFR$_9$]
SPNFR-S-Backlog$_4$	[SPNFR$_{19}$, SPNFR$_5$, SPNFR$_{10}$, SPNFR$_{15}$, SPNFR$_{20}$]

SUB-TABLE 6.8.1 SPFR Sprint$_4$ - SPFR-S-Backlog$_4$

Requirements	Tasks	Schedule WK	Schedule D	Resource	Deliverable	Review	Ship/ Deploy	Retrospective
SPFR$_{18}$	SPFR$_{18}$.T$_1$	16	1	RTM$_1$	SPFR.DLV$_{16}$	WK$_{18}$.D$_1$	WK$_{18}$.D$_1$	WK$_{18}$.D$_5$
	SPFR$_{18}$.T$_2$	16	2	RTM$_1$				
	SPFR$_{18}$.T$_3$	16	3	RTM$_1$				
	SPFR$_{18}$.T$_4$	16	4	RTM$_1$				
	SPFR$_{18}$.T$_5$	16	5	RTM$_1$				

(Continued)

Requirements	Tasks	Schedule		Resource	Deliverable	Review	Ship/ Deploy	Retrospective
		WK	D					
SPFR$_{23}$	SPFR$_{23 \cdot T1}$	16	1	RTM$_2$	SPFR.DLV$_{17}$	WK$_{18}$.D$_1$	WK$_{18}$.D$_1$	WK$_{18}$.D$_5$
	SPFR$_{23}$.T$_2$	16	2	RTM$_2$				
	SPFR$_{23}$.T$_3$	16	3	RTM$_2$				
	SPFR$_{23}$.T$_4$	16	4	RTM$_2$				
	SPFR$_{23}$.T$_5$	16	5	RTM$_2$				
SPFR$_{28}$	SPFR$_{28}$.T$_1$	16	1	RTM$_3$	SPFR.DLV$_{18}$	WK$_{18}$.D$_1$	WK$_{18}$.D$_1$	WK$_{18}$.D$_5$
	SPFR$_{28}$.T$_2$	16	2	RTM$_3$				
	SPFR$_{28}$.T$_3$	16	3	RTM$_3$				
	SPFR$_{28}$.T$_4$	16	4	RTM$_3$				
	SPFR$_{28}$.T$_5$	16	5	RTM$_3$				
SPFR$_4$	SPFR$_4$.T$_1$	16	1	RTM$_4$	SPFR.DLV$_{19}$	WK$_{18}$.D$_1$	WK$_{18}$.D$_1$	WK$_{18}$.D$_5$
	SPFR$_4$.T$_2$	16	2	RTM$_4$				
	SPFR$_4$.T$_3$	16	3	RTM$_4$				
	SPFR$_4$.T$_4$	16	4	RTM$_4$				
	SPFR$_4$.T$_5$	16	5	RTM$_4$				
SPFR$_9$	SPFR$_9$.T$_1$	16	1	RTM$_5$	SPFR.DLV$_{20}$	WK$_{18}$.D$_1$	WK$_{15}$.D$_1$	WK$_{18}$.D$_5$
	SPFR$_9$.T$_2$	16	2	RTM$_5$				
	SPFR$_9$.T$_3$	16	3	RTM$_5$				
	SPFR$_9$.T$_4$	16	4	RTM$_5$				
	SPFR$_9$.T$_5$	16	5	RTM$_5$				

SUB-TABLE 6.8.2 SPNFR Sprint$_4$ - SPNFR-S-Backlog$_4$

Requirements	Tasks	Schedule		Resource	Deliverable	Review	Ship/ Deploy	Retrospective
		WK	D					
SPNFR$_{19}$	SPNFR$_{19}$.T$_1$	17	1	RTM$_1$	SPNFR.DLV$_{16}$	WK$_{18}$.D$_1$	WK$_{18}$.D$_2$	WK$_{18}$.D$_5$
	SPNFR$_{19}$.T$_2$	17	2	RTM$_1$				
	SPNFR$_{19}$.T$_3$	17	3	RTM$_1$				
	SPNFR$_{19}$.T$_4$	17	4	RTM$_1$				
	SPNFR$_{19}$.T$_5$	17	5	RTM$_1$				
SPNFR$_5$	SPNFR$_5$.T$_1$	17	1	RTM$_2$	SPNFR.DLV$_{17}$	WK$_{18}$.D$_1$	WK$_{15}$.D$_2$	WK$_{18}$.D$_5$
	SPNFR$_5$.T$_2$	17	2	RTM$_2$				
	SPNFR$_5$.T$_3$	17	3	RTM$_2$				
	SPNFR$_5$.T$_4$	17	4	RTM$_2$				
	SPNFR$_5$.T$_5$	17	5	RTM$_2$				

(Continued)

Requirements	Tasks	Schedule WK	Schedule D	Resource	Deliverable	Review	Ship/Deploy	Retrospective
SPNFR$_{10}$	SPNFR$_{10}$.T$_1$	17	1	RTM$_3$	SPNFR.DLV$_{18}$	WK$_{18}$.D$_1$	WK$_{18}$.D$_2$	WK$_{18}$.D$_5$
	SPNFR$_{10}$.T$_2$	17	2	RTM$_3$				
	SPNFR$_{10}$.T$_3$	17	3	RTM$_3$				
	SPNFR$_{10}$.T$_4$	17	4	RTM$_3$				
	SPNFR$_{10}$.T$_5$	17	5	RTM$_3$				
SPNFR$_{15}$	SPNFR$_{15}$.T$_1$	17	1	RTM$_4$	SPNFR.DLV$_{19}$	WK$_{18}$.D$_1$	WK$_{18}$.D$_2$	WK$_{18}$.D$_5$
	SPNFR$_{15}$.T$_2$	17	2	RTM$_4$				
	SPNFR$_{15}$.T$_3$	17	3	RTM$_4$				
	SPNFR$_{15}$.T$_4$	17	4	RTM$_4$				
	SPNFR$_{15}$.T$_5$	17	5	RTM$_4$				
SPNFR$_{20}$	SPNFR$_{20}$.T$_1$	17	1	RTM$_5$	SPNFR.DLV$_{20}$	WK$_{18}$.D$_1$	WK$_{18}$.D$_2$	WK$_{18}$.D$_5$
	SPNFR$_{20}$.T$_2$	17	2	RTM$_5$				
	SPNFR$_{20}$.T$_3$	17	3	RTM$_5$				
	SPNFR$_{20}$.T$_4$	17	4	RTM$_5$				
	SPNFR$_{20}$.T$_5$	17	5	RTM$_5$				

6.3.5 The Fifth Cluster of Sprints' Backlogs of Requirements

In reference to Tables 6.1–6.4, Sub-Table 6.9.1 presents the breakdown structures, schedules, resource allocations, deliverables, Review schedules, ship and deploy schedules, and Retrospective schedules for the backlogs of the fifth cluster's Sprint as follows.

Sub-Table 6.9.1 presents the plan for carrying on the fifth set of software product functional requirements (i.e., SPFR fifth Sprint backlog: SPFR-S-Backlog$_5$, including five SPFRs: SPFR$_{14}$, SPFR$_{19}$, SPFR$_{24}$, SPFR$_{29}$, and SPFR$_5$). It presents the tasks needed to carry out these requirements (i.e., SPFR$_{14}$.T$_1$–T$_5$, SPFR$_{19}$.T$_1$–T$_5$, SPFR$_{24}$.T$_1$–T$_5$, SPFR$_{29}$.T$_1$–T$_5$, and SPFR$_5$.T$_1$–T$_5$), their schedules (i.e., week number and day number), their allocated resources (i.e., of RTM$_1$ through RTM$_5$), their anticipated deliverables (i.e., SPFR.DLV$_{21}$ through SPFR.DLV$_{25}$), their anticipated Review dates (i.e., week number and day number, WK$_#$.D$_#$), their anticipated ship and deploy dates (i.e., week number and day number, WK$_#$.D$_#$), and their anticipated Retrospective dates (i.e., week number and day number, WK$_#$.D$_#$).

TABLE 6.9 Cluster$_5$ of Sprints' backlogs of requirements

SPFR-S-Backlog$_5$	[SPFR$_{14}$, SPFR$_{19}$, SPFR$_{24}$, SPFR$_{29}$, SPFR$_5$]

SUB-TABLE 6.9.1 SPFR Sprint$_5$ - SPFR-S-Backlog$_5$

Requirements	Tasks	Schedule WK	Schedule D	Resource	Deliverable	Review	Ship/ Deploy	Retrospective
SPFR$_{14}$	SPFR$_{14}$.T$_1$	19	1	RTM$_1$	SPFR.DLV$_{20}$	WK$_{20}$.D$_1$	WK$_{20}$.D$_1$	WK$_{20}$.D$_5$
	SPFR$_{14}$.T$_2$	19	2	RTM$_1$				
	SPFR$_{14}$.T$_3$	19	3	RTM$_1$				
	SPFR$_{14}$.T$_4$	19	4	RTM$_1$				
	SPFR$_{14}$.T$_5$	19	5	RTM$_1$				
SPFR$_{19}$	SPFR$_{19}$.T$_1$	19	1	RTM$_2$	SPFR.DLV$_{21}$	WK$_{20}$.D$_1$	WK$_{20}$.D$_1$	WK$_{20}$.D$_5$
	SPFR$_{19}$.T$_2$	19	2	RTM$_2$				
	SPFR$_{19}$.T$_3$	19	3	RTM$_2$				
	SPFR$_{19}$.T$_4$	19	4	RTM$_2$				
	SPFR$_{19}$.T$_5$	19	5	RTM$_2$				
SPFR$_{24}$	SPFR$_{24}$.T$_1$	19	1	RTM$_3$	SPFR.DLV$_{22}$	WK$_{20}$.D$_1$	WK$_{20}$.D$_1$	WK$_{20}$.D$_5$
	SPFR$_{24}$.T$_2$	19	2	RTM$_3$				
	SPFR$_{24}$.T$_3$	19	3	RTM$_3$				
	SPFR$_{24}$.T$_4$	19	4	RTM$_3$				
	SPFR$_{24}$.T$_5$	19	5	RTM$_3$				
SPFR$_{29}$	SPFR$_{29}$.T$_1$	19	1	RTM$_4$	SPFR.DLV$_{23}$	WK$_{20}$.D$_1$	WK$_{20}$.D$_1$	WK$_{20}$.D$_5$
	SPFR$_{29}$.T$_2$	19	2	RTM$_4$				
	SPFR$_{29}$.T$_3$	19	3	RTM$_4$				
	SPFR$_{29}$.T$_4$	19	4	RTM$_4$				
	SPFR$_{29}$.T$_5$	19	5	RTM$_4$				
SPFR$_5$	SPFR$_5$.T$_1$	19	1	RTM$_5$	SPFR.DLV$_{24}$	WK$_{20}$.D$_1$	WK$_{20}$.D$_1$	WK$_{20}$.D$_5$
	SPFR$_5$.T$_2$	19	2	RTM$_5$				
	SPFR$_5$.T$_3$	19	3	RTM$_5$				
	SPFR$_5$.T$_4$	19	4	RTM$_5$				
	SPFR$_5$.T$_5$	19	5	RTM$_5$				

6.3.6 The Sixth Cluster of Sprints' Backlogs of Requirements

In reference to Tables 6.1–6.4, Sub-Table 6.10.1 presents the breakdown structures, schedules, resource allocations, deliverables, Review schedules, ship and deploy schedules, and Retrospective schedules for the backlogs of the sixth cluster's Sprint as follows.

Sub-Table 6.10.1 presents the plan for carrying on the sixth set of software product functional requirements (i.e., SPFR sixth Sprint backlog:

SPFR-S-Backlog$_6$, including five SPFRs: SPFR$_{10}$, SPFR$_{15}$, SPFR$_{20}$, SPFR$_{25}$, and SPFR$_{30}$). It presents the tasks needed to carry out these requirements (i.e., SPFR$_{10}$.T$_1$–T$_5$, SPFR$_{15}$.T$_1$–T$_5$, SPFR$_{20}$.T$_1$–T$_5$, SPFR$_{25}$.T$_1$–T$_5$, and SPFR$_{10}$.T$_1$–T$_5$), their schedules (i.e., week number and day number), their allocated resources (i.e., of RTM$_1$ through RTM$_5$), their anticipated deliverables (i.e., SPFR.DLV$_{26}$ through SPFR.DLV$_{30}$), their anticipated Review dates (i.e., week number and day number, WK$_\#$.D$_\#$), their anticipated ship and deploy dates (i.e., week number and day number, WK$_\#$.D$_\#$), and their anticipated Retrospective dates (i.e., week number and day number, WK$_\#$.D$_\#$).

TABLE 6.10 Cluster$_6$ of Sprints' backlogs of requirements

SPFR-S-Backlog$_6$	[SPFR$_{10}$, SPFR$_{15}$, SPFR$_{20}$, SPFR$_{25}$, SPFR$_{30}$]

SUB-TABLE 6.10.1 SPFR Sprint$_6$ - SPFR-S-Backlog$_6$

Requirements	Tasks	Schedule WK	Schedule D	Resource	Deliverable	Review	Ship/ Deploy	Retrospective
SPFR$_{10}$	SPFR$_{10}$.T$_1$	21	1	RTM$_1$	SPFR.DLV$_{20}$	WK$_{22}$.D$_1$	WK$_{22}$.D$_1$	WK$_{22}$.D$_5$
	SPFR$_{10}$.T$_2$	21	2	RTM$_1$				
	SPFR$_{10}$.T$_3$	21	3	RTM$_1$				
	SPFR$_{10}$.T$_4$	21	4	RTM$_1$				
	SPFR$_{10}$.T$_5$	21	5	RTM$_1$				
SPFR$_{15}$	SPFR$_{15}$.T$_1$	21	1	RTM$_2$	SPFR.DLV$_{21}$	WK$_{22}$.D$_1$	WK$_{22}$.D$_1$	WK$_{22}$.D$_5$
	SPFR$_{15}$.T$_2$	21	2	RTM$_2$				
	SPFR$_{15}$.T$_3$	21	3	RTM$_2$				
	SPFR$_{15}$.T$_4$	21	4	RTM$_2$				
	SPFR$_{15}$.T$_5$	21	5	RTM$_2$				
SPFR$_{20}$	SPFR$_{20}$.T$_1$	21	1	RTM$_3$	SPFR.DLV$_{22}$	WK$_{22}$.D$_1$	WK$_{22}$.D$_1$	WK$_{22}$.D$_5$
	SPFR$_{20}$.T$_2$	21	2	RTM$_3$				
	SPFR$_{20}$.T$_3$	21	3	RTM$_3$				
	SPFR$_{20}$.T$_4$	21	4	RTM$_3$				
	SPFR$_{20}$.T$_5$	21	5	RTM$_3$				
SPFR$_{25}$	SPFR$_{25}$.T$_1$	21	1	RTM$_4$	SPFR.DLV$_{23}$	WK$_{22}$.D$_1$	WK$_{22}$.D$_1$	WK$_{22}$.D$_5$
	SPFR$_{25}$.T$_2$	21	2	RTM$_4$				
	SPFR$_{25}$.T$_3$	21	3	RTM$_4$				
	SPFR$_{25}$.T$_4$	21	4	RTM$_4$				
	SPFR$_{25}$.T$_5$	21	5	RTM$_4$				

(Continued)

Requirements	Tasks	Schedule		Resource	Deliverable	Review	Ship/ Deploy	Retrospective
		WK	**D**					
SPFR$_{30}$	SPFR$_{30}$.T$_1$	21	1	RTM$_5$	SPFR.DLV$_{24}$	WK$_{22}$.D$_1$	WK$_{22}$.D$_1$	WK$_{22}$.D$_5$
	SPFR$_{30}$.T$_2$	21	2	RTM$_5$				
	SPFR$_{30}$.T$_3$	21	3	RTM$_5$				
	SPFR$_{30}$.T$_4$	21	4	RTM$_5$				
	SPFR$_{30}$.T$_5$	21	5	RTM$_5$				

6.3.7 Calculations

SUB-TABLE 6.10.2 Case study calculations

Project Period	Initiation period + implementation period + project Retrospective period
Initiation Period	The project initiation lasts for as long as needed.
Implementation Period	22 weeks
Project Retrospective Period	1 day (typically)
Project Base Cost	Overhead cost + Product Owner cost + RHSI Master cost + RHSI Team cost
	$30,000.00 + 4 * $5,000.00 + 4 * $4,000.00 + 5 * 4 * $3,000.00
	$126,000.00
	$30,000.00 + 22 weeks * ($5,000.00 per month *12 months per year / 52 weeks per year) + 22 weeks * ($4,000.00 per month * 12 months per year / 52 weeks per year) + 22 weeks * ($3,000.00 per month * 12 months per year / 52 weeks per year) * 5 members = $30,000.00 + $25,384.62 + $20,307.70 + $76,153.85 = $151,846.17
Overall Cost	Base cost + risks contingency fund (3%) = 1.03 * Base cost = $156,401.56
Price	Overall cost + profit (20%) = 1.2 * 156,401.56 = $187,681.87

6.4 SUMMARY

This chapter provided a detailed case study applying the RHSI methodology, showcasing its symbolic implementation.

This chapter built upon the concepts introduced in Chapters 4-5 and offered the following:

- An overview of the case study artifacts (Section 6.2), encompassing given user stories, requirements, prioritization (Section 6.2.1), time-boxing (Section 6.2.2), project staffing (Section 6.2.3), financials (Section 6.2.4), requirements' prioritization (Section 6.2.5), and the creation of PPBacklogs and S-Backlogs (Section 6.2.6).
- The clustering of Sprint backlogs into meaningful groups (Section 6.3), including the detailed breakdown for each cluster (Sections 6.3.1–6.3.6).
- The calculations of periods, costs, and price estimations (Section 6.3.7).

The chapter exemplified the application of the RHSI methodology in symbolic scenarios, facilitating a better understanding of its practical use in organizing and executing projects effectively.

References and Reading Material

1. Pierre Bourque and Richard E. Fairley, SWEBOK V3 Guide to the Software Engineering Body of Knowledge V3.0. IEEE COMPUTER SOCIETY. *https://ieeecs-media.computer.org/media/education/swebok/swebok-v3.pdf*

2. Hironori Washizaki, SWEBOK V4.0 Guide to the Software Engineering Body of Knowledge v4.0. A PROJECT OF THE IEEE COMPUTER SOCIETY. *https://ieeecs-media.computer.org/media/education/swebok/swebok-v4.pdf*

3. Moh'd A. Radaideh, Software Project Management: With PMI, IEEE-CS, and Agile-SCRUM. DE GRUYTER 2024. *https://www.degruyter.com/document/doi/10.1515/9783111206868/html?lang=en*

4. Moh'd A. Radaideh. (2024). Evaluating the Software Engineering Curriculum at JUST: A Comparative Analysis with IEEE Knowledge Areas. International Journal of Intelligent Systems and Applications in Engineering, 12(4), 583–593. Retrieved from *https://ijisae.org/index.php/IJISAE/article/view/6262*

5. Moh'd A. Radaideh, & Al-Haija, Q. A. . (2024). A Blended Learning Approach for Educating Software Project Management. International Journal of Intelligent Systems and Applications in Engineering, 12(3), 490–498. *https://ijisae.org/index.php/IJISAE/article/view/5279.*

6. Moh'd A. Radaideh, Mohammad, N., and Mukbil, M., "A proposed cloud-based platform for facilitating donation Services in support to

needy students". The Springer's Journal of Supercomputing. January 2023. *https://link.springer.com/article/10.1007/s11227-023-05062-0*

7. Moh'd A. Radaideh, and Abdel-Qader, R., "A PROPOSED CLOUD-BASED PLATFORM OF INFORMATION TECHNOLOGY SER-VICES DELIVERY MANAGEMENT". The Springer's Journal of Supercomputing. June 2022. *https://link.springer.com/article/10.1007/s11227-022-04600-6*

8. Radaideh, M., "Benchmarking the software engineering undergraduate program curriculum at Jordan University of Science and Technology with the IEEE software engineering body of knowledge: (software engineering knowledge Areas #11-15)". IEEE CPS - Benchmarking the software engineering undergraduate program curriculum at Jordan University of Science and Technology with the IEEE software engineering body of knowledge: (software engineering knowledge Areas #11-15) | IEEE Conference Publication | IEEEXplore.

9. Radaideh, M., "Shifting the Paradigms from Teaching Project Management to Teaching Software Project Management at the Jordan University of Science and Technology According to the IEEE Software Engineering Management Knowledge Area." IEEE CPS - Shifting the paradigms from teaching project management to teaching software project management at Jordan University of Science and Technology based on the IEEE software engineering management knowledge area | IEEE Conference Publication | IEEEXplore.

10. Radaideh, M., "Benchmarking the Software Engineering Undergraduate Program Curriculum at Jordan University of Science and Technology with the IEEE Software Engineering Body of Knowledge (Software Engineering Knowledge Areas #1–5)". SPRINGER NATURE Research Book Series: Advances in Software Engineering, Education, and e-Learning, pp 747-768, September 2021 (https://link.springer.com/chapter/10.1007/978-3-030-70873-3_53).

11. Radaideh, M., "Benchmarking the Software Engineering Undergraduate Program Curriculum at Jordan University of Science and Technology with the IEEE Software Engineering Body of Knowledge (SWE Knowledge Areas #6–10)". Published in the SPRINGER NATURE Research Book Series: Advances in Software Engineering, Education, and e-Learning, pp 85-100, September 2021 (https://link.springer.com/chapter/10.1007/978-3-030-70873-3_7).

INDEX